Complicated Grief, Attachment, &Art Therapy

THEORY, TREATMENT, AND
14 READY-TO-USE PROTOCOLS

of related interest

Dying, Bereavement and the Healing Arts
Edited by Gillie Bolton
ISBN 978 1 84310 516 9
eISBN 978 1 84642 680 3

Grief Unseen
Healing Pregnancy Loss through the Arts
Laura Seftel
ISBN 978 1 84310 805 4
eISBN 978 1 84642 479 3

Digital Art Therapy
Material, Methods, and Applications
Edited by Rick L. Garner
ISBN 978 1 84905 740 0
eISBN 978 1 78450 160 0

DBT-Informed Art Therapy
Mindfulness, Cognitive Behavior Therapy, and the Creative Process
Susan M. Clark
ISBN 978 1 84905 733 2
eISBN 978 1 78450 103 7

Mindful Art Therapy
A Foundation for Practice
Barbara Jean Davis
ISBN 978 1 84905 426 3
eISBN 978 0 85700 791 9

Integrating Art Therapy and Yoga Therapy
Yoga, Art, and the Use of Intention
Karen Gibbons
ISBN 978 1 84905 782 0
eISBN 978 1 78450 023 8

Complicated Grief, Attachment, & Art Therapy

Theory, Treatment, and
14 Ready-to-Use Protocols

Edited by Briana MacWilliam

Jessica Kingsley *Publishers*
London and Philadelphia

First published in 2017
by Jessica Kingsley Publishers
73 Collier Street
London N1 9BE, UK
and
400 Market Street, Suite 400
Philadelphia, PA 19106, USA

www.jkp.com

Library of Congress Cataloging in Publication Data
Title: Complicated grief, attachment, and art therapy : theory, treatment,
and 14 ready-to-use protocols / [edited by] Briana MacWilliam.
Description: London ; Philadelphia : Jessica Kingsley Publishers, 2017.
Identifiers: LCCN 2016056992 (print) | LCCN 2017006711 (ebook) | ISBN
9781785927386 (alk. paper) | ISBN 9781784504588 (ebook)
Subjects: LCSH: Grief therapy. | Attachment behavior. | Arts--Therapeutic use.
Classification: LCC RC455.4.L67 C63 2017 (print) | LCC RC455.4.L67 (ebook) |
DDC 616.89/1656--dc23
LC record available at https://lccn.loc.gov/2016056992

British Library Cataloguing in Publication Data
A CIP catalogue record for this book is available from the British Library

ISBN 978 1 78592 738 6
eISBN 978 1 78450 458 8

Printed and bound in Great Britain

Contents

Part III. Applications

Introduction

Briana MacWilliam

Intersections of attachment and grief

The meaning making of memories, the weaving of symbol into story:
this is the work of grief. In the therapeutic practice of the art therapist,
it is essential to understand the healing aspects of this process, when
exploring how disturbances in attachment impact grief and loss.

Attachment is a bio–psycho–social process by which affectional
bonds are formed between human beings, most critically examined
through the earliest phases of development. What qualifies as a
"disturbance" is further explored throughout this text, but generally
speaking, when a child receives such messages as "you make me
proud," "you make me angry," or "don't hurt your sister's feelings," he
realizes the power he wields over others—including his more capable
adult caretakers—and this is anxiety inducing. Equally, he realizes
the opposite must be true: if he can make others feel something and
act accordingly, then they can make him feel something and act
accordingly as well. In this way, the child falls into blame games that
quickly spiral into complicated relationships, fraught with tension
and unresolved issues. He then carries those loose ends into other
aspects of life, compounding his "unfinished business" (James and
Friedman, 2009).

Finally, when a great loss occurs, the child is put to the task of
unwinding this tangled web for himself—a responsibility he must

learn, perhaps, for the first time in his life. No, you cannot control the rain that ruined your picnic, or the delayed flight that cost you a promotion, or the philandering activities of your ex-boyfriend, or the abusive nature of your stepfather, or the cancer that killed your mother, nor the car accident that took your child, but you can control how you move on from it. You *can* make a decision about how these horrible events will continue to shape your experience of the present moment. It is bad enough when terrible things happen to us, but to succumb to these events and their influence through self-inflicted perpetuity is to always feel pain.

"Easier said than done," you might say, and you would be right. But it begins with making the choice, with realizing that holding onto a lovely fantasy that only causes you heartache is not a way of honoring the dead or the lost, but a form of self-punishment. Equally, beating yourself up over things you might have said or done, or failed to say and do, is to place the work of forgiveness in other people's hands, and absolve yourself of responsibility. In this vein, the work of grief is the work of growth, defined by a revisiting and revising of our attachments, through the process of integration. It is a choice between contracting into a victimized identity, or "discovering grace" on the other side of helplessness and surrender (Tolle, 2004).

What is integration? In essence, integration is how we observe, understand, interact with, create, and communicate our life story. Integration has been defined through various stage theories, models of change and research methodologies, many of which you will find illuminated in this text. Less important is discerning which of these approaches to dealing with grief is the "right" one; more important is discovering which one resonates for the individual. Like a thumbprint, no two persons are the same, and so it is with how we make meaning of our stories. Integration is the work of discovering what is ours, and what was given to us. What we want to keep and what we want to change. It is not finding the missing pieces of a puzzle—we are already whole and always have been—it is a reshaping of the puzzle to include all the pieces that need fit.

Integration doesn't happen overnight. Relying solely on time to heal a wound, however, inadequately bandages an untreated infection. Only through a concerted effort to confront the depths of our pain and the origins of its structure is it possible to feel the sun on our face. In C.S. Lewis's (1961, pp.52–53) *A Grief Observed* he notes, there was no sudden transition from fear, anger, grief and pain to warmth and light. It was "like the warming of a room or the coming of daylight. When you first notice them, they have been already going on for some time."

Art therapy and short-term treatment

If the work of integration is equivalent to reshaping our psychic puzzles to fit all the necessary pieces, then art therapy challenges us to create that puzzle in a tangible way. A theory may suggest a particular outcome based on an educated guess, but it is only through experimentation that an extraneous variable makes itself known, serving to validate, disprove and/or revise our original thinking. Through a willing suspension of disbelief, creative acts allow for this element of the unknown; we accept, for a moment, we don't know everything, and are willing to try a new way of perceiving. This suspension allows us to watch a film, read a book, gaze at an abstract painting, or play a song and experience emotional resonance, which may be derived of fictional content, but nonetheless helps us solve real life quandaries.

In the context of art therapy, we might refer to these "extraneous variables" as sensations, metaphors, images and/or personal symbols that bubble up from the unconscious to deliver their own critiques of our conscious "self" theories. It is the responsibility of the art therapist to contain, assist, and mirror, in this fantastic "transitional space," what reconciliation lies between the client's inner and outer worlds (Winnicott, 1970). To meet this challenge, the art therapy student and working professional benefits from three things: knowledge of theory, an experiential understanding of its applications, and a mastery of implementation. Adhering to this philosophy, the content of this book was divided into three parts:

> *Part I*: Examines grief and attachment, including definitions and key terms, existing change and recovery models, a developmental framework, a bio–psycho–social–spiritual perspective, and a discussion of directive and non-directive art therapy approaches.

> *Part II*: Examines through the *art-based self-studies of art therapists* the intra-psychic journey of addressing the grieving process. Methods, procedures, and a discussion of themes are organized in an instructional manner for ease of replication.

> *Part III*: Examines through the implementation of *art therapy interventions with various populations* the observable journey of integration in the grieving process. Methods, procedures, and a discussion of themes are organized in an instructional manner for ease of replication.

According to its website, the American Art Therapy Association (AATA) represents more than 5000 professional art therapists across the globe (and others who hold the belief that the creative process involved in art making is healing and life enhancing). A survey conducted of its members in 2013 revealed over two-fifths (41.9%) of respondents work with "Mood or Anxiety Disorders," and "Posttraumatic Stress Disorder" was chosen by 30.7 percent of respondents. The American Psychological Association offers four "psychological effects" of mood disorders and PTSD: depression, generalized anxiety, survivor's guilt, and grief and loss. Additionally, risk factors for complicated grief, which is a prolonged, dysfunctional experience of grief, include being a woman, a history of mood disorders, low social supports, insecure attachment style, positive care giving with the deceased, and pessimistic temperament and personality correlates—all of which "suggests common underlying vulnerability" (Shear *et al.*, 2011). It is the argument of this author that the "underlying vulnerability" quite clearly relates to one's fundamental attachment dynamics, and this has predictive and possibly protective implications for the experience of grief.

Much of the psychotherapeutic literature consists of studies and case examples that have been conducted over a long period of time, and in private practice. But many art therapists working in institutional settings engage their clients on a short-term basis, due to the terms of their employment (per diem work, volunteer positions, or internships are typically limited in their scope), the nature of the setting (such as in acute care, hospice, rehabilitation centers, foster care programs, or transitional programs and residencies), or because the clients are ambivalent about engagement and have no external incentive to participate (such as in community-based programs, outpatient programs, and harm reduction programs). A short-term treatment model was selected for this reason.

Studies of brief interventions and short-term treatment models have been conducted in a wide range of healthcare settings, from hospitals and primary healthcare locations (Babor et al., 1994; Chick, Lloyd, and Crombie, 1985; Fleming et al., 1997; Wallace, Cutler, and Haines 1988) to mental health clinics (Harris and Miller, 1990). Because they are timely, focused, and client centered, short-term treatment models can quickly enhance the overall working relationship with clients and can be useful for addressing specific behavior change issues in treatment settings. Interventions administered in short-term treatment are usually structured and focused. Its primary goals are to raise awareness of problems and then to recommend a specific change or activity that moves a client towards a new conception and/or experience of their problems (in the context of this text, the experience of grief and loss, and related attachment disturbances).

Additionally, while scholarly in nature, this book provides its readers with hands-on activities for working with grief. It is my fantasy that when the art therapist working in an institutional setting is asked to create a "billable" treatment plan, he or she will be able to pull out this book and feel up to the task, fearing the auditors and regulatory bodies who are ignorant to the benefits of art therapy no more.

How to read this book

If you have picked up this book and perused the introduction, grief has likely touched you or your clients in some fashion. My recommendations for considering its contents are as follows:

> *If you are a student in training,* I ask you to consider your motives for exploring the topic of grief, and examine what unfinished business you may still harbor. I would encourage you to pay particular attention to Parts I and II, which will help frame your theoretical understanding and illuminate the processes of self-examination and discovery. This is essential to the teasing out of "what is ours and what was given to us," allowing the professional in training to become a better facilitator of this process for his or her clients.

> *If you are a working professional,* already you have a command of early developmental theory and have witnessed firsthand the effects of attachment disturbances in grief. I would invite you, however, to approach this book with a willingness to suspend pre-existing theoretical frameworks, and consider an integrated approach that expands upon them. Part II may be useful in processing any vicarious trauma or counter-transferential material, while Part III provides practical short-term treatment interventions.

> *If you are grieving* and are interested in creative approaches to healing, this text is intended to be a useful addition to your toolbox. Whether your loss occurred in the distant past, recent past, or is anticipated to occur in the near future, it is never too late or too soon to engage in this work. In confronting the task of rebuilding your life story, I would encourage you to pay attention to Parts I and II, which provide a helpful frame of

reference and examples of how others have navigated this path. Part III provides additional options for materials, methods, and procedures that may inspire. Please note, this book is intended to promote therapeutic practices but is *not* intended to replace therapy. I highly recommend seeking professional support as you embark on this journey.

References

Babor, T.F., Grant, M., Acuda, W., Burns, F.H., *et al.* (1994) 'A randomized clinical trial of brief interventions in primary health care: Summary of a WHO project.' *Addiction* 89, 6, 657–660.

Chick, J., Lloyd, G., and Crombie, E. (1985) 'Counseling problem drinkers in medical wards: A controlled study.' *British Medical Journal 290*, 965–967.

Fleming, M.F., Barry, K.L., Manwell, L.B., Johnson, K., and London, R. (1997) 'Brief physician advice for problem drinkers: A randomized controlled trial in community-based primary care practices.' *JAMA 277*, 13, 1039–1045.

Harris, K.B. and Miller, W.R. (1990) 'Behavioral self-control training for problem drinkers: Components of efficacy.' *Psychology of Addictive Behaviors 4*, 2, 90–92.

James, J. and Friedman, R. (2009) *The Grief Recovery Handbook, the Action Program for Moving beyond Death, Divorce, and Other Losses including Health, Career, and Faith.* New York: Harper Collins Publishers.

Lewis, C.S. (1961) *A Grief Observed.* New York: Harper Collins.

Shear, M.K., Simon, N., Wall, M., Zisook, S., *et al.* (2011) 'Complicated grief and related bereavement issues for DSM-5.' *Depression and Anxiety 28*, 2, 103–117.

Tolle, E. (2004) *The Power of Now: A Guide to Spiritual Enlightenment.* Novato, Canada: Namaste Publishing.

Wallace, P., Cutler, S., and Haines A. (1988) 'Randomised controlled trial of general intervention in patients with excessive alcohol consumption.' *British Medical Journal 297*, 663–668.

Winnicot, D.W. (1970) *Playing and Reality.* New York: Basic Books.

PART I

Theory

1

The Language of Grief

When There Are No Words

Briana MacWilliam

What you never get over

Many times, I have heard the expression, "Some things you never get over, you just learn to carry them." It's a phrase that rings both true and false for me. Yes, old patterns of relating affect the ways we interact with new people. And yes, some wounds cut so deep we are left with scarring. But there is a difference between climbing over something and/or dragging it behind you, and stopping to cut it up into itty-bitty pieces, cook it over a campfire and then eat it, so you can keep going, unencumbered. Sitting down to write this book, I found myself banging my head against the wall, trying to take a definitive position on whether or not there are some losses you just can't get over. Ultimately, the stand I decided to take is this: I don't know.

I don't know if grief is something a person will ever be rid of, or if it is something he or she will simply learn to carry. Or if it is something you think you've gotten over, and then it shows up again at your back door. The truth is, no one else can tell you either. Only you can answer that question for yourself. I can tell you from my own experience and the experiences of others, *loss* is something that will never go away.

And in that vein, here's another quote for you, "Attachment is the root of all suffering." I saw this as I was happily researching articles on attachment theory, looking for clinical support for this book. It stopped me in my tracks. There I was, with the aim of offering hope to grievers and clinicians alike, and Buddha had to throw a wrench in the works. At first, I took the meme as a personal criticism; "You're steering people towards suffering," it told me. But then I realized it was a thumbs up that I was headed in the right direction. After all, how can we overcome suffering—or learn to carry it, or cut it up into itty-bitty pieces—if we are unwilling to address it?

As an art therapist, I have been largely trained in the psychoanalytic tradition, which, in its modern configuration, is a humanistic clustering of theories aimed at examining the machinations of our biological drives, the ego and its relationship to early attachment "objects," and the development of a self-identity. While analysis has been criticized for being a horse of a different color, with no unifying vernacular or streamlined modus operandi (unlike behavioral sciences, which are often based on a single and uniformed model), I would argue its strength lies in this varied approach. Examining psychic phenomena—such as the experience of grief—from within numerous frameworks allows us to see alternate patterns and transfer our point of view, according to the needs of the individual (Pine, 1990).

But one need not accrue the student loan debt that I have to grasp the common thread throughout all of these theories, which is this: relationships are important. Chances are, you already knew that (because everybody knows that) but how they are important, and in what way for *each* and every individual, slips into a gray area that has kept many an analyst well fed and living on the Upper West Side (at least, in New York City). It is not my intention with this book to paint a black and white picture, or to suggest formulaic solutions, but to illuminate just how foggy it all is, and offer a small but steady nightlight.

The title of this chapter, "When there are no words," alludes to an experience of loss that shakes us to our very core. From our earliest beginnings, we form a sense of self through what are called "identifications," which is a fancy word for saying, "in relationship to others" (or more specifically, our perception of others). As infants, we are prompted to respond to a collection of sounds, and eventually learn that these sounds are called "words." The first word a child is encouraged to learn is his or her name, and hot on its heels, the use of a first person pronoun: "I," "me," "mine," "myself," etc. A mastery of these words allows us to think abstractly and thus identify with this concept of "self" in relationship to others (both animate and inanimate objects). Thus, we think we know who we are based on our affiliations and the things we own (literally and figuratively). This is when the ego—our thinking self—assumes its throne.

My last name, MacWilliam, is Scottish and it means, "son of William." The name, which has lasted for generation upon generation, exemplifies this defining of one's self in relation to (or in belonging to) another person. But what happens if we lose that person? What happens if I assume someone else's last name? What meaning does a name have then? What meaning does the "I" have, if I no longer have an identification to tell me? Who am "I" now?

Perhaps, I am without words. Without a name. But I still *am*. And I have experienced a shift in self-consciousness: I am not my thoughts, but my awareness of them. Albert Einstein referred to the "illusory sense of self" as an "optical illusion of consciousness." Spiritualist Eckhart Tolle assures us, however, "The recognition of illusion is also its ending. In seeing who you are not, the reality of who you are emerges by itself" (2005, p.28). I am not suggesting the only way to be your authentic self is to leave all your loved ones behind and live in isolation for the rest of your life. I am suggesting that the illusion grief creates—a feeling as if you cannot go on, or your life is irreparably damaged—is one that prevents you from inhabiting a more whole sense of self. It's true, you may never be the same; you might find ways to grow! You might also crash around butting up against whatever external people, places, and things help you recreate that illusion—until it dissolves again. And it will. Because, as I said before, loss is here to stay.

Six myths about grief

At a national conference for writers, I attended a workshop in which a presenter posed the question, "What is it about love that we can't get enough of?"

A woman in the audience raised her hand and said, "Love heals."

Immediately, I thought, "Why isn't that a bumper sticker?" Then my thoughts circled around the experience of grief—of love lost; a void that is not always felt in the physical sense, but in the absence of spirit. Sometimes loneliest of all when the lost love object is standing right next to you, a living reminder of what once was. "Love heals" is not a bumper sticker because when we think about love we cannot help but think about the pain the loss of it causes, and who wants to be reminded of *that* at every red light?

As a society, we do not know how to talk about or handle our grief. And this affects all aspects of life, even the most trivial. To cope, we develop myths about the appropriate ways to handle grief. There are many myths out there; some may be specific to an individual's family dynamic, while others might be reflective of cultural values, or some combination of the two. John W. James and Russell Friedman, founders of The Grief Recovery Institute, identify six most commonly held myths about grief in the Western world, and the negative impact they have on the bereavement process. In their book, *The Grief Recovery Handbook*, James and Friedman (2009) explore several scenarios to illustrate this point. Here are a few common phrases associated with each myth.

1. *Don't feel bad.* "Pull yourself together."

2. *Replace the loss.* "Let's go to the pet store tomorrow. I'll buy you a new puppy."

3. *Grieve alone.* "She just needs her space. She'll get over it."

4. *Just give it time.* "Time heals all wounds."

5. *Be strong for others.* "Gotta keep a stiff upper lip for your mother and your sister."

6. *Keep busy.* "If you wallow in here, you'll never get over it. Get back out there. Find something to do."

The problem with each of these myths is that they involve a form of repression and disregard of painful feelings that otherwise become stuck in the body, which can lead to significant diagnoses, such as anxiety and depression. This might also leave us feeling deeply disconnected from our inner life and vitality, resulting in a feeling of numbness, emptiness, and purposelessness. While it may be contrary to popular belief, I suggest the following instead:

1. Feel as bad as you do.

2. Don't replace the loss.

3. Find someone who shares your pain.

4. Take all the time you need to acknowledge the loss and take stock of its meaning.

5. Let others take care of themselves and/or know your limits.

6. Don't burn out on distractions.

Grief is the normal and natural reaction to loss of any kind, though we have been socialized to believe that these feelings are unattractive and disruptive to others. More than that, to be willing to grieve properly is to be willing to feel pain. The irony is that in an avoidance of pain, we only compound it. So why do we do it?

Somewhere along the line, these patterns of avoidance served a protective function. Through various interactions with his parents, a child learns certain thoughts and feelings are unacceptable and should be eliminated. Through the upheavals of grief, those repressed creative parts of the self are unearthed, offering an opportunity to finally express their contents, in order to become a whole person.

An understanding of the relationship between creativity and paradox helps illuminate this process. This is explored in more depth in the body of this text.

The nature of unfinished business: A bio–psycho–social–spiritual perspective

Life is full of losses. Some might be "little losses," as Kübler-Ross (1969) described them, while others make your whole life feel like the Titanic. And loss can take on many forms, such as the death of a loved one, a major transition, a romantic heartbreak, divorce, loss of a job, estrangement from a family member, loss of a friend, death of a pet, and so on. One might assume the nature of the loss defines the depth of your grief, and recent studies regarding violent death would support that assumption (see Chapter 3). But why might a mourner suffering the loss of a long-anticipated death of a family member caused by a slow-moving cancer display complicated grief symptoms, while the mourner of a violent and deadly attack on her spouse is able to pick herself up and move on after a "normal" period of grief?

It is the thesis of this text that the underlying mechanisms of grief are uniquely related to our earliest attachment models. Thus, often it is the nature of your *unfinished business* that defines the despair, qualifying each individual's grief as a distinctive experience, one that cannot be neatly tucked into specific stages or lumped into a population of mourners with a special *type* of loss.

James and Friedman (2009) describe grief as "the conflicting feelings caused by the end of or change in a familiar pattern of behavior" (p.3). Unfinished business can be thought of as "unfinished emotions attached to a living person with whom you have a less than fulfilling relationship" (p.9). If grief is like reaching out for someone who has always been there, and they are no longer there, then unfinished business is like reaching out for someone who has never been there for you, and *still* isn't—be he dead or alive.

To begin, let us examine four dimensions of experience including the physical, mental and emotional, social, and spiritual realms. Please keep in mind, these dimensions are inextricably intertwined, but sometimes it helps to consider the color of each woven thread in its own right when examining the larger tapestry.

What happens to us biologically when we grieve?

In its earliest forms, loss was *sensed* before it was articulated, defined by those awful moments of unbearable hunger, before your mother was able to feed and soothe you. It was also inevitably quelled by her smiling, cooing and caressing embrace, which assured you all was well with the world. In the present, loss rips open those pangs of our initial blissful fantasies and violent deprivations, shining a light on the nuances of those original attachment and bonding dynamics. It is a cell memory—as is the lost object of our affections—a part of our very bodily existence.

For example, according to neuro-psychiatrist Dr. Amen (2007), there are four phases of romantic attachment—attraction, infatuation, commitment, and detachment—each phase with its own chemical trigger. When we love someone, eventually, he will become imbedded in the limbic part of our brains (his smell, the touch of his skin, the sound of his voice, the beat of his heart, etc.). When we cannot interact with our love object as we are used to, that part of the brain becomes inflamed, looking for him. This inflammation is associated with low serotonin levels, which leads to depression, trouble sleeping, feeling obsessed, loss of appetite, and wanting to isolate ourselves. Additionally, a deficit in endorphins, which modulates pain and pleasure pathways in the brain, may be responsible for why we feel physical pain during a breakup. Your heart literally aches. The pathways in the brain associated with non-romantic attachments function in much the same way (Hass-Cohen and Findlay, 2015).

We attach ourselves to the relics of our partners because they function as "transitional objects." These physical items are popularly understood to be a stand-in for the missing loved one, like a teddy bear for a child who misses his or her mother. But they are symbols for not only the absent person, but *your version* of the absent person—the image you have of him in your head. The actual person was likely a close approximation, but your fantasies for the relationship were probably founded on whatever image of him you still cling to in your mind (Winnicott, 1970).

HOW DO PHYSICAL EXPERIENCES COMPLICATE UNFINISHED BUSINESS?

Our physical needs are a powerful force that demands immediate attention. Often, the pain of grief is unbearable and so we seek short-term escapes from it. These escapes are usually effective distractions because they are characterized by their ability to alter our physical experience of pain. Perhaps they simply numb the pain, or they might replicate the feeling of "oneness" that our love object provided, be it sex, affection, food, medication, drugs, alcohol, excessive exercise, mind-altering meditation practices, and the like (Fromm, 1956; Viorst, 1986). Such distractions only serve to perpetuate unfinished business because they prevent an acknowledgement of its existence. Like putting a Band-Aid on an infected wound and expecting it to heal.

It is also important to be aware of the physiological changes that occur in our bodies if the lost love object was a sexual partner. Both men and women experience chemical changes in their bodies that have a calming and stabilizing effect on mood through repeated sexual intercourse with the same person, which promotes healthy physiological function (in fact, having sex a minimum of three times per week can make you look ten years younger). Hormonal balance also plays a role, particularly for women (Amen, 2007). All of these physiological experiences serve to complicate our experience of grief.

What happens to us mentally and emotionally when we grieve?

I purposely did not divide "mental" aspects from "emotional" aspects because from a developmental perspective, their relationship is too tightly intertwined. If the physical, social, and spiritual realms of experience were the primary colors of red, blue, and yellow, mental and emotional aspects together would be a secondary blend, like purple, green, or orange.

James and Friedman (2009) are vehement in their assertions that grief is not purely a mental or "intellectual" problem: "Grief is a broken heart, not a broken brain. All efforts to heal the heart with the head fail because the head is the wrong tool for the job. It's like trying to paint with a hammer—it only makes a mess" (p.5). I would emphasize, however, that your emotions have a reciprocal relationship with your perceptions and cognitive decision making. Strong emotions, sometimes referred to as "affects," can be stimulated by significant loss, knocking your rational self off its throne. Thus, you are not always in your "right mind" when you are grieving (Stein, 2004). This can lead to the utilization of short-term escapes I mentioned earlier, which serve to temporarily stave off the emotions that fuel cyclical negative thoughts.

HOW DO MENTAL AND EMOTIONAL STRESSORS COMPLICATE UNFINISHED BUSINESS?

The problem with taking a purely intellectual approach to recovery is that though it may be well meaning, it could be unintentionally abusive and belittling to one's emotions. For example, if a person is suffering a bad breakup and a close friend says, "Don't feel bad, he was a jerk anyway. Plenty of fish in the sea." The observance of maltreatment and the individual's ability to find a new partner, while factually correct, are emotionally barren. They also indirectly criticize the griever for still loving someone that has been deemed unworthy, putting the griever in the position of feeling attacked and defending the lost love object, which is confusing and can lead to emotional isolation and withdrawal from social supports.

Another example of intellectualizing and rationalizing is the tendency to compare and minimize: "Well, I may be sad and alone, but at least I'm not down and out on the street." Again, while factually accurate, this attitude only serves to push the emotions you have *a right to feel and express* by the wayside, to remain ignored and unacknowledged. This is a function of internalized ideas about shame and "selfishness." Please take this to heart; it is *not* selfish to grieve, nor is it selfish to *move on*. Wolfelt (2014) makes this point most eloquently: "To honor your grief is not self-destructive or harmful, it is life sustaining and life-giving, and it ultimately leads you back to love again. In this way, love is both the cause and the antidote...it is a great gift that we can openly mourn our life losses." This is further illuminated in the "six myths about grief."

What defines a social context for grief?

There are three things that define a social context for grief: 1) how others react to you and your grief on an individual level, 2) socially accepted rituals for grieving in a group context, and 3) the political labels we assign the griever.

1. How others react to you and your grief on an individual level is deeply revealing of all personality constructs involved. How you generally respond to obstacles in life will likely reflect your response to significant loss, on an intensified level. For example, if you are quiet by nature, you may express grief quietly, while your brother prods, "Cry it out!" If you are naturally outgoing, you might express your grief openly, prompting your stuffy aunt to roll her eyes and harshly whisper, "Put a lid on it." If loved ones criticize your coping skills on a regular day, they will respond in equal measure to the intensity of your grief.

2. Socially accepted rituals for grieving in a group context can help or hinder your grief experience. There is a wealth of

research that supports the importance of ritual in creating a context of meaning. A funeral or similar ceremony is a time and place to express your feelings about death, thus legitimizing them. A funeral can also bring you closer to your social supports in a collaborative effort, which has been shown to aid in the surpassing of individual differences and conflicts (Hansen, 2009). Public acknowledgement and support also affirms that life goes on, and can serve to bring one back to his or her religious, spiritual, and/or philosophical beliefs in a positive fashion (James and Freidman, 2009; Matthews and Clark, 1998; Wolfelt, 2004).

3. The political labels we assign the griever depend upon the type of loss a person experiences. For example, there are many support groups and organizations centered around the circumstances of loss, such as suicide, murder, AIDS and other chronic illnesses, death of a child, military service, divorce, rape, substance abuse, and so on. Self-help groups centered around a type of loss not only serve you in your ongoing journey towards integration and recovery from grief feelings, but they help you acknowledge the myths about grief you may be unconsciously perpetuating, as you listen to someone describe the tricks he used to play in avoiding his feelings. Loss-specific support groups also provide a safe place in which to express yourself, because you anticipate an empathic response (James and Freidman, 2009; Jung, 2001; Maisel and Raeburn, 2008; Matthews and Clark, 1998; Wolfelt, 2004).

HOW DO SOCIAL STRESSORS COMPLICATE UNFINISHED BUSINESS?

1. Friends, family members, lovers, and other community members cannot help but project their own ideas about how to handle grief onto your situation. Because we are ill equipped as a society with knowing how to acknowledge, confront, and

process loss, your pain will inevitably conjure the echoes of *their* repressed pain and unacknowledged losses. This complicates grief because it illuminates pre-existing interpersonal dynamics that may have been left unresolved with *remaining* loved ones. Thus, the "six myths about grief" surface to unendingly irritate, exasperate, manipulate, cajole, bully, and/or persuade us away from our own personal experience and processing of grief (James and Friedman, 2009). This is, however, why grief is such an opportunity for transformation. Because it opens up the possibility for not only recontextualizing your life as it pertains to the lost love object, but also as it pertains to your *ongoing* relationships.

2. Socially accepted rituals for grieving may hinder and/ or complicate unfinished business, if it is experienced as a de-legitimizing, ostracizing, conflictual, and/or meaningless event. While everyone accepts a funeral is the appropriate time and place to express grief (even if your form of expression rubs a few the wrong way), it may be perceived as the *only* time and place in which it is appropriate, thus compartmentalizing and disqualifying the expression of those feelings in a different context. In the planning of a funeral, family members have to come together to divvy up the responsibilities. Inevitably, someone must be appointed or elected the leader and the rest must follow. More often than not, this is bound to cause conflict, stirring up those long ignored interpersonal dynamics, and for some, leading to feelings of being devalued and ostracized, which negatively impacts the "meaning making" aspect of the public ritual. Additionally, if the ritual or funeral is conducted in a religious manner that differs from the griever's beliefs, this can detract from the experience as well.

3. The problem with assigning labels to grievers is that the grievers may then develop a sense of identity surrounding

the loss, rather than integrate their feelings and move on from it. For example, "survivor" is a term typically used in a context of loss and bereavement, and while it is intellectually accurate it causes the griever to constantly revisit the circumstances of his or her loss. The griever may get caught up in defining himself and his pain, rather than in completing his unfinished business (James and Freidman, 2009). We might also include the word "veteran" in this discussion, as the word basically means "once a soldier always a soldier"; depending upon the solider's experience of military service, this could encourage an identity forever defined by trauma and warfare, and any attempts to revise that definition to be perceived as disloyal or dishonorable.

Additionally, while loss-specific self-help groups can be advantageous in the short term, in the long term, their infrastructures can become too rigid and potentially ostracizing. For example, Alcoholics Anonymous (AA) requires an admission of helplessness and the acceptance of a higher power (Jung, 2001; Maisel and Raeburn, 2008; Matthews and Clark, 1998). But what about the incurable atheist? Grievers are already segregated in our society. Defining identity by circumstance only serves to further isolate them, which impedes long-term solutions.

What happens to us spiritually when we grieve?

James and Friedman (2009) assert there are two distinct possibilities following loss: 1) regardless of the nature of the loss, your spiritual or religious faith is undamaged, or 2) your spiritual or religious faith may be shattered or shaken. On this topic, we must delineate between spirituality and religiosity. Virgina Satir (1988) described spirituality as "a pipeline to universal intelligence and wisdom through our intuition, which can be tapped through meditation, prayer, relaxation, awareness, the development of high self-esteem, and a reverence for life" (p.338). Maisel and Raeburn (2008, p.149) describe spirituality as:

> a more honest self-relationship, where the desire to be authentic replaces the idle hope to exert complete control...it means that you move on from an egoistic defensiveness...to an acceptance of the demands of personal responsibility...a leap from pride and isolation to mindfulness and connection to the larger whole.

In other words, spirituality is an existential leap towards taking responsibility for authoring your own life's narrative, and achieving a sense of meaning by sharing that narrative with others. Religiosity is an adherence to external tenets established by a group ethos and unquestioned tradition. To practice religious adherence without spiritual awareness is to absolve oneself of personal responsibility, and use external constructs as an auxiliary ego: "It's bad because the Bible says so," not because you know it to be morally wrong, based on personal principle.

When we experience loss we may question both our religious and spiritual convictions, and find ourselves asking "How?" and "Why?" questions. "How could God let this happen?" "Why me? Why now?" This speaks to a fundamental sense of helplessness and lack of control, in the face of loss. Blaming God and punishing Him/Her by withdrawing a belief in His/Her existence (if it was ever previously present) are common reactions. If you take the existentialist perspective, you are responsible for answering those questions for yourself. You could also consider the same notion in a more religious context: as much as God is an omnipotent force, He/She is also present in each and every one of us. In short, "God helps those who help themselves."

HOW DOES SPIRITUALITY COMPLICATE UNFINISHED BUSINESS?

In the context of loss, faith and religion can play a protective role in the healthy navigation of grief. For example, in a 1983 study of

92 families who had lost a child, 70 percent of the parents said their religious beliefs gave them comfort at the time of their child's funeral. A year later, 80 percent of the parents had found strength and solace in their religion, and 40 percent felt their religious commitment was actually *stronger* after the child's death (Matthews and Clark, 1998, p.25). But it is in a discerning examination of the word "stronger" that the spiritual complications for unfinished business become apparent. Wolfelt (2003, p.43) points out:

> Mistakenly, people may think that with faith, there is no need to mourn. If you buy into this misconception, you will set yourself up to grieve internally but not mourn externally. Having faith does not mean you do not need to mourn. It does mean having the courage to allow yourself to mourn.

While the respondents to the study above may have self-reported a stronger religious commitment, we must take into consideration the degree of personal insight into the underlying mechanisms of their faith: is it truly the result of spiritual integration, or of an exaggerated adherence to external structures in order to avoid internal pain?

When it comes to the benefits of spiritual and religious practices in dealing with grief, grievers and practitioners working with grievers must take into account "spiritual bypassing." Spiritual bypassing is a tendency to use spiritual and religious practices as a way to bypass or avoid dealing with emotional unfinished business. Welwood (2000) states, "While struggling to find themselves, many people are introduced to spiritual teachings and practices that urge them to give themselves up. As a result, they wind up creating a new "spiritual" identity, which is actually an old dysfunctional identity— based on avoidance of unresolved psychological issues—repackaged in a new disguise" (p.12). In this way, spiritual and religious teachings become a way to rationalize and reinforce old defenses, including and exemplified by the "six myths about grief."

Key terms and definitions

At this point, it may be useful to examine a few key terms that are used in everyday vernacular, but perhaps are not so clearly understood.

Attachment

Attachment is a deep and enduring emotional bond that connects one person to another across time and space (Ainsworth, 1973; Bowlby, 1969). Attachment theory in psychology originates with the work of John Bowlby, who defined attachment as a lasting psychological connectedness between human beings, which is motivated by a need for physical proximity, includes appraisals of the primary caretaker's availability, and is intended to stimulate "felt security" (Fonagy, 2001). Wallin (2007, p.1) identified three findings which he felt had "profound and fertile implications" for psychotherapy: 1) attachment relationships are the key context for development, 2) preverbal experience makes up the core of the developing self, and 3) the stance of the self towards experience (a person's innate predisposition or *temperament*) predicts attachment security better than the facts of personal history. In this text, a developmental view of attachment largely influenced the frame in which grief is discussed. Attachment styles are also discussed.

Loss

Loss is a broad term used to encompass any number of real-life experiences, the result of which leads to feelings of grief. It may include the death of a loved one, divorce, loss of a job, a big move and/or lifestyle adjustment, the ending of a romantic relationship, estrangement of a family member, the dissolution of a friendship, receiving a chronic and debilitating diagnosis, surviving an assault, and so on. Typically, what qualifies a loss event is that it negatively impacts our sense of emotional and mental wellbeing, and may even threaten our sense of self-efficacy and identity. In fact, loss can change our worldview entirely, leaving us feeling insecure in its wake.

Trauma

Trauma is the result of a profound loss. Traumatic events are extraordinary, not because they occur rarely, but rather because they overwhelm the ordinary human adaptations to life (Herman, 1990). "Trauma theory" is a relatively recent concept that emerged in the healthcare environment during the 1970s, mostly in connection with studies of Vietnam veterans and other survivor groups (Holocaust survivors, abused women and children, disaster survivors, refugees, victims of sexual assault). Post-traumatic stress disorder (PTSD) was added as a new category in the American Psychiatric Association official manual of mental disorders in 1980. Chronic post-traumatic stress disorder (C-PTSD) has also become an area of study for individuals with prolonged exposure to traumatic experiences. Trauma theory represents a fundamental shift in thinking from the idea that those who have experienced psychological trauma are either "sick" or deficient in moral character, to the reframe that they are "injured" and in need of healing. The impact of trauma is discussed throughout this text.

Grief, bereavement, and mourning

While some people tend to use the three words interchangeably, there is a difference. Grieving is a multifaceted response to loss, particularly to the loss of someone or something to which a bond was formed. Although conventionally focused on the emotional response to loss, it also has physical, cognitive, behavioral, social, and philosophical dimensions. In the context of this text, grief is understood to encompass one's reaction to any major loss that causes a disruption to the attachment system. Bereavement is a period of sadness following the loss experience; it refers specifically to the state of loss. Mourning is best understood as the way we express our grief in front of others. Religious practices and cultural customs (such as funerals, memorials, ancestral altars, etc.) are frequently the most obvious examples of this expression.

Complicated grief

Sometimes called "persistent complex bereavement disorder," complicated grief is differentiated from "normal" grief, in that the symptoms last for a prolonged period of time (from a diagnostic perspective, longer than six months), and severely impact the ability of an individual to resume healthy functioning and maintain a quality of life. Complicated grief is like being in an ongoing, heightened state of mourning that keeps you from healing. There are many similarities between complicated grief and major depression, but there are also distinct differences. In some cases, clinical depression and complicated grief occur together. Signs and symptoms of complicated grief may include: intense sorrow and pain at the thought of your loved one, focus on little else but your loved one's death or absence, extreme focus on reminders of the loved one or excessive avoidance of reminders, intense and persistent longing or pining for the deceased or absent, problems accepting the death or absence, numbness or detachment, bitterness about your loss, feeling that life holds no meaning or purpose, irritability or agitation, lack of trust in others, and inability to enjoy life or think back on positive experiences with your loved one.

Integration

In essence, integration is how we observe, understand, interact with, create, and communicate our life story. Integration has been defined through various stage theories, models of change and research methodologies, many of which you will find illuminated in this text. It is not finding the missing pieces of a puzzle—we are already whole and always have been—it is a reshaping of the puzzle to include all the pieces that need to fit.

References

Ainsworth, M.D.S. (1973) 'The development of infant–mother attachment.' In B. Cardwell and H. Ricciuti (eds) *Review of Child Development Research* (Vol. 3). Chicago: University of Chicago Press.

Amen, D. (2007) *The Brain in Love: 12 Lessons to Enhance Your Love Life.* New York: Random House Publishing.

Bowlby, J. (1969) *Attachment. Attachment and Loss: Vol. 1. Loss.* New York: Basic Books.

Fonagy, P. (2001) *Attachment Theory and Psychoanalysis.* New York: Other Press.

Fromm, E. (1956) *The Art of Loving.* New York: Harper & Row.

Hansen, M. (2009) *Collaboration: How Leaders Avoid the Traps, Build Common Ground, and Reap Big Results.* Boston, MA: Harvard Business Review Press.

Hass-Cohen, N. and Findlay, J.C. (2015) *Art Therapy and the Neuroscience of Relationships, Creativity, and Resiliency: Skills and Practices.* New York: W.W. Norton.

Herman, J.L. (1990) *Trauma and Recovery: The Aftermath of Violence—from Domestic Abuse to Political Terror.* New York: Basic Books.

James, J. and Friedman, R. (2009) *The Grief Recovery Handbook: The Action Program for Moving beyond Death, Divorce, and Other Losses including Health, Career, and Faith.* New York: Harper Collins Publishers.

Jung, J. (2001) *Psychology of Alcohol and Other Drugs: A Research Perspective.* Thousand Oaks, CA: Sage.

Kübler-Ross, E. (1969) *On Death and Dying: What the Dying Have to Teach Doctors, Nurses, Clergy, and Their Own Families.* New York: Scribner.

Maisel, E. and Raeburn, S. (2008) *Creative Recovery: A Complete Addiction Treatment Program That Uses Your Natural Creativity.* Boston, MA: Shambalah.

Matthews, D. and Clark, C. (1998) *The Faith Factor: Proof of the Healing Power of Prayer.* New York: Penguin.

Pine, F. (1990) *Drive, Ego, Object and Self.* New York, NY: Basic Books.

Satir, V. (1988) *The New People Making.* Mountain View, CA: Science and Behavior Books.

Stein, M. (2004) *Jung's Map of the Soul: An Introduction.* Chicago: Open Court.

Tolle, E. (2005) *A New Earth: Awakening to Your Life's Purpose.* New York: Namaste Publishing.

Viorst, J. (1986) *Necessary Losses: The Loves, Illusions, Dependencies, and Impossible Expectations That All of Us Have to Give up in Order to Grow.* New York: Simon & Schuster.

Wallin, D. (2007) *Attachment Psychotherapy.* New York: Guilford.

Welwood, J. (2000) *Toward a Psychology of Awakening: Buddhism, Psychotherapy, and the Path of Personal and Spiritual Transformation.* Boston, MA: Shambalah.

Winnicott, D.W. (1970) *Playing and Reality.* New York: Routledge.

Wolfelt, A. (2003) *Understanding Your Grief: Ten Essential Touchstones for Finding Hope and Healing Your Heart.* Fort Collins, CO: Companion Press.

Wolfelt, A. (2014) 'The capacity to love, the reason we grieve.' TAPS Magazine, 20, 3. Retrieved from http://www.taps.org/magazine/article.aspx?id=12513, accessed on February 27, 2017.

2

The Origins of Attachment

Briana MacWilliam

The origins of attachment

Attachment theory rests on two fundamental principles: 1) a well-functioning attachment relationship provides a secure base that optimizes autonomy and provides support and comfort under stress, and 2) attachment relationships inform the development of "internal working models," which are the basis for how we perceive and organize experience, like a script that is performed over and over again with new and various actors. Attachment figures are individuals to whom we seek proximity, from whom we resist separation, to whom we turn when in distress, and from whom we garner support and encouragement as we explore the world, engage in meaningful activities, and strive to master new challenges (Fraley and Davis, 1997). Loss of such a person creates a great disruption that is easily recognized as acute grief. Resolution of acute grief requires successful adjustment to far-reaching effects of the loss, both practical and psychological. Complicated grief occurs when resolution is impeded (see Chapter 3 for more detail).

Often, attachment and bonding are discussed interchangeably, but they are not one and the same. Neufeld and Mate describe attachment as "a force of attraction pulling two bodies toward each other." Attachment is at "the heart of relationships and of social functioning...[it is] the pursuit and preservation of proximity, of closeness and connection: physically, behaviorally, emotionally, and psychologically" (2004, p.17). Harville Hendrix describes attachment as a physical and spiritual yearning for the early symbiotic union of the womb. He uses the term "Eros" to describe it, a Greek word we equate with romantic love, but which originally had the broader meaning of "the life force" (1988, p.17). Sigmund Freud would describe such a force as a "libidinal drive." Simply put, attachment is motivated by an instinctual need to orient oneself, a turning towards the "other" in an attempt to make sense of the world and one's place in it.

In the pursuit of attachment, however, we are paradoxically driven towards a state of independence. Having blissfully enjoyed a sense of intimate "oneness" with our mothers for about the first 12 to 16 months of life, the advent of crawling and walking propel us towards a state of independence, a process Margaret Mahler called "separation individuation." A child's state of feeling both distinct from and connected to its mother has a profound impact on all later relationships. If a child is fortunate, he will be able to make clear distinctions between himself and other people, maintaining flexible boundaries that he can open or close at will (Hendrix, 1988). Mahler suggested that a child suffers greatly if this individuation process is not handled with care, leading to profound confusion about who one is: What is self and what is other? What is me and what is not me? Early arrestments in this time of life can make for a complicated and intensely painful experience of grief in adulthood.

Less widely known, but perhaps more easily understood, Neufeld and Mate identify six "ways of attaching," ascending from the more simplified to complex:

1. *Senses.* The emphasis is placed on physical proximity. A child needs to feel attached through smell, sight, sound, or touch.

2. *Sameness.* Usually in evidence by toddlerhood, the child seeks to be like those he or she feels closest to.

3. *Belonging and loyalty.* To be close to someone is to feel possessive of him or her, and to be obedient and faithful to that person.

4. *Significance.* Needing to matter to the person we are closest to, and seeking to please him or her and win his or her approval.

5. *Feeling.* Marked by a seeking to be emotionally open and vulnerable with an attachment figure; a willingness to share one's feeling states.

6. *Being known.* Usually observable by the time a child enters school, this is when a child seeks to share his or her secrets and insecurities in the hopes of being completely seen, heard, and embraced, in spite of them.

Essentially, Neufeld and Mate describe the dynamics of intimacy: the integration of both good and bad feelings—loving someone, even though they have disappointed you, and continuing to love yourself, when you have disappointed someone else—which allows for the vulnerable experience of more complex emotions, and enhances one's capacity to think and learn. Integration also happens to be the work of grief, the ability to make sense of what we've lost. One's conscious reflection upon the mysteries of one's unconscious processes and pressures is essential to this work.

Bonding

Bonding characterizes the nature of the emotional connection established between the child and the "other" he or she has attached him or herself to, usually whoever is established as the primary caregiver—often the mother. Feeding is the first collaborative effort in which both mother and child engage, thus it has a significant impact on the quality of the earliest bond formed. But an adequate exchange of nutrients alone does not a healthy emotional connection make.

While Abraham Maslow's hierarchy of needs originally suggested food was our first and foremost priority on the road to self-actualization, Harry Harlow (who worked with Maslow) later determined contact-comfort and attachment to be primary when it comes to cognitive and emotional development, after conducting controversial social isolation experiments on infant monkeys. Furthermore, Renee Spitz studied infants in orphanages who were adequately fed and held but failed to bond with their caretakers, which resulted in "a failure to thrive." Spitz thus determined *bonding* to be an important aspect of attachment, and a benchmark of development that allows for growth on all spectrums.

WHAT MAKES FOR A HEALTHY BOND?

If the feeding experience is a pleasurable one—consisting of snuggles, smiles, caresses, and cooing—the infant is able to establish a sense of security and begin to formulate a mental picture of a loving mother, described by object relations theorists as a "libidinal object" (Winnicott, 1970). As previously discussed, this will help the child develop and later sustain a sense of self in his mother's absence; he has achieved what Margaret Mahler would describe as *object constancy*, which is similar to developmentalist Jean Piaget's concept of *object permanence*. The child comes to understand that the mother is a separate individual with her own identity, and continues to exist whether or not he can perceive her physical presence. The child has found a "compass point" from which to properly orient himself psychologically and emotionally (Neufeld and Mate, 2004).

Achieving an optimal, healthy bond is reliant upon a variety of factors, both internal and external. Edith Jacobson felt that biology and experience mutually influenced each other and continue to interact throughout development. She also emphasized *affective perception*: because experience is subjective, there is no such thing as an objectively good mother, only mothering that *feels* good to a particular baby (Tyson and Tyson, 1990). This raises the issue of *temperament* and resulting *styles of attachment*.

Temperament

When the temperament of the babe and the disposition of the mother are in sync, they are considered "attuned." Temperament is a term used to describe a child's innate disposition, as evidenced by observable behaviors. Thomas, Chess and Birch began the classic New York longitudinal study in the early 1950s regarding infant temperament, by rating infants on nine temperamental characteristics. Ultimately, they found the infants fell into one of three major categories: the easy child, the difficult child, and the slow-to-warm-up child (1968). They found these attributes to exist across cultures, and determined about 65 percent of children fell into one of these three categories (the rest had temperaments that were not so distinctly determined).

Mary K. Rothbart (Rothbart and Hwang, 2005) defines temperament as individual differences in reactivity and self-regulation that manifest in the domains of emotion, activity, and attention. She identified three underlying dimensions of temperament, using factor analysis on data from 3- to 12-month-old children: surgency/extraversion (the degree to which a child is generally happy, active, and enjoys vocalizing and seeking stimulation), negative affect (the degree to which a child is shy and not easily calmed), and effortful control (the degree to which a child can focus attention, is not easily distracted, and employs planning).

Jerome Kagan and his colleagues (2007) studied the temperamental category of "reactivity" in infants ages 14–21 months. Children with high reactivity experienced intense fear to novel events, and children with low reactivity were minimally fearful. Intervening family experiences were shown to mediate the infants' "expected profiles" by age five. Those that remained highly reactive at age five, however, were at higher risk for developing anxiety and conduct disorders. Parents and family members who were able to compensate for the child's initial high or low reactivity allowed for the infant's innate disposition to change and improve.

Furthermore, Solomon Diamond described temperaments based upon characteristics found in the animal world: fearfulness, aggressiveness, affiliativeness, and impulsiveness. H. Hill Goldsmith and Joseph Campos used emotional characteristics to define temperament, originally analyzing five emotional qualities: motor activity, anger, fearfulness, pleasure/joy, and interest/persistence, but later expanding to include other emotions (Zentner and Bates, 2008).

The ongoing list of theorists and supporting research for temperament speaks to the importance of its acknowledgement and its impact on the bond between mother and child. When mother and child are mismatched in temperament, it can lead to difficulties in attachment and misperceptions of characterological "disturbances" in the child—a mistake, if unchecked, that could lead to actual disturbances, through *projected introjects*.

For example, if an introverted child is born into an extroverted family, he may be perceived as depressed and withdrawn. Similarly, if an excitable and physically active child is born into a calm and more sedentary family, he or she may be perceived as hyperactive and distractible. If the parents and family members deliver and reinforce (project) either of these depreciative messages (introjects) frequently enough, the child may come to identify with (internalize) these misinterpretations as his own truth. This creates a psychic dissonance between what self psychologists would describe as the "true self" and "false self," leading to feelings of low self-esteem, anxiety and rigidity, meaninglessness and alienation, what is sometimes called a "narcissistic wound." Heinz Kohut's treatment for these early childhood injuries is *vicarious introspection*, which suggests the only way to truly understand a person is from within his or her subjective experience, via empathy. However, if left untreated, such disturbances can lead to significant obstacles when confronted with the task of grieving later in life, particularly in the realm of relationships (Mitchell and Black, 1995). How can one go about the task of reshaping of one's perception of reality, in order to integrate one's self into it, if one does not have an essential sense of self to begin with?

The evolving bond
Styles of attachment

Our style of attaching from an early age impacts our relationships later in life. For example, Allan and Barbara Pease (2009) attribute the adult's romantic inclinations to his childhood "love map." A "love map" is a blueprint that contains the things we think are attractive determined by the brain's hardwiring and a set of criteria formed in childhood. Similarly, Freud believed a child's amorous interest in his parents fixes his attraction to later lovers. His repressed memories and emotions remain in pristine condition, to be exhumed at a later date, unchanged. Freud wrote, "The unconscious, at all events, knows no time limit" (as quoted in Lewis, Amini, and Lannon, 2000). Indeed, many scientists believe love maps begin forming around age six, and are firmly in place by age 14 (Lewis *et al.*, 2000). For the purposes of this chapter, I will expand the definition of one's love map to include all attachment relationships, romantic and otherwise.

Mary Ainsworth is best known for devising "the strange situation" to study attachment and separation/reunion behavior between mothers and their infants. Mary Main (Main, Kaplan and Cassidy, 1985) expanded on this work, examining the connections between parenting styles and the resulting attachment styles of their children, in a longitudinal study (Wallin, 2007). The results of Main's study were categorized into four pairings:

1. *Autonomous parenting typically leads to a secure attachment style, in the child.* When parents display an autonomous parenting style, they are flexible enough to stand both inside and outside their experiences as they are having them; they are reflective, responsive, thoughtful, and in control of their emotions. Their children, in infancy, demonstrate a flexible balance between seeking comfort in proximity to mother, and exploring on their own. They are warmly welcoming to their mothers in a "strange situation," and are easily soothed post absence. When Main observed these children at six years of age, she found them to

be emotionally open, able to find solutions to scenarios of separation, would create realistic and healthy family drawings (with figures close together and arms outstretched, making contact), and enjoyed looking at a family Polaroid.

2. *Dismissive parenting typically leads to an insecure/avoidant attachment style, in the child.* The dismissive parent minimizes the importance of love relationships, has a lack of recall of childhood experiences, and idealizes problematic relationships. This parent is typically emotionally constricted and dismissing of feeling states and bids for emotional and/or physical contact.

In infancy, this parent's child engages in exploration to the exclusion of attachment behaviors, avoids mother to prevent feeling rejected or overwhelmed by intrusive behaviors, emotional expression is limited to investment in play objects, and the child is seemingly oblivious to mother's return in a "strange situation." When Main observed a child like this at six years of age, the child appeared emotionally restricted and sullen, and could not find solutions to scenarios of separation. Family drawings had dissociated figures that were far apart with no arms, and/or floating in the air with stereotypical happy faces. The child also refused to look at or engage with a family Polaroid.

3. *Preoccupied parenting typically leads to an insecure/ambivalent (sometimes called "insecure-anxious") attachment style, in the child.* Preoccupied parents are deeply concerned about their own attachment relationships, discouraging of independent strivings in the child (to the point of enmeshment), are deeply anxious and fearful of abandonment, and swamped by the effects of their childhood. They are inhibited in their capacity for recall, reflection, and to be fully present. For the child, avoidance is over-regulation of affect, ambivalence is under-regulation, resulting in hyper-reactivity.

In infancy, Main observed the child focuses only on the mother, clinging and angrily resistant one minute, then passively helpless the next. The child is anxiously preoccupied with mother's whereabouts and inconsolable upon her return, unable to explore. At six years of age, Main observed these children to have intense expressions of need and anger. Solutions to separation scenarios were both rewarding and punishing (e.g. buy the parents flowers, then hide their clothes). Figures in family drawings were very large and very small, very close together, and featuring vulnerable, intimate parts of the body. Reactions to a family Polaroid were deeply absorbed and disturbed, setting off tics, and anxieties about being abandoned.

4. *Unresolved parenting typically leads to a disorganized (sometimes called "anxious–avoidant") attachment style in the child.* Unresolved parents have experienced trauma and/or losses that were unresolved. Most important was not the experience they endured, but the way they'd integrated it into their understanding. Notably, the degree to which the experience lay unresolved impacted the degree to which their child became disorganized. In infancy, children of unresolved parents displayed bizarre, overtly conflicted, dissociated, or inexplicable behaviors. This was the result of a breakdown in the attachment system: the child has an inherent push to attach to someone that is simultaneously a threat and frightening.

At six years of age, Main observed these children to be inexplicably afraid and unable to do anything about it. When presented with separation scenarios, they fell silent, were too disturbed to respond, predicted catastrophic outcomes, or became disorganized in language and behavior. Upon reunion with their parents, children displayed parentified behaviors—either caretaking or punitive and controlling—in order to maintain proximity, while dealing with the threat the parents posed. Family drawings included skeletons, dismembered body parts, or figures scratched out. When presented with a Polaroid, they became wordless, irrational, or distressed.

THE RELATIONSHIP BETWEEN PARENTING STYLES AND ATTACHMENT STYLES

In laymen's terms, as adults, we set ourselves up by finding relationships that confirm our early models, even when these patterns are not in our own self-interest. For example, in a romantic relationship, the person with an ambivalent attachment may need to be with his or her partner all the time to gain reassurance. To support this perception of reality, they choose someone who is isolated and hard to connect with: "See? If I didn't hound him all the time, he'd *never* express his feelings or show me affection." The person with a model of avoidant attachment has the tendency to choose someone who is possessive or overly demanding of attention, from whom he or she constantly needs to escape: "See? I *have* to be distant, otherwise her constant hounding would suck me dry." These cyclical patterns leave one in a constant state of grief over lost and/or failed relationships. They also render us susceptible to complicated grief, particularly in the event of death and/or severe trauma.

Implicit versus explicit learning and attachment

These theories would seem to suggest that we spend our whole adult lives reliving our childhood dramas, like a song stuck on repeat. But this supposition is flawed for two reasons. First, memory is not a thing. Your heart is an object but the pulse it generates is a physiological event; it occupies no space and has no mass. Second, memory is not only mutable, but the nature of the brain's storage mechanisms dictates that memories must change over time (Lewis *et al.*, 2000). Our love maps are determined at the crossroads of implicit versus explicit learning. Lewis *et al.* (2000, p.103) state:

> The physiology of memory determines the heart of who we are and who we can become…the plasticity of the mind, its capacity

to adapt and learn, is possible only because neuronal connections can change... The stability of an individual mind—what we know as identity—exists only because some neural pathways endure.

Explicit learning encodes memories of events including autobiographical recollections and discrete facts. This is commonly described as our conscious perceptions. However, there is a wealth of learning human beings absorb without being consciously aware of it; this is implicit learning. We tend to give greater credence to explicit knowledge of facts, but this is misplaced, as evidenced by distorted eye-witness accounts, and those small moments of, "Huh, I remember it differently."

For example, Mr. Underwood suffered catastrophic damage to his hippocampus, destroying his explicit memory and leaving him perpetually living in the present. Researchers taught Mr. Underwood to braid, a skill he did not have prior to suffering brain damage. After he had mastered it, researchers asked him if he knew how to braid. He replied, "No," a truthful statement from his perspective. But when three strips of cloth were placed in front of him, he wove them together without hesitation.

When it comes to engaging in relationships, overwhelmingly, it is this mysterious, implicit learning mechanism—our unconscious knowledge—that tends to take charge. If your parents have a dysfunctional relationship, this will produce implicit schema, planting an erroneous generality in a child's brain. Your unconscious knowledge "distills but does not evaluate" how applicable the early lessons of family life are to the larger adult world. Recall, Hendrix pointed out that a person's composite imago image only etches certain data "onto a template," without interpretation. This appears detrimental, because a child, in the absence of understanding his love map in the context of its conception, might grow up to make poor decisions in love. However, it also creates an opportunity for the adult to *re*contextualize his love map with the help of mature experiences.

In other words, as an adult, you might act childish at times, but you are no longer a child. Parts of you have grown and matured in spite of those wounds you still carry, and those mature parts provide you with the tools required to achieve personal insight. Insight allows for change. And change allows for the revision and integration of maladaptive patterns. And that will guide you through the quicksand of grief.

The essential artist
Where talk therapy alone falls short

I've described the grieving process as an opportunity for the "revision" of attachment disturbances several times, but what exactly does that mean? A reasonable person might assume analyzing pivotal moments in childhood will resolve his troubles, turning talk therapy into "a treasure hunt for the explicit past." Autobiographical memories are useful, but "explicit memory is not a shrine" (Lewis *et al.*, 2000). People rely on the rational mind to solve problems, and are naturally baffled when it proves useless to effect emotional change (Lewis *et al.*, 2000).

Recounting a timeline of your past alone will not navigate you out of these muddy waters. You have to engage in relationships, see what comes up *in the present*, and be able to withstand the discomfort of when your wires cross with your partner's—long enough, at least, to determine the origin of the conflict, and whether or not it is rectifiable. Keep in mind, those wires *can* change, but not when left alone in isolation. And not if you only talk about it. Talk therapy alone falls short for three reasons:

1. *Most talk therapies are ego based, which means they rely on your conscious mind to have insight.* But insight alone is passive, it doesn't change patterns, merely allows for the *possibility* of change. Because it is partly unconscious, your *true self* is by nature unknowable in its entirety, and thus you cannot think and talk your way to wholeness. Yet the thinking self is

obsessed with remaining in control and struggles to accept what it does not understand. If given free reign, it will spin around in passive, insightful circles rather than allowing an intuitive, implicit awareness to become a transformative *libidinal* force.

2. *Because most talk therapies are ego based, they are ill equipped to provide affective learning experiences.* Affective experiences are those that stimulate us physically and emotionally. Emotions are always connected to the body because sensations are the first form emotions take, and are often expressed through the body (such as with anxiety). Affective learning thus becomes *meaningful* learning, which is essential to mental and emotional growth. This in turn bolsters the ego in a positive way, making it more flexible and better able to hold opposing ideas at the same time, which allows for abstraction, complex emotions, and a deeper understanding of those emotions. Unless therapy activates and/or acknowledges the body in some fashion, it won't be affectively effective (Maisel and Raeburn, 2008; Ogden, Minton, and Pain, 2006; Satir, 1988; van der Kolk, McFarlane and Weisaeth, 1996).

3. *The language of talk therapy is subject to "the reductionism of words."* It is easiest to understand this concept when comparing the language of the ego to the language of the unconscious, which is one of somatic experiences, images, symbols, and metaphors. We go to therapy to examine pressures and motivations we experience but do not understand, using ineffective tools. It's like trying to repair a leaky roof with a hammer that has no head. Or going to a foreign country where you do not speak the language and make no effort to learn it, but still expect one day to wake up fluent. Words are essential to integrating unconscious symbols into our conscious awareness, but we must first be willing and able to set aside the thinking-mind (sometimes referred to as "monkey mind"), which communicates

in a language of words, in order for unconscious material to emerge, through an entirely different form of communication (Robbins, 1994; Welwood, 2000).

Creative arts therapists have been working with a language that appeals to the unconscious and provides affective experiences for years. It is a language of the body, metaphors, images, and symbols. Arthur Robbins (1994, p.4), author of *A Multi-Modal Approach To Creative Art Therapy*, states:

> Symbol and image have become the inner codifications of my experiences. They defy the reductionism of words as they hold and mirror the complexity of my early attachments, link past to present, and point to my future. As organizer of my past, this world of symbol and image holds my polarities of hate and love, bad and good.

It is the vocabulary of creativity that allows for ego flexibility and the revision of seemingly unchangeable patterns of loving and mourning.

References

Fraley, R.C. and Davis, K.E. (1997) 'Attachment formation and transfer in young adults' close friendships and romantic relationships.' *Personal Relationships 4*, 2,131–144.

Hendrix, H. (1988) *Getting the Love You Want: A Guide for Couples.* New York: St. Martin's Griffin.

Kagan, J., Snidman, N., Kahn, V., Towsley, S., Steinberg, L., and Fox, N.A. (2007) 'The preservation of two infant temperaments into adolescence.' *Monographs of the Society for Research in Child Development 72*, 2, 1–95.

Lewis, T., Amini, F., and Lannon, R. (2000) *A General Theory of Love.* New York: Random House Publishing.

Main, M., Kaplan, N., and Cassidy, J. (1985) 'Security in infancy, childhood, and adulthood: A move to the level of represenatation.' *Monographs of the Society for Research in Child Development 50*, 1–2, 66–104.

Maisel, E. and Raeburn, S. (2008) *Creative Recovery: A Complete Addiction Treatment Program That Uses Your Natural Creativity.* Boston, MA: Shambalah.

Mitchell, S. and Black, M. (1995) *Freud and Beyond.* New York, NY: Basic Books.

Neufeld, G. and Mate, G. (2004) *Hold on to Your Kids: Why Parents Need to Matter More Than Peers.* New York: Ballantine Books.

Ogden, P., Minton, K., and Pain, C. (2006) *Trauma and the Body: A Sensorimotor Approach to Psychotherapy.* New York: W.W. Norton.

Pease, A. and Pease, B. (2009) *Why Men want Sex and Women Need Love.* New York: Broadway Books.

Robbins, A. (1994) *A Multi-Modal Approach to Creative Art Therapy.* London: Jessica Kingsley Publishers.

Rothbart, M.K. and Hwang, J. (2005) 'Temperament and the development of competence and motivation.' In A.J. Elliot and A.C. Dweck (eds) *Handbook of Competence and Motivation.* New York: Guilford Press.

Satir, V. (1988) *The New People Making.* Mountain View, CA: Science and Behavior Books.

Thomas, A., Chess, S. and Birch, H. (1968) *Temperament and Behavior Disorders in Children.* New York: New York University Press.

Tyson, P. and Tyson, R. (1990) *Psychoanalytic Theories of Development: An Integration.* New York: Vail-Ballou Press.

van der Kolk, B., McFarlane, A., and Weisaeth, L. (1996) *Traumatic Stress: The Effects of Overwhelming Experience on Mind, Body, and Society.* New York: Guilford.

Wallin, D. (2007) *Attachment Psychotherapy.* New York: Guilford.

Welwood, J. (2000) *Toward a Psychology of Awakening: Buddhism, Psychotherapy, and the Path of Personal and Spiritual Transformation.* Boston, MA: Shambalah.

Winnicott, D.W. (1970) *Playing and Reality.* New York. Routledge.

Zentner, M. and Bates, J. (2008) 'Child temperament: An integrative review of concepts, research programs and measures.' *European Journal of Developmental Science 2,* 1/2, 7–37.

3

Complicated Grief

Briana MacWilliam and Dina Schapiro

A brief history

Complicated grief occurs when an individual experiences prolonged, unabated grief. The neural mechanisms distinguishing complicated grief from non-complicated grief are unclear, but hypothesized mechanisms include both pain-related pathways, related to the social pain of loss, and reward-related pathways, related to attachment behavior (O'Connor *et al.*, 2008). Four principles of attachment functioning are helpful in understanding complicated grief (Shear *et al.*, 2007):

1. Attachment relationships provide support for healthy physical, mental, and emotional functioning.

2. Mental representations of attachment figures shape our expectations for caregiving.

3. Stress activates a need to be close to our attachment figures and receive loving attention, while inhibiting our desire to explore and seek novel stimulation.

4. Among adults, providing care is valued equally or even more so than receiving care.

Acute grief and the process of integrating the loss usually occur naturally and without the need for active effort. Once the loss is integrated, yearning and searching diminish, grief intensity declines, and there is often a deep feeling of connection to the deceased. Individuals suffering from complicated grief fail to experience reprieve from pain and longing. Caught in a loop of prolonged grief symptoms and complicating psychological and/or life problems, time seems to stand still, frozen at the time of the loss or death. Complicated grief also appears most prevalent in individuals engaging in grief-related avoidance behaviors, such as refraining from activities they enjoyed performing with the lost or deceased attachment figure, because of the fear of intensifying sadness and yearning for the person (Shear *et al.*, 2011). For brief periods, this may be helpful in mediating acute distress, but over a prolonged period it could lead to a dysfunctional turning away from reality (see "Six myths about grief," in Chapter 1).

The concept of pathological mourning has been around since Sigmund Freud's seminal paper "Mourning and Melancholia," but it began receiving formal attention more recently. In the 1980s and 1990s, researchers noticed that antidepressant medications relieved such depressive feelings as sadness and worthlessness but did nothing for other aspects of grief, such as pining and intrusive thoughts about the deceased. The finding suggested that complicated grief and depression arise from different circuits in the brain (Hughes, 2011).

Two models of grief have been hypothesized: a detachment model and a reunion model (Bowlby, 1980). In *the detachment model*, the grief emotion is believed to play a role in the acceptance of the reality of the death and therefore assist in recovery from the loss. In *the reunion model*, the grief is a form of protest against separation from the deceased, and serves to promote reunion with the lost person, not detachment. Freed and Mann (2007) hypothesize that if the detachment model is correct, the pangs of grief would occur with reduced activity in the brain's reward system over time, as the acceptance of the loss leads to detachment. If the reunion model is correct, the pangs of grief would continue to occur simultaneously with reward activity in the brain, when exposed to "cues of the deceased" (such as memories, photos, etc.), motivating reunion with the deceased.

In 2008, Mary-Frances O'Connor and a team of researchers scanned the brains of women who had lost their mother or a sister to cancer within the past five years, and compared the results of women who had displayed typical grief with those suffering from complicated grief. While both groups displayed activity in neural pathways related to pain, for those with complicated grief their reward centers lit up as well. This is the part of the brain that lights up on imaging scans when addicts look at photographs of drug paraphernalia and when mothers see pictures of their newborn infant. This doesn't necessarily mean women are addicted to their feelings of grief, but rather they still feel attached to the deceased. This is significant, because it not only supports the hypothesis that attachment activates reward pathways, but also suggests complicated grief is a result of maladaptive attachment patterns and behaviors (the thesis for this text). It also suggests the detachment model may apply to "normal" grief (a slow process of acceptance and integration of the loss), and the reunion model applies to complicated grief (a paradoxical experience where both the pain and pleasure pathways of the brain are activated in grief, because you still feel attached).

Finally, in 2009, Holly G. Prigerson published data collected from nearly 300 grievers she had followed for more than two years. By analyzing which of some two dozen psychological symptoms tend to cluster together in these participants, she finally devised the criteria for complicated grief, which were added to the *Diagnostic and Statistical Manual of Mental Disorders* (DSM) in 2013. Sometimes called "persistent complex bereavement disorder," complicated grief is differentiated from "normal" grief in that the symptoms severely impact the ability of an individual to resume healthy functioning and maintain a quality of life, similar to depression.

Although some symptoms of grief and depression overlap (fluctuations in mood, appetite, activity level, sleep patterns, etc.), the two conditions are thought to be distinct. Grief is tied to a particular event, for example, whereas the origins of a bout of clinical depression are often more obscure. Antidepressants do not ease the longing for the deceased that grievers feel. So in most cases, treating grieving people for depression is ineffective. However, grief may trigger a major depressive episode, in the way that other major life stressors do. Whittling out the differences between normal grief, complicated grief, and depression reflects the fundamental dilemma of psychiatry: mental disorders are diagnosed using subjective criteria. Any definition of where normal ends and abnormal begins will be the object of individual opinion (Hughes, 2011).

Scope

In the general population, the prevalence of complicated grief in those who have experienced loss of significant others has been reported as 2.4 percent to 6.7 percent, which is relatively low, but prevalence is higher among those bereaved by violent death. For example, in a sample of 126 respondents bereaved by the Bosnian conflict, 31 percent expressed complicated grief; in a sample of 704 respondents bereaved by the September 11th attacks, 43 percent expressed complicated grief; and in a study of 128 respondents bereaved by suicide, 75 percent expressed complicated grief symptoms (Kersting *et al.*, 2011). Rynearson (2001) claimed that violent death comprised three Vs—violence, violation, and volition. These interfere with acceptance of death, because of the intentional use of physical force or power, threatened or actual, against oneself, another person, or a group or community (Norris, 1992). Furthermore, violent death caused by disaster is sudden and unexpected, and sometimes includes additional trauma, such as facing life-threatening situations and witnessing damaged corpses. Raphael, Martinek, and Wooding (2004) called these bereavements "traumatic loss," which is more stressful, complicated, and difficult to recover from than the bereavement of natural death.

The factors affecting the prevalence of complicated grief are considered to be comorbid mental disorders, lack of readiness for the death, difficulty in making sense of the death, high level of negative appraisal about the self and others, and various social stressors. Post-traumatic stress disorder is, in particular, considered to contribute to the development of complicated grief by suppressing function of the medial prefrontal cortex and the anterior cingulate cortex, which works at facilitating the normal mourning process, when grief distress is activated and interrupts acceptance of death (Nakajima *et al.*, 2012).

For example, Murphy *et al.* (2003) studied PTSD among bereaved parents following the violent deaths of their 12- to 28-year-old children in a longitudinal prospective analysis. This study examined the prevalence of PTSD among parents bereaved by the violent deaths of their 12- to 28-year-old children. A community-based sample of 171 bereaved mothers and 90 fathers was recruited by a review of Medical Examiner records and followed for two years. Four important findings emerged: both parents' gender and children's causes of death significantly affected the prevalence of PTSD symptoms. Twice as many mothers and fathers whose children were murdered met PTSD full diagnostic criteria, compared with accident and suicide bereavement. Symptoms in the re-experiencing domain were the most commonly reported. PTSD symptoms persisted over time, with 21 percent of the mothers and 14 percent of the fathers who provided longitudinal data still meeting criteria two years after the deaths. Parents who met criteria for PTSD, compared with those who did not, were significantly different on multiple study variables (Murphy *et al.*, 1999).

Although research has confirmed that violent losses can exacerbate grief reactions, few investigations have explored underlying mechanisms. Why is it harder for some, and not others? In this study, the authors used a dataset on bereaved spouses and bereaved parents at 4 and 18 months post loss to examine the mediating effects of self-worth and worldviews (benevolence and meaningfulness beliefs). Individuals bereaved by violent causes had significantly more PTSD, grief, and depression symptoms at 4 and 18 months post loss than persons bereaved by natural causes. Moreover, self-worth—not worldviews—mediated the effects of violent loss on PTSD and depression symptoms cross-sectionally, and PTSD symptoms longitudinally. Findings underscore that self-views are a critical component of problematic reactions to violent loss (Mancini *et al.*, 2011). And where do self-views originate? In our earliest attachment relationships.

Attachment hunger and addiction

To the extent that the individual is able to achieve a sense of mental and emotional separation from the early mother–child union, he will experience his "true self." But if he never fully achieved this, his feeling of wholeness will depend on someone else. If this is the case, his parents probably provided a distorted mirror, bent by their need to see him as an extension of themselves, or how they wanted to see him, steering him towards any one of three insecure attachment styles we discussed in Chapter 2: ambivalent (sometimes called "anxious"), avoidant, or disorganized (sometimes called "anxious–avoidant").

For most adults, the "someone else" is no longer mother; you may have broken from that feeling of "oneness" with her long ago. But when faced with the prospect of losing or breaking away from whomever you found to replace that vacancy, a terrible desperation and panic ensues. This, Halpern (1982) refers to as "attachment hunger," which he believes is akin to an addict's need for a fix. It is composed of "powerful primitive feelings that are lodged deeply in your musculature and the reactions of your body's chemistry" (p.31). In his book *Love and Addiction*, Stanton Peele concludes that "the addicting element is not so much in the substance, but in the person who is addicted" (Peele and Brodsky, 1975 as cited by Halpern 1982, p.7). Indeed, according to the recent brain research mentioned above, attachment experiences are felt in the reward centers of the brain associated with addiction—but also, potentially, with pain. Why might that be?

If attachment theory has taught us anything, it is that children are naturally predisposed to love and affection; it is an innate, bio–psycho–social–spiritual capacity. However, as John Bradshaw asserts, "A child's healthy growth depends on someone loving and accepting him unconditionally. When this need is met, the child's energy of love is released so he can love others" (1990, p.39). If a child is not loved for his essential self, his egocentricity sets in, and his true self never emerges. The child may become arrested emotionally at any number of phases of development, and grow up to harbor what Bradshaw calls a "wounded inner child."

These arrestments may be the result of the three insecure parenting styles we discussed in Chapter 2: dismissive, preoccupied, and unresolved. These parenting styles in their extreme forms manifest in abusive and traumatic experiences, such as sexual abuse, physical abuse, emotional abuse, and the proliferation of toxic shame, reinforced by educational, social, and cultural institutions. The wounded inner child contaminates the adult's life in a variety of ways, including co-dependency, offender behaviors, narcissistic disorders, trust issues, acting out or acting in behaviors, magical thinking, intimacy dysfunctions, "nondisciplined" behaviors, addictive and/or compulsive behaviors, thought distortions, and feelings of emptiness, apathy, and depression. Treating the inner child involves addressing the "original pain," and allowing yourself to *feel* the repressed feelings in the present. Bradshaw states that:

> Grief involves the whole range of human emotions. The original pain is an accumulation of unresolved conflicts whose energy has snowballed over time. The wounded inner child is frozen because there was no way he could do his grief work. (1990, p.76)

According to Bradshaw, the work of grief involves reclaiming your inner child at every phase of development, and includes such interventions as letter writing, and guided meditations.

With respect to the addictive and/or compulsive contaminates, Bradshaw concludes that all addicts (including those addictively attached to unhealthy relationships) have been emotionally abandoned, and to a child "abandonment is death." Basic survival needs associated with attachment are "my parents are okay" and "I matter." If the messages and behaviors the parents deliver to the child do not reflect this sentiment, there is a pathological turning inwards and distorting of the self, to somehow make this true: "Dad is in a rage and beat me again. I must have done something wrong to provoke it. I must be bad. I must be worthless." In this scenario, the father is preserved as a "good" figure, and to receive punishment is evidence that one matters enough to be punished.

For the purposes of this discussion, let's consider attachment hunger a "feeling addiction" (including *all* of the aforementioned dimensions: rage, "awfulizing," sadness, grief, and love) that has the added potency of an ingestive addiction, because it directly and quickly activates the most primal parts of our brains associated with pleasure, pain, and survival. To put it more succinctly, it is my belief that *all addictions* are secondary to attachment hunger. And attachment hunger is a precursor to complicated grief.

Art therapy and addiction

In Chapter 2, we discussed how faulty internal working models built upon internalized projected introjects interact with our attachment styles to replicate unhealthy patterns of relating (notably, anxious–ambivalent individuals and avoidant individuals are usually drawn to each other for this reason). When this happens, feelings of grief and loss could potentially be perpetual, if the underlying mechanisms of basic security and attachment issues are left unacknowledged and unaddressed. In other words, anxious–ambivalent individuals have to learn the benefit of setting boundaries and being alone, and avoidant individuals have to learn the benefit of giving and being in relationships. These lessons, once learned, may be the only things capable of buffering the unavoidable losses and grief feelings we all must endure.

Art therapy is particularly useful in this endeavor because it works towards healing self-splits, and can substitute for the rituals that are involved in the addictions that distract us from them. The art is the object, so whatever the addict projects onto the drug can instead be projected onto the art. Let's say a man's mood and affect state have been stimulated by a loss and/or grief feelings that are unconscious and/or preverbal, causing diffuse feelings of anxiety and depression seemingly "out of nowhere." He turns to his drug of choice to feel something different or to be distracted, which is truly an attempt to feel nothing in the face of his powerlessness. When an addict starts to make art he or she is being trained to make choices for themselves: "Why did you choose that color? What draws you to this material? Where would you like to place this collage piece on the page?" The art therapist is teaching the addict to have a sense of self-awareness. And when one is more conscious, one's reality testing improves and the individual starts realizing the choices available. Imagine a client who smooshes pastels all over the paper and art space, says "That's fun," and walks out of the room without washing his hands. Then imagine the same patient, months later, returns, does same thing, but then before leaving the room realizes, "Oh, I have to wash my hands." It's an expansion of conscientiousness.

The impact of trauma and abuse

To understand the impact of trauma and abuse on attachment and grief, we must take into consideration the severity of the abuse and/or trauma, and at what phase of development it occurred, especially with respect to neurological development. The innate capacities for a child to grow and thrive in all dimensions are dependent upon the availability of an average expectable environment, when the timing is right (Tyson and Tyson, 1990). If stress and hypervigilance are prolonged and unrelenting, leading to such conditions as C-PTSD, it may affect neurological changes that could have a lasting and debilitating impact on learning (King-West and Hass-Cohen, 2008). This may lead to failures in achieving certain developmental goals, resulting in low self-esteem, loss of efficacy, and poor affect regulation—all of which have the potential to manifest in adulthood as the contaminants identified by Bradshaw, above.

From the art therapist's perspective, we may see evidence of developmental progress and arrestments in children's art-making process and products. Victor Lowenfeld (1957) used the term "art education therapy" to describe the therapeutic and educational use of art with children, and provided us with a normal trajectory of children's drawings, what we can expect to see at certain ages, based on bio–psycho–social–spiritual development. These stages move from scribbling (18 months to 3 years), to basic forms (3–4 years), to human forms (4–6 years), to the development of a visual schema in which scenes of the environment are depicted (9–12 years), followed by increasing levels of realism (adolescence and beyond). Elizabeth Koppitz (1968) offers in-depth methods of interpreting the significance of children's human figure drawings, Burns and Kaufman (1970) help us understand children's Kinetic Family Drawings (KFD), and DiLeo (1983) offers interpretive suggestions for drawing directives such as "draw a man in a boat" (examining cognition), "draw a house" (examining affect) and "draw a tree" (examining self image). It was Williams and Woods (1977) who coined the term "developmental art therapy" and gave name to the many other clinicians examining how art expression can be used to recognize and understand how cognitive and developmental abilities evolve in the child ("normal" and/or otherwise impaired) and the adult (Malchiodi, Kim, and Choi, 2003).

The list of various arts-based assessments goes on, and there are many existing texts that explore this topic, beyond the scope of this book. Additionally, emerging paradigms in this area attempt to address disorders of extreme stress that are resistant to change, like C-PTSD, through the frame of attachment and neuroscience. Hass-Cohen and

Findlay (2015) expand upon this in their Art Therapy Relational-Neuroscience (ATR-N) approach, which is described in greater detail in Chapter 5.

In sum, the impact of trauma and abuse on grief feelings relies upon the severity of the trauma and abuse, the context in which it occurred, the age at which the trauma and abuse occurred, the resulting attachment style, and a comprehensive understanding of underlying developmental factors (pertaining to both the age at which a developmental arrestment might have occurred, and the developmental phase in which the client currently examines it).

References

Bowlby, J. (1980) *Attachment and Loss. Vol III. Loss, Sadness and Depression.* New York: Basic Books.

Bradshaw, J. (1990) *Homecoming: Reclaiming and Championing your Inner Child.* New York: Bantum Books.

Burns, R.C. and Kaufman, S.H. (1970) *Kinetic Family Drawings (K-F-D): An Introduction to Understanding Children through Kinetic Drawings.* New York: Brunner/Mazel.

DiLeo, J.H. (1983) *Interpreting Children's Drawings.* New York: Brunner/Mazel.

Freed, P.J. and Mann, J.J. (2007) 'Sadness and loss: Toward a neurobiopsychosocial model.' *American Journal of Psychiatry 164,* 1, 28–94.

Halpern, H. (1982) *How to Break Your Addiction to a Person.* New York: Bantam Books.

Hass-Cohen, N. and Findlay, J.C. (2015) *Art Therapy and the Neuroscience of Relationships, Creativity, and Resiliency: Skills and Practices.* New York: W.W. Norton.

Hughes, V. (2011) 'Shades of grief: When does mourning become a mental illness?' *Scientific American,* June 1. Available at www.scientificamerican.com/article/shades-of-grief, accessed on November 16, 2016.

Kersting, A., Brähler, E., Glaesmer, H. and Wagner, B. (2011) 'Prevalence of complicated grief in a representative population-based sample.' *Journal of Affective Disorders 131,* 1–3, 339–343.

King-West, E. and Hass-Cohen, N. (2008) 'Art therapy, neuroscience and complex PTSD.' In N. Hass-Cohen and R. Carr (eds) *Art Therapy and Clinical Neuroscience.* London: Jessica Kingsley Publishers.

Koppitz, E. (1968) *Psychological Evaluation of Children's Human Figure Drawings.* New York: Grune & Stratton.

Lowenfield, V. (1957) *Creative and Mental Growth.* Third edition. New York: Macmillan.

Malchiodi, M., Kim, D., and Choi, W. (2003) 'Developmental art therapy.' In C. Malchiodi (ed.) *The Handbook of Art Therapy.* New York: Guilford Press.

Mancini, A.D., Prati, G., and Black, S. (2011) 'Self-worth mediates the effects of violent loss on PTSD symptoms.' *Journal of Traumatic Stress 24*, 1, 116–120.

Murphy, S.A., Braun, T., Tillery, L., Cain, K.C., Johnson, L.C., and Beaton, R.D. (1999) 'PTSD among bereaved parents following the violent deaths of their 12- to 28-year-old children: A longitudinal prospective analysis.' *Journal of Traumatic Stress 12*, 2, 273–291.

Murphy, S.A., Johnson, L.C., Wu, L, Fan, J.J., Lohan, and J. (2003) 'Bereaved parents' outcomes 4 to 60 months after their children's deaths by accident, suicide, or homicide: A comparative study demonstrating differences.' *Death Studies, 27*, 39–61.

Nakajima, S., Masaya, I., Akemi, S., and Takako, K. (2012) 'Complicated grief in those bereaved by violent death: The effects of post-traumatic stress disorder on complicated grief.' *Dialogues in Clinical Neuroscience 14*, 2, 210–214.

Norris, F.H. (1992) 'Epidemiology of trauma: Frequency and impact of different potentially traumatic events on different demographic groups.' *Journal of Consulting and Clinical Psychology 60*, 409–418.

O'Connor, M.-F., Wellisch, D.K., Stanton, A.L., Eisenberger, N.I., Irwin, M.R., and Lieberman, M.D. (2008) 'Craving love? Enduring grief activates brain's reward center.' *NeuroImage 42*, 2, 969–972.

Peele, S. and Brodsky, A. (1975) *Love and Addiction*. New York: Taplinger Publishing.

Raphael, B., Martinek, N., and Wooding, S. (2004) 'Assessing traumatic bereavement.' In J.P. Wison and T.M. Keane (eds) *Assessing Psychological Trauma and PTSD*. Second edition. New York: Guilford Press.

Rynearson, E.K. (2001) *Retelling Violent Death*. New York: Taylor & Francis.

Shear, K., Monk, T., Houck, P., Melhem, N., *et al.* (2007) 'An attachment-based model of complicated grief including the role of avoidance.' *European Archives of Psychiatry & Clinical Neuroscience 257*, 8, 453–461.

Shear, M.K., Simon, N., Wall, M., Zisook, S., *et al.* (2011) 'Complicated grief and related bereavement issues for DSM-5.' *Depression and Anxiety 28*, 2, 103–117.

Tyson, P. and Tyson, R. (1990) *Psychoanalytic Theories of Development: An Integration*. New York: Vail-Ballou Press.

Williams, G. and Wood, M. (1977) *Developmental Art Therapy*. Baltimore, MD: University Park Press.

4

The Impact of Culture and Community

Briana MacWilliam, Anne Briggs, Maya Rose Hormadaly, and Dana George Trottier

Cultural influences

Culture and grief

A white, middle-class, female student of mine approached me one day with a clinical concern. She worked primarily with black children of varied ethnic backgrounds, ages 11 to 13, in an urban, school-based setting. Her client was a young girl whose father had passed away the previous year. In a recent art therapy session, the normally defensive and reticent little girl had finally opened up to my student, describing the events of her father's funeral. In particular, she noted feeling overwhelmed and fearful of the dramatic, emotional outbursts of her aunties. One auntie had even flung herself on the coffin, requiring several male family members to tear her off of it. My student's concern was that the young girl had created outlandish memories as a way of using fantasy to dissociate herself from the painful feelings of her father's loss. She feared this might impede the little girl's ability to successfully navigate the grieving process.

I smiled softly, touching my student's hand, "You've never been to a black funeral, have you?" Indeed, she hadn't.

In an article entitled "The difference between white funerals and black funerals" a black, South African, male author offers an anecdotal account of the ways in which white people and black people grieve. The nuances he describes are hard to measure and qualify through empirical research and study, but are frequently observed and appreciated through the frame of humor.

> The first time I attended a white person's funeral, I thought I had landed on another planet. The service was meant to start at 9am and by 8:45am everyone was seated, all 27 of us. At promptly 9am, the organ started and everyone rose. Besides the priest, three other people spoke for about three minutes each. Around 9:30am, things were wrapped up and the family proceeded to the crematorium while we went outside to the lawn and grabbed some sandwiches. By 10:15am I was back at my desk at work as if nothing had happened.
>
> Oh no, not our funerals... The first big event on the day of the funeral is when the casket is brought out of the house and the mourners can fully appreciate it in its glory. There's always that aunt who takes out a hanky, dabs at her eyes and murmurs approvingly, "At least my uncle's child is going to rest inside a beautiful 'house'. It must have cost at least 80k." Towards the end of the whole rigmarole comes the most dramatic part, the viewing of the body. There is always some woman—a cousin of the deceased, thrice removed—who waits until everyone has seen the body before she approaches. She's already wailing at 200 decibels by the time [she approaches] the front, and then she truly opens her voice box and emits bloodcurdling screams that seem to part the roof of the Lord's house, before she collapses at the feet of the casket stand and is promptly whisked away. The most curious thing about her is that her grief tends to miraculously dissipate and she's usually spotted later in the "after-tears" tent, gyrating with a Smirnoff in her hand (Ngcobo, 2015).

Importantly, the tone in which this author examines cultural influences over grieving processes is somewhat sarcastic. This raises the important issue of understanding the group ethos when participating in the rituals of grief, as opposed to one's personal grieving process; there might be cultural norms for ethnic groups and how they grieve, but each individual will have their own relationship to and opinion of that cultural norm.

Perhaps it was presumptuous of me to assume the little girl had better reality testing than my student gave her credit for, because one cannot assume *all* black funerals (let alone this little girl's father's funeral) involve displays of emotion that, in comparison to white funerals, appear "outlandish." Even my choice to use the term "black" as opposed to "African–American" was a conscientious one, because not all black Americans think of themselves as African, and not all Africans are black. On the other hand, to use the term "black" may also be perceived as (once again) stripping a populace of their cultural and ethnic heritage. "Black," in this context, refers to a specific phenotype, as it is understood in a racist American perspective. But take what we might call a "black American" and place him in certain countries in Africa, and he might be considered "white" because of his American ethnicity.

National identities can also impact the ways in which we perceive grief and loss. I was walking past various retail shops in New York City, accompanied by a Jewish Israeli friend and veteran. He kept staring at the Memorial Day signage and shaking his head when sales clerks, positioned at the entrances of these shops, would try to hand him a flyer and say, "Happy Memorial Day!"

"You seem upset," I prompted.

"In Israel, Memorial Day is a solemn occasion. A siren goes off and everything just stops. Even the cars in the street. People just get out in the middle of an intersection and share a moment of silence. War isn't happy. Death isn't happy. And it's not an occasion for a 40-percent-off discount."

In this section, I have provided examples of how important it is to examine grief in the context of culture, but these are by no means the only comparisons that can be made. An awareness of cultural norms for the rituals of grief is essential to ethical and responsible clinical practice, lest we make erroneous interpretations. This is particularly important for the art therapist and clinician in his or her role as a gatekeeper of services within institutions.

Culture and attachment

It's worthwhile to mention the influence of culture over the socialization methods of parents in dealing with their children, which impacts the way children learn how to attach and grieve. In this context, *culture* is defined as the intersection of one's socially assigned gender role, racial and ethnic identity, socioeconomic status, religious beliefs, national identity, and the physical products and observable manifestations of those things. Most of us are socialized to use culture (or certain aspects of it) as a cue for perceptions about temperament, sexuality, intelligence, athletic ability, aesthetic preferences, and so on.

For example, a white, middle-class, American child may be encouraged to "cry it out" as a way of promoting self-regulation (Erikson, 1980, pp.59–60), and conforming to a democratic culture that "insists on self-made identities" (Erikson, 1980, p.99). Their healthy development therefore depends upon "a certain degree of choice, hope for an individual chance, and a conviction in freedom of self-determination" (Erikson, 1980, p.99). Any loss of identity, however, exposes the individual to childhood conflicts. Erikson points out the neuroses among men and woman during WWII, who could not stand the displacement of their careers and the other special pressures of war, as an example of this (Erikson, 1980).

Additionally, we must consider the intersections of race, class, and gender in the formation of healthy attachments, and one's reaction to the inevitable loss of those attachments. Pressure to conform, according to Orbe's co-cultural theory, encourages minorities to adopt a variety of verbal and nonverbal communication practices, such as "mirroring" dominant appearances and language styles. They may also cognitively rehearse in extensive preparation, prior to interacting with dominant groups, and/or censor themselves. It is as if they have to create not only one, but two (if not more) "false selves" in order navigate everyday life (Allen, 2004).

Culture impacts relationships in a variety of ways, particularly for minority groups who must contend with the persistent standards of a dominant group. The chapter contributions in Part III of this text are intended to provide an overview of specific populations and their experiences of grief. As a matter of practice, I would encourage the art therapist and practicing clinician to *always* research the cultural influences of the population he or she works with, including his or her own.

Paradigms in working with diversity

Paradigms in working with diversity are ever changing and evolving. The psychologists of the multiculturalism movement wanted to challenge the Euro–American cultural values and norms found in traditional psychotherapy approaches, which rarely addressed issues of power, privilege, and social context. This multicultural approach would give "meaning to minority and majority group identities as rooted in the context of particular social (gendered and racialized) interactions" (Tummala-Narra, 2013). And while it is important to investigate the cultural norms of the population you work with, we must also avoid the notion that once we have learned enough "facts" we are "culturally competent." To assume so is the equivalent of slapping a label on someone: "I've read all there is to know about you and where you come from, so now I can comfortably put you in this box, having fulfilled my ethical duty."

This is not to demean researching particular cultures or to dissuade someone from doing their due diligence. Each and every art therapist should be well informed. However, as I mentioned above, there might be cultural norms for ethnic groups and how they grieve, but each individual will have their own relationship to, and opinion of, that cultural norm. Learning all there is to know about every culture on the planet is not only an impossible task, but an unnecessary one. In working with diversity, it is more important to adhere to guiding principles that show us how to access our essential humanness in a sensitive, honest, and respectful way, while being aware of our own cultural influences and contexts.

Tummala-Narra (2013) offers an approach that builds on existing psychoanalytic contributions, such as self-examination, indigenous narrative, language and affect, social oppression, and cultural identifications. Her approach consists of five elements:

1. *Self-examination.* Explore the effects of historical trauma and neglect of sociocultural issues in psychoanalysis on present and future psychoanalytic theory and practice.

2. *Indigenous narrative.* Recognize clients' and therapists' indigenous cultural narrative, and the conscious and unconscious meanings and motivations accompanying these narratives.

3. *Language and affect.* Recognize the role of contest in the use of language and the expression of affect in psychotherapy.

4. *Social oppression.* Attend to how the client's and therapist's experience of social oppression and stereotypes of the other influence the therapist, the client, and the therapeutic process and outcome.

5. *Cultural identifications.* Recognize that culture itself is dynamic, and that individuals negotiate complex, intersecting cultural identifications in both creative, adaptive ways, and self-damaging ways, as evidenced in the use of defense.

To truly be culturally competent, we need to balance an appreciation and validation of the differences among us, with the "common forces of our humanity," in equal measure. Additionally, in their text, Ethnicity and Family, McGoldrick, Giordano and Pearce (1996, p.7) warn that "It is only when the exclusion of outsiders becomes primary to group identity that one's group identity reflects something dysfunctional— namely a negative identity: defining oneself as a part of a group that excludes others."

The beliefs and behaviors—of both the art therapist and the client—regarding grief are shaped by factors, including gender, race, ethnicity, political views, economic status, geographic region, religion, sexual orientation, physical appearance, disabilities, and age. As art therapists we must be mindful that a group whose characteristic response to illness is different from the dominant culture is likely to be labeled "abnormal." McGoldrick *et al.* (1996) cite many studies demonstrating how people differ along the following lines, specifically:

- their experience of pain

- what they label as a symptom

- how they communicate about their pain or symptoms

- their beliefs about its cause

- their attitudes towards the helpers (doctors and therapists)

- the treatment they desire or expect.

Lastly, it is important not to rely on the false assumption that art is a "universal language" (Moon, 2000). Symbols and metaphor may be the language of the soul and the unconscious, but their shape and meaning are influenced by our cultural contexts. And it is the art therapist's ethical responsibility to deepen their understanding of their own cultural prejudices and assumptions.

Art therapy and community

Collective mourning: Grief as motivating connection

COLLECTIVE MOURNING

In the "Culture and grief" subsection above, I referenced a conversation I had with a friend and Jewish Israeli veteran. He went on to publish his own article regarding his experience of collective mourning, which he refers to as "parallel mourning." I have included a quote from his article here, as an introduction into this topic:

> Americans, as a nation, don't mourn their soldiers. While military families might mourn the loved ones they lost, there is no national camaraderie, no shared language of loss, no parallel mourning. But then I experienced the anniversary of 9/11. It was a somber day. The air felt different outside. There was a weight to people's movement. American flags were hanging outside stores and apartments. There was a memorial service on almost every channel. Every name of every victim was read out loud. Why did Americans seem to mourn the victims of 9/11, but not the soldiers who died in Iraq and Afghanistan in the resulting war? Was it the proximity of the attack? Was it the realization that any American could be killed in a terror attack in the United States? The questions loomed large as I experienced the anniversary of the September 11 attacks, the day that—as a nation—America mourns. (Bezalel, 2014)

The answers to the questions Bezalel raises may be varied, but I would argue that the posing of the questions is of greatest significance. When you have an individual asking questions about collective norms is when you begin to see healing transformations in those norms.

Art therapy, in particular, is an effective intervention when healing from communal trauma and grief. For example, Fitzpatrick (2002) studied a group of female Bosnian refugees living in Australia who were struggling with significant attachment ruptures:

> To find home—a feeling of belonging in a known social and geographic space—is fundamental to our sense of who we are. For refugees, many of whom have experienced war, oppression, and poverty, the need to seek an experience of home is a primary yearning. (p.151)

Whether or not these women had faced problems with their earliest attachments, their sense of security in the world was undoubtedly shaken by the war in Bosnia. Together they had lived through a horrific experience that involved rape, imprisonment, destruction, and death—all of which were carried out in the "efforts to create an ethnically pure state" (p.151). After their attachments with their homeland were suddenly severed, they were left trying to recreate some sort of stability in an alien land. Fitzpatrick explained how art enabled those who were touched by the trauma to approach themselves, each other, and the world with fresh eyes:

> Art offers the maker as well as the viewer an opportunity to look at and experience the world in a new way, and to be challenged, moved, stimulated, and soothed. Ultimately, art explores what it is to be human. (Fitzpatrick, 2002, p.152)

Furthermore, Fitzpatrick also found that the art gave the participants of her study a safe distance from their pain—a "veil of denial" that let them face memories in tolerable ways without being overly flooded with feeling (Howard cited by Fitzpatrick 2002, p.153). In guiding these women on a creative journey back through their war-torn pasts, Fitzpatrick observed how art therapy empowered them not only to revisit but also reconstruct their individual traumatic experiences.

GRIEF AS MOTIVATING CONNECTION

Art's healing potential reaches far beyond the personal. Research has shown that offering art therapy interventions not just to individual clients but also to broader communities can lead to social action and transformation (Kapitan, Litell and Torres, 2011). Kapitan *et al.* assert that "community" can be interpreted in various ways but always involves looking beyond a single life and seeking to influence a broader system:

> "Community" in art therapy usually refers to the surrounding social environment of the individuals and groups with whom art therapists practice. For some social activist art therapists, however, the community itself is the "client" by being the primary focus of intervention. Art therapy on the macro level of practice may be defined as the purposeful design of therapeutic or transformative arts interventions directed toward community and organizational needs. A characteristic approach is to form collaborative partnerships with community organizations that have a social advocacy mission. (2011, p.65)

More interest in using art to effect widespread change has led to the development of participatory action research (PAR), a methodology that calls upon community members to co-design and co-conduct research studies so that they closely fit the community's needs and goals. Instead of an outside researcher assuming he or she knows what will benefit the community, the community participates in assessing itself and devising a plan to progress towards its goals.

Kapitan *et al.* (2011) witnessed how a PAR intervention significantly strengthened a Nicaraguan community's sense of empowerment, capacity, and equity in sustainable ways. Reflecting on the outcomes of their project, they encouraged art therapists across the world to broaden our vision and see both the therapeutic *and* transformational potential of our work:

> [This] cross-cultural collaboration conceptualizes creative art therapy as an emancipatory process for strengthening the development of the whole person—psychoeducational, spiritual, relational, and political—that exerts a positive transformational impact on a person's family, community, and oppressive societal structures. (Kapitan *et al.*, 2011, p.71)

One particular example of community building was the World Trade Center Children's Mural Project (WTCCMP), an extensive endeavor facilitated by art therapist Marygrace Berberian that included 3100 children's self-portraits. In the days following 9/11, Berberian sensed that children across the city were expressing a deep need "to symbolically rebuild the Twin Towers, to rebuild what was destroyed" (Levy *et al.*, 2002, p.107). Driven to respond, she developed an art directive with concrete guidelines so that schoolteachers could present it to hurting children without doing harm. The project was embraced by young people throughout New York City, as well as those living in 14 other states and 22 countries. As the collaborative art piece developed, Berberian witnessed firsthand how art making infused a time of mourning with hope and strength:

> The capacity to express oneself through line, color, and form is a rebirth process. Art is a recreation of past representations significant to the artist in the moment. Creativity allows for describing, building, and reconfiguring an injured object so mourning can begin. People need to keep alive what is lost and destroyed so they can begin to let it go on their own terms. (Levy *et al.*, 2002, p.107)

When offered a safe space, simple instructions, and basic art materials, children who felt powerless were given the opportunity to join together and creatively channel healing to both themselves and their city. Each child's unique self-portrait added strength to the mural's visual declaration of resilience and peace—a declaration that was stirring in the hearts of minds of people across the world.

Overall, while art undoubtedly can foster positive change within an individual, it also has the potential to support larger communities in need of healing and growth. Fortunately, helpers and healers around the world passionately believe in positive change, and have dedicated their lives to working towards that end.

Intergenerational transmission of trauma and grief

Recent longitudinal research suggests that those with significant trauma histories have increasing insecure attachment styles. Not only do insecure attachment styles inhibit life-giving relationships, but they may also "impede the development of effective strategies for regulating negative affect and coping with stress" (Ogle, Rubin and Siegel, 2014, p.329). Sadly, trauma survivors often face years of struggle due to intense conscious and/or unconscious anxiety about the very thing they need to survive: close human connections. Survivors of acute trauma are not the only ones who suffer. Larsson (2012) explains how parenting plays a vital role in an infant's development of a sense of self and others, suggesting that inadequate or absent caregiving leads to long-term consequences (p.10) and potential intergenerational transmission of grief and trauma affects.

How one perceives death (or loss), both of her loved ones and that of herself, will ultimately shape her experience of life and love. Parkes (2006) points out the cross-generational effect of unprocessed grief stating that "bereavement in adult life reflects and, to some extent, repeats the experience of earlier losses and gives rise to grief, both for the person lost and for earlier losses" (p.135). Given the cross-generational passage of loss, bereavement patterns and attachments styles have been reinforced and solidified. Cross-generational trauma, therefore, is a perpetuation of maladaptive attachment styles.

In the following subsection, co-author and contributor to this text, Maya Rose Hormadaly, has offered her story as anecdotal support for the use of expressive arts therapies in the transmission of intergenerational grief and loss. While this text is primarily focused on the specific modality of art therapy, Maya describes this process as achieved through drama therapy. The interplay between images, art making, script-writing, role-play, and performance all work in tandem, however, to give a creative voice to the experience of intergenerational grief, in multiple modalities.

Maya Rose's story: The motherless daughter integrates a "good enough" mother

My mother did not speak much of her mother. During the silences that plagued my mother's constant laughter, a void lingered from above her, above us, threatening to consume everything. This void dangled above her through most of her life, a constant reminder of the shadow of her own mother that could destroy everything offhandedly in a moment, even from her years of absence in the physical world. I could tell when my mother's face was being poisoned by this fear. It was the left corner of her mouth that would tilt downward at first, then her mouth would quiver and I would know that her mother had come yet again to visit.

"Your mother was crazy, wasn't she?" I asked my mother when I was 11, on a mundane afternoon in the supermarket. She looked around to see if anyone was listening, looked me straight in the eyes, and said bluntly, "She was wonderful." Not many stories were told about my grandmother; only that she was wonderful, hilarious, and brilliant. I wondered how such a wonderful being could hold such dark powers over my mother. Over us.

My mother was fixated on assuming her role as my mother. As her only girl, I was assigned the role of having a corrective mother–daughter experience, even if she herself was playing the role of mother this time. Any gaps and insecurities my mother experienced from her childhood seemed to be overcompensated with me. I was destined to become the first "fixed" female in a lineage of hurt women. So she wove us together, and I, recognizing her fragility, tied the strings tighter, terrified of the power I knew I had over her.

My mother's mother, the duchess of the void above, was an artist. Her paintings and sculptures are haunting with their realistic portrayal of agony, female agony. Aside from being wonderful and being an artist, she also lived with a diagnosis of schizophrenia. She was both a force of nature and a cracked soul that needed to be tended to. I felt then, and still do, a strong connection to her. I knew that someone brave had to be holding that paintbrush and kneading that clay.

A month before my mother died in a car accident, I found her sniffling in front of the computer screen, typing as if she were possessed. I looked over her shoulder to peak at the screen, resting my hand on her back. At first she covered the screen, and then she looked at me with torn eyes, and told me that she was writing a book about her mother. It was the first time I saw a glimmer of life when mentioning her mother. I hugged her tight and told her I was proud of her, not knowing that 12 years from that moment I would be in her position, writing about my wonderful, dead mother, and juggling tears of unbearable grief and unfathomable love.

My mother is to me what her mother was to her—the ultimate source of love and fear—an attachment that is entangled in trauma, beauty, and survival. I have always wondered if I, too, would give my future daughter this painful gift of love and fear. This question—will I be like my mother? —is the reason for this self-exploration. Three generations of unprocessed grief seek a different form of inheritance in this thesis. If theater is to me what paint was to my grandmother and words were to my mother—a personal outlet that allowed some sun to come in through the dark void above—creativity is the way to transform my family's trauma into art and healing.

A performance of intergenerational loss

An arts-based research performance was created to explore the influence of creativity over the transmission of intergenerational trauma and the ability to integrate a good enough mother. To achieve this, Maya explored this transmission of trauma by embodying the attachment triad of grandmother (Florence), mother (Jane), and daughter (Maya).

The artist-researchers engaged in a rehearsal process, examined video recordings of rehearsals, the script, the performance, and the video recording of the performance. Playing the dead, playing herself, and saying goodbye to mother and grandmother were the three most pivotal milestones during this process. These milestones mark evident transformation and profound insight, which ultimately contributed to the integration of the good enough mother in an effort to halt continued transmission of intergenerational loss.

Playing the dead

The embodiment of Florence, Maya's grandmother, whom she had never met, was a prolonged and pleasurable experience as the amount of physical and emotional distance from her character was significantly greater than embodying the other two characters: mother and Maya herself. The distance from Florence gave Maya freedom and a sense of play while she imitated her character as perceived through stories heard about Florence. There was little commitment to absolute truth as her portrayal was not based on her own memory of her grandmother. The result of embodying Florence was an empathic understanding of the way her mental illness protected her. Additionally, the role of art making became clearer to Maya, as both Florence and she utilize a shared artistry as a means of coping with experiences that cannot be otherwise expressed. Florence, who Maya began this process fearing and resenting as the source of mental illness in her family, became more delicate and Maya began responding to her much like a mother would respond to a child. This transition helped Maya form a healthier bond to her memory and eased the anxiety and ambivalence she initially felt in regards to resembling Florence. At the end of the rehearsal process, Maya felt connected to her and evidently took pride in having shared qualities with her grandmother.

The embodiment of Jane, Maya's mother, was significantly more challenging. Jane, who passed 12 years ago, was hard to embody and when embodied Maya could only tolerate it for short periods of time. In those embodiments, there was less flexibility and spontaneity as Maya continuously attempted to maintain absolute truth to the memory of her mother; this experience was triggering to Maya as she failed to uphold the authenticity of her mother. Embodying Jane was also somewhat of a revival of her mother which was at times extremely painful as it was a reminder of Maya's unfulfilled fantasy of her return; this was most present during a viewing of a recording where Maya became aware of her acute physical resemblance to her mother. As the embodiments became more frequent and Maya spent more time inhabiting the role of her dead mother, Maya was able to find more of a sense of play and take joy in the shared love of art and humor. It was a combination of repetition (ritual) and the incorporation of her mother's music making (art) that allowed Maya to fully try on and play out this role. At the end of the rehearsal process Maya felt that Jane existed within her in a way that was accessible and less tender. Maya's connection to her dead mother was no longer just a painful recollection; rather it was experienced almost as the beginning of a new relationship to her—the beginning of integration.

Playing herself

The embodiment of Maya, as herself, was by far the most challenging task. Maya experienced a sense of being stifled and speechless when playing herself. At times, she was completely dissociated from her own character and curious as to why this was occurring. The director, Dana, redirected this dissociation by reversing roles and taking on the role of Maya. This gave Maya the opportunity and the distance necessary to direct herself vicariously and have empathy for what she was experiencing. Playing the role of director in this rehearsal was essentially the first time in this process that Maya felt like the good enough mother. As the good enough mother in the role of director, Maya exhibited strength, empathy, and stability necessary to mother herself. At the end of the rehearsal process, Maya was the character she enjoyed playing the most as she discovered freedom in performing the integration of selected qualities of both her mother and grandmother.

Saying goodbye

One particular rehearsal stands out as a definitive moment in this process. This rehearsal emerged from the intent to place a movement piece at the end of the performance. This movement piece was an embodiment of the car accident Maya's mother died in. Maya was unable to improvise and kept returning to rigid roles such as commander, boss, and fetus; all three of these roles were subject to the demands of others. While rehearsing this piece, it became clear that Maya was performing the trauma cycle. Rather than finding the necessary roles to move forward, she was pulled back in by the comfort of her inherited grief and trauma response. Additionally, the energy and arousal she experienced around performing the trauma was indicative of the unprocessed emotions Maya held towards the finality of her mother's death. The act of playing out the passing of her mother provided Maya with a sense of thrill and control in that she was able to embody a scene that had been the most pivotal moment in her life and took place in her absence.

Moreover, the physicality of playing in a car, the vehicle responsible for her mother's death, was a performance of her own fear of driving, as well as frustration at, and resentment towards, being a passenger in her life. Control was the most evident element in this rehearsal and it manifested in Maya's holding of the safety belt in several moments and fashions during the rehearsal. The director then suggested that she perform the movement piece in the car with the intention to exit it. This resulted in recognition that there was unfinished business and unprocessed grief. Through this enactment, Maya was able to say goodbye to both her mother and her grandmother, two women she never was privileged to say goodbye to in reality. Ultimately, it was decided not to incorporate the movement piece into the performance as the rehearsal sufficiently served its purpose of providing closure and promoting forward movement.

The performance

The performance was the culmination of four months of investigation and crafting of the script. By playing all three women Maya was able to find that the intergenerational trauma was not the transmission of mental illness or the fear of it, or sudden deaths. It was the attachments that were formed as a response to unprocessed grief. The performance gave Maya insight into the ways grief can be inherited when unprocessed and repressed. Additionally, the role of art as a coping mechanism used by all three characters was unveiled in performance: Florence's painting and sculpting, Jane's writing and music, and Maya's theater.

In summation, integration occurred after playing a multitude of roles and selecting the roles that best served the desired role as a good enough mother. The experience of playing all the roles facilitated the identification of roles that are needed as well as roles that do not serve the purpose of integration. The performance was the integration of all three characters, as well as three facets of Maya's self that have been explored throughout this process. Ultimately, the integration occurred because the performance allowed the space for all three women to create a combined repertoire of roles that make up a good enough mother. And as Florence says in the play, "Put a frame around a wound and it has a different meaning."

References

Allen, B. (2004) *Difference Matters: Communicating Social Identity.* Long Grove, IL: Waveland Press.

Bezalel, O. (2014) 'Parallel mourning.' Available at http://ewp.cas.nyu.edu/docs/ IO/39266/bezalelparallel.pdf, accessed on November 17, 2016.

Erikson, E. (1980) *Identity and the Life Cycle.* New York: W.W. Norton.

Fitzpatrick, F. (2002) 'A search for home: The role of art therapy in understanding the experiences of Bosnian refugees in Western Australia.' *Art Therapy: Journal of the American Art Therapy Association 19*, 4, 151–158.

Kapitan, L., Litell, M., and Torres A. (2011) 'Creative art therapy in a community's participatory research and social transformation.' *Art Therapy: Journal of the American Art Therapy Association 28*, 2, 64–73.

Larsson, P. (2012) 'How important is an understanding of the client's early attachment experience to the psychodynamic practice of counselling psychology?' *Counselling Psychology Review 27*, 1, 10–21.

Levy, B.A., Berberian, M., Brigmon, L.S.V., Gonzalez, S.N., and Koepfer, S.R. (2002) 'Mobilizing community strength: New York art therapists respond.' *Art Therapy 19*, 3, 106–114.

McGoldrick, M., Giordano, J., and Pearce, J. (1996) *Ethnicity and Family Therapy.* New York: Guilford Press.

Moon, B. (2000) *Ethical Issues in Art Therapy*. Springfield, IL: Charles C. Thomas Publishers.

Ngcobo, N. (2015) 'The Difference between White Funerals and Black Funerals.' *Rand Daily Mail*, March 8, 2015. Available at www.rdm.co.za/lifestyle/2015/03/08/the-difference-between-white-funerals-and-black-funerals, accessed on November 17, 2016.

Ogle, C., Rubin, D., and Siegel, I. (2014) 'The relation between insecure attachment and posttraumatic stress: Early life versus adulthood traumas.' *Psychological Trauma: Theory, Research, Practice, and Policy 7*, 4, 324–332.

Parkes, C.M. (2006) *Love and Loss: The Roots of Grief and Its Complications*. New York: Taylor & Francis.

Tummala-Narra, P. (2013) 'Psychoanalytic applications in a diverse society.' *Psychoanalytic Psychology 30*, 3, 471–487.

5

Concepts in Treatment

Briana MacWilliam, Danielle Klingensmith,
Lauren D. Smith, Melissa Meade, Julie Day,
Romona Mukherjee, and Karen Gibbons

Treating grief
Kübler-Ross and the five stages of death and dying

In her seminal work *On Death and Dying*, Dr. Elisabeth Kübler-Ross
(1969) described the path that terminally ill patients travel as five
stages of death and dying: denial, anger, bargaining, depression,
and acceptance. Most consider Kübler-Ross's stages as linear, but
she acknowledges that the stages involve feelings that last a varying
amount of time and often do not represent a linear progression.

Kübler-Ross, along with David Kessler (2005), in their book
On Grief and Grieving, applied the five stages to those grieving the
loss of a loved one. In the Anniversary Edition, Maria Shriver stated
in the foreword, "We are a grief-illiterate nation, and Kübler-Ross
dedicated her life to helping people find peace in challenging losses.
She gave us permission to grieve..." The American culture tends to
deny death as a part of life. Kübler-Ross opened the dialogue on the
concept of grief.

Kübler-Ross's first stage of death and dying, denial and isolation,
serves to isolate the patient from the unimaginable news of their
impending death and enables them to move to engaging other more
serving defenses. Denial can exhibit as searching for other doctors

and expecting other results. The first stage of denial for the grieving individual left behind appears as disbelief, the inability to believe that they will not see the loved one again. Denial may exhibit as numbness or being paralyzed. As with the dying individual, denial serves the griever as a defense mechanism to allow for surviving on a day-to-day basis and protecting from the overwhelming truth. The individual may retell the story repeatedly in an attempt to make sense of the situation and incorporate the trauma. Denial serves as a temporary defense that will gradually be replaced with anger, rage, envy, and resentment.

Patients exhibiting anger may displace the anger and direct it at those caring for him/her, making caretaking difficult. Counseling patients in this stage of death and dying can prove difficult as the patient may act dismissively or aggressively; the therapist can provide the crucial opportunity to express the anger. The patient and the grieving caretaker may experience this stage by directing anger inward, outward, or in a dispersed manner. The grieving individual may experience anger at themselves or at the deceased. They may blame doctors or God or others, or may feel angry that life continues on without their loved one.

Anger surfaces when the grieving individual feels that, despite the pain of loss, they will survive, and serves as a powerful emotion, enabling the individual to experience underlying feelings of pain. With the power of anger, the individual has structure to the feelings associated with the loss. As with other emotions, the grieving must allow themselves the experience of anger, because through experiencing the anger, it will dissipate. Anger will often appear misplaced or disproportionate to onlookers. Regardless of appearances, anger serves the griever and provides a step toward healing. If anger turns inward, it can exhibit as guilt; the therapist should console the griever that he/she is not to blame. The anger serves as a reminder that they can feel, they did love, and helps acknowledge the loss. The therapist should support the griever in the anger, not diminish it, allowing the individual to move through the feelings.

Anger transitions into the third stage of bargaining. When anger does not result in the desired outcome, bargaining serves as the nicer approach, a potential reward for good behavior. Most bargaining involves requests from a higher power and/or a request to postpone the inevitable. Patients and grieving individuals may experience guilt as a result of such requests and the therapist should exhibit sensitivity to this possibility. The "if only" thoughts haunt the individual and they attempt to negotiate in an effort to avoid the pain. Bargaining serves to keep pain in the distance and allows the individual to feel some control over uncontrollable feelings.

Depression follows bargaining as the patient begins to sense great loss. While this stage appears painful, it serves as a necessary step in the patient's transition. The therapist should avoid attempts to cheer the patient up, in favor of acknowledging and honoring the patient's position and feelings. Allowing the patient to feel the losses and express sorrow will facilitate moving into acceptance.

For the grieving individual, the move into the present moment results in depression. The emptiness and sadness engulf the individual leaving feelings of great loss. The depression involved in grief does not represent mental illness but serves as an opportunity for the griever to experience a natural response to a real loss. Getting through daily activities, including getting out of bed, can seem insurmountable. The feeling seems endless and hope is scarce. Kübler-Ross and Kessler suggest viewing depression as a visitor to help the griever experience the loss and come to terms with the emptiness. Depression enables the griever to slow down, process the experience and rebuild.

By expressing the feelings of each of the previous stages, patients can then reach the final stage of acceptance. For the patient facing death, this stage does not appear as a happy emotion, but as devoid of feelings with a sense of peace. Often family members need the most support at this stage as the patient turns more inward and sits in silence. For the grieving individual, acceptance also follows depression. While acceptance sounds like feeling okay with the loss, that does not represent reality. Acceptance refers to dealing with the reality and adapting to a new reality. It allows the griever to find a new place, a new path in life without the loved one. It allows the griever to find peace in light of the knowledge that life will never be the same again.

Kübler-Ross determined that hope existed throughout the stages. Hope served the patients throughout their suffering with thoughts that the experience provides some meaning or mission which enables them to endure. Therapists working with terminally ill patients and grieving individuals should allow for hope, even in the direst circumstances, to provide the strength they need to continue in their struggle.

These stages provided a foundation for future work and have been applied to many aspects of grief, such as divorce. Dr. Colin Murray Parkes expanded on this foundation describing overlapping stages of numb disbelief, yearning for the deceased, disorganization and despair, and finally reorganization. Dr. J. William Worden describes grieving related to four tasks that must be accomplished in order to heal: 1) accepting the loss, 2) experiencing the resulting pain, 3) putting the loss in some perspective and adjusting to a changed world without the person who has died, and 4) altering ties with the deceased enough that they are able to invest their love and energy in others. Each of these theories reflect their origin in Kübler-Ross's work (Harvard Mental Health Letter, 2011).

CRITICISMS

Ruth Davis Konigsberg (2011) strongly criticizes the stage theory of grief in her book *The Truth About Grief: The Myth of Its Five Stages and the Five Stages of Loss*, stating that considering the stages as discrete steps to complete has delayed the healing of grief. She discusses research that describes resilient grievers as having a more positive worldview and chronic grievers to have been more dependent on their lost loved one and having fewer coping mechanisms; the difference between these two groups has nothing to do with the stages. One risk identified regarding the stage theory is the concept that an individual must complete that stage of grief before moving on. Although Kübler-Ross did not intend that belief, her theory has been misconstrued in this manner. One could consider the stages to provide self-fulfilling prophesies. When someone is lost in the grieving process, they could consider that they should feel a certain way, postponing dealing with existing feelings. Charles Corr (2015) also criticized the stage theory, noting that individuals experience more than five emotions and responses in grief. Both Corr and Konigsberg note that empirical research has not supported Kübler-Ross's theory.

Despite her criticism, Konigsberg acknowledges that the public has taken Kübler-Ross's stages more literally than intended. Additionally, Corr states that Kübler-Ross identified key insights into the process of death and dying that underpin understanding, including the fact that dying patients have unmet needs and the need for caregivers to actively listen to patients' concerns. Corr discusses Kübler-Ross's impact by humanizing and normalizing the experiences of the emotions associated with grief. Additionally, Corr recognizes the practical advice offered in Kübler-Ross's publications regarding coping with death. Overall, Kübler-Ross greatly contributed to the understanding of individual experiences when coping with death and opened the discussion of loss in our society. Criticism of her work emphasizes the fundamental of counseling regarding respect for the client and meeting the client where he/she is.

Approaches to grief resolution

Over the 30 years since their introduction, these stages, have often been misinterpreted to imply a clear-cut process of grieving. Kübler-Ross (2005) later reiterated that: "[The stages] were never meant to help tuck messy emotions into neat packages. They are tools to help us frame and identify what we may be feeling. But they are not stops on some linear timeline in grief" (p.7). Indeed, there is no step-by-step recipe for grief. Grief is a "circular staircase" and thus any new loss can "unstitch mercilessly the scars of old wounds" (Bertman, 1999, p.9). We might be better served if we can think about the stages of grieving not as something we *must* go through, but something that "*illuminates* what we are going through. Perhaps [then] we can come to understand why sorrow turns out to be not a state but a process" (Viorst, 1986, p.238). Bertman also supported this standpoint.

Though useful from descriptive "snapshot" points of view, stage theories tend to be oversimplified, lead to false expectations (too much of a recipe or "cookbook" approach, too rigidly sequential), and are often misunderstood. We must be careful not to trivialize or minimize the profundity and uniqueness of a personal or communal grief by reducing it to mere explanation or method. We must curtail our reliance on jargon: not everyone needs to "work through" or achieve "closure" or even express anger. Thus, trusting the process, a phrase commonly heard within the art therapy community when describing art making, also holds true for grief. Where we are in the grieving process is where we need to be until ready to move forward.

Rather than seeking closure from grief, a more helpful approach might be to work towards grief *resolution*. Sherebrin (1999) likens resolution to the "progression of a chord from dissonance to consonance—in other words, as *integration*" (p.238). Musically, dissonance is "a mingling of discordant sounds; especially a clashing or unresolved musical interval or chord."[1] The listener might cringe at the keys played because they sound unpleasant. Conversely, musical consonance, or concordance, is "a simultaneous occurrence of two or more musical tones that produces an impression of agreeableness or resolution on a listener."[2] The notes sound harmonious. A better goal than working towards "getting over" a loss would be to learn to "integrate the loss into our lives so that we can continue in harmony" (p.238). The music will never be quite the same as before

---

1   www.merriam-webster.com/dictionary/dissonance
2   www.merriam-webster.com/dictionary/concord

the loss, but the growth and experience that come through grieving can produce new, rich melodies.

However, Bertman (1999) argued that grief resolution may not be necessary or even helpful:

> Human grief exists both in time and timelessness. There is a healing trajectory and periodic revisits of grief—planned and unexpected—are part of the process. Grief, therefore, is not "resolved" in the medical sense of the work; rather it becomes a repositioning and revival of the loved one in an inner space and time, accessible forever, whenever one needs, wants or is forced to feel the connection. This is the paradox—the healing power of grief. At that moment of connection, the emptiness and void are gone, or at least temporarily held at bay. (p.15)

For all of these theorists, grief is a fluid and unpredictable process which most will experience as a result of forming expectations and connections with those around us. "Grief is a life-cycle event." It is a "subjective experience" that we are only able to understand as we "filter and interpret it through our own experience" (Bertman, 1999, p.15).

Patient and family-centered bereavement support models

The patient and family-centered care (PFCC) philosophy reflects current best practice in the healthcare environment, and is implemented particularly within medical/surgical settings. However, within the broader context of psychotherapeutic treatment models, its philosophy spans ethical, humanistic, and relational domains.

According to the American Academy of Pediatrics (AAP), Family Voices, The Institute for Patient and Family-Centered Care, and the Maternal and Child Health Bureau (MCHB) and similar organizations, the development of a PFCC standard reflect the following tenets (Arango et al., 2011, p.298):

- *Information sharing:* The exchange of information is open, objective, and unbiased.

- *Respect and honoring differences:* The working relationship is marked by respect for diversity, cultural and linguistic traditions, and care preferences.

- *Partnership and collaboration:* Medically appropriate decisions that best fit the needs, strengths, values, and abilities of all involved are made together by involved parties, including families at the level they choose.

- *Negotiation:* The desired outcomes of medical care plans are flexible and not necessarily absolute.

- *Care in the context of family and community:* Direct medical care and decision making reflect the child within the context of his/her family, home, school, daily activities, and quality of life within the community.

The PFCC model echoes the predominant teaching of Carl Rogers and humanistic psychology, the belief that human beings are experts in their own lives. By extension, we can apply this theory and acknowledge that human beings are also experts in their own experience of grief.

In providing bereavement support we accept that there is no "right way" to grieve. The spectrum of human response to grief and loss shifts like a tide—passing through non-linear iterations of pain, denial, guilt, regret, depression, anger, rationalization, complication, etc., and we often repeat or revisit feeling states as the process unfolds over time. We must also acknowledge that the constellation of every "family" is diverse, and within a family system there exist myriad coping styles, patterns of grief, and individual approaches to processing loss. So we depart from Kübler-Ross here, and look instead at alternatives that make room for integration of the memory or relationship to the deceased into a new daily pattern of living.

In this way, the art therapist working from a PFCC-model creates room for modes of adaptive grieving, for the intuitive and instrumental griever alike. The intuitive griever is more likely to allow for the open expression of affect, reflecting outwardly their inner grief experience (Umphrey and Cacciatore, 2014), whereas the instrumental griever may demonstrate "a more cognitive, behavioral, and problem-solving style. They may feel discomfort when experiencing and expressing emotions and prefer to be more task-oriented in their coping style" (Umphrey and Cacciatore, 2014, p.6).

Thus, the art therapist is uniquely qualified to respond through supportive interventions that accommodate a range of mourning styles. Bereavement interventions for adaptive grief models include:

- legacy building through hand printing/plaster casting

- life review (multimedia intervention—photo, video, etc.)

- containment (clay work, sculpture, construction)

- sensory-stimulating (fiber, textiles)

- narrative and externalization (letter writing, storytelling).

As relevant literature has noted (and previously discussed here), the nature of traumatic loss impacts the brain's ability to create cohesive memories and formulate responsive language surrounding the traumatic event. In crisis the "higher verbal regulatory functions in the cerebral cortex are out of reach" (King-West and Hass-Cohen, 2008, p.33), possibly restricting a person's ability to verbalize his or her experience. In the crisis of bereavement, particularly for instrumental grievers, the utilization of art materials as central to the processing of loss may activate the motor system functions of the cortex, the brainstem, and the spinal cord—all integral to the experience of "taking action." This may contribute to a family's sense of action in the face of helplessness after a death.

Through an ethical lens, clinicians have a responsibility to care for the entire family when providing bereavement support.

Practiced most frequently in palliative healthcare environments, this culture of inclusion acknowledges all members of the family as part of the dying process and deserving of care (Jones, Contro, and Koch, 2014, S9). The strong relational framework of art therapy practice likewise acknowledges the centrality of "connection" in the face of loss, and through the symbolism of forging new connections, either with art material itself or through the creative process or within the therapeutic alliance itself, new relational pathways might be explored even in the most isolating face of grief and loss.

A treatment model for complicated grief

When calls for a loved one go unanswered, the result is intensified proximity-seeking, which becomes the central preoccupation of the bereaved person. Shear *et al.* (2007) suggest there are two fundamentally different forms of traumatic experience, one that occurs following a violent incident, and the other related to the demise or permanent loss of a love object. The subsequent stress response syndrome has some shared features, but differs if it is traumatic *stress* or traumatic *loss*. Failure to integrate information about a violent event results in PTSD while failure to integrate the permanent loss of an attachment figure produces complicated grief. Death of a loved one can trigger either reaction.

Prior to the inclusion of complicated grief in the DSM-5, two main diagnostic criteria for complicated grief were studied. First, the Prigerson *et al.* (1999) consensus criteria differentiated between two categories of symptoms:

1. *separation distress*: preoccupation with thoughts of the deceased, longing and searching for the deceased, loneliness

2. *traumatic distress*: feeling disbelief about the death, mistrust, anger, feeling shocked by the death, and the experience of somatic symptoms of the deceased.

In addition, there must be disturbance that causes clinically significant impairment. Horowitz *et al.* (1997) differentiated three categories of symptoms:

1. *intrusion*: unbidden memories, emotional spells, strong yearning

2. *avoidance*: avoiding places that are reminders of the deceased, emotional numbness towards others

3. *failure to adapt symptoms*: e.g. feeling lonely or empty, having trouble sleeping.

While Horowitz *et al.* (1997) regarded avoidance as an important criterion for complicated grief, Prigerson and Jacobs (2001) removed the avoidance item in order to improve the internal consistency and diagnostic accuracy of the traumatic distress category. This decision was based on a finding by Raphael and Martinek (1997) that in contrast to PTSD patients who avoid reminders of the trauma, complicated grief patients avoid reminders *of the absence* of the person and hence *actively seek* reminders of the deceased person. Another difference between Horowitz's model and Pigerson and Jacob's model pertains to the "disturbance item." Disturbance in social living is one possible item in the avoidance cluster of the Horowitz *et al.* criteria that does *not* necessarily have to be fulfilled for a diagnosis, whereas the presence of functional disturbance is considered an integral part within the Prigerson *et al.* consensus criteria (Forstmeier and Maecker, 2007).

Studies gathered evidence in favor of both criteria (Jacobs, Mazure, and Prigerson, 2000; Lichtenthal, Cruess, and Prigerson, 2004). Forstmeier and Maecker (2007) compared the two diagnostic systems in a representative sample of 570 elderly people. Features of bereavement, diagnoses of complicated grief, and related symptoms were assessed. The Horowitz *et al.* criteria set were found to be more inclusive and less strict than the Prigerson *et al.* criteria set. The importance of functional impairment and the number of symptoms needed account for this difference (Forstmeier and Maecker, 2007).

In 2008, Prigerson, Horowitz, and others collaborated on a clinical study to enhance the detection and potential treatment of bereaved individuals at risk for complicated grief, which ultimately found complicated grief is a clinically significant form of psychological distress associated with substantial disability.

INTEGRATION OF LOSS

Integration of loss seems to occur through a process of swinging back and forth between avoiding thoughts and memories of the deceased, and turning towards them. The magnitude of this oscillation is initially very large, but over time it is gradually minimized to a comfortable rhythm of engagement with, and then setting aside, thoughts and memories of the lost love object. Shear *et al.* (2007) assert that this naturally oscillating process is optimal for effecting a revision of the working model of the attachment figure. The enticement of ongoing life provides "the motivation for comprehending the death, while increasing comprehension of the death frees motivational and attentional resources." When the loss has been incorporated into the working model, trauma-like symptoms resolve, proximity-seeking recedes and grief intensity abates.

Stroebe and Schut (1999) maintain that resolution of acute grief must proceed hand in hand with coping with associated life stresses. They propose a "dual process" coping model, which suggests effective coping requires addressing both loss and restoration-related stress. The model postulates that the two groups of stressors are best addressed simultaneously; if coping with important life problems is ineffective, this complicates the grief. This coping model extends Horowitz's model (Horowitz *et al.*, 1997), which is focused more narrowly on the intrinsic biobehavioral process of integrating trauma.

In a clinical trial, Shear *et al.* (2007) developed a treatment approach for complicated grief, based on the dual process model, which attempts to address both ends of grief's pendulum swing. They developed an assessment and specific goals related to loss-focused strategies and restoration- focused strategies. These strategies are quite compatible with expressive arts therapy interventions. For example, for loss-focused strategies, the goal was to "move the loved one from the mind to the heart." Loss-focused interventions included:

- imaginal revisiting exercises

- working with memories and pictures

- imaginal conversations with the deceased

- situational revisiting exercises.

For restoration-focused strategies, the goal was to "restore satisfying activities and relationships," and included such interventions as:

- self-care and personal goals work

- working on interpersonal disputes

- role transitions.

All of these strategies lend themselves to existing art therapy techniques. Imaginal conversations and revisiting exercises are well explored and expanded upon by the work of Sean McNiff and gestalt art therapists. In examining the technique of talking to your artwork and allowing it to talk back (imaginal dialogues), and other such interventions as "hot seat" and "empty chair," we can draw these comparisons. Working with memories and pictures is a rudimentary definition of "art therapy" as a whole, but could more specifically lend itself to phototherapy interventions, collage, visual journals, life lines, "cognitive mapping" exercises, memory boxes, and more (all of which can be found in Parts II and III of this text).

In working with complicated grief, it is important for the art therapist to honor not only the periods of engagement with grief material, but also the swings away from it. In fact, this oscillation is part of the natural grieving process, and essential to it. The art therapist must be sensitive to the orientation of their client while in session: "Is my client engaged with grief material today? Or does my client need a break from it?" Corresponding interventions will assist with the process of integration.

Mindfulness and the embodiment of treatment

Several decades ago, researchers discovered that our thoughts could drive our moods. But it wasn't until the 1980s that we discovered the reverse is also true; mood can drive our thoughts. And our moods—closely tied to our emotions—are housed in the body. The mind does not exist in isolation from the body; much of what the body feels is colored by our thoughts, and much of what we think is informed by the body. Think about the infectiousness of yawning, laughing, or smiling, for example; tiny shifts in the body can change our whole outlook.

Now let's consider this in the context of grief. In the "six myths about grief," discussed in Chapter 1, we see a common implication: grief is a "problem" that has to be "fixed." Being solution focused is not in and of itself a bad thing, if we are applying it to the external world. It's how we've managed to develop the technology we have, and address many of the world's problems. However, it becomes detrimental when we turn that mechanism inward. Williams and Penman illustrate this concept beautifully (2011, p.28):

> tension, unhappiness or a exhaustion aren't "problems" that need to be solved. They are emotions. They reflect state of mind and body. As such, they cannot be *solved*, only *felt*. Once you have felt them—that is, acknowledged their existence— and let go of the tendency to explain or get rid of them, they are much more likely to finish naturally, like the mist on a spring morning.

When you try to solve the "problem" of happiness (or any other "negative" emotion) you deploy one of the mind's most powerful tools: rational critical thinking. You see yourself as unhappy and want to be happy. Your mind then analyzes the gap and tries to figure out the best way to bridge it. To do this, it switches into "doing" mode (Williams and Penman, 2011). And this is the worst thing for an internal conflict or unhappy mood. Because to analyze a gap between how you are and how you want to be is to become critical of the self, and *what is* (which is to become critical of everything, because "what is" is the present moment, and that is all we have). Then you start asking yourself, "What's wrong with me? Why do I keep making the same mistakes?" Suddenly, you are not only unhappy, but unhappy about being unhappy.

Wallin (2007) refers to this over-identification with emotion as being "embedded in experience." He states, "It's as if we are the experience as long as the experience lasts" (p.135). To be mindful is to be able to observe your emotions, regulate them, and make good use of them. For the individual who is over-identified with their emotions, what might otherwise be useful *information* has become the whole of reality; there are no beliefs that are not also facts. Parents in the grip of such states, perhaps triggered by a crying child, for example, may too easily fall into a rage, terrifying the child who can neither turn toward nor away from their attachment figure, "who has become both the source of danger and sole haven of safety" (Wallin, 2007, p.95). And this gives rise to a disorganized or anxious–avoidant attachment style in the next generation.

According to Wallin (2007), a securely attached individual reflects coherently on experience and has the capacity for a "reflective" and "mentalizing" stance. Fonagy's term "mentalizing" essentially refers to the ability to be aware of our own reactions to things and thereby grasp the deeper meaning of our experiences (Fonagy and Target, 2006). For example, feeling put off by a friend's insecurity and neediness has meaning that can only be understood in the context of your own anxieties about being vulnerable. Important to note, the securely attached individual's sense of "self" is capable of three things:

1. making sense of things, rather than being riddled with inconsistencies

2. experiencing her- or himself as an integrated whole, rather than fractured by dissociations and disavowals

3. collaborating with other "selves."

In sum, to be mindful is to be fully engaged in the present and receptive to whatever experience arises, without getting caught up in any specific aspect of that experience. It is the ability to avoid over-identifying with the "I," and be aware of experience without judging or evaluating it. This achievement relates to a secure attachment, and is made possible through engagement with the body and meditation practices. Furthermore, to be mindful is to both experience and understand your grief in its context, which will ultimately allow it to "finish naturally, like the mist on a spring morning" (Williams and Penman, 2011, p.28). Emerging paradigms in treatment take into account the importance of mindfulness, including Dialectical Behavior Therapy (DBT) and Art Therapy Relational Neuroscience (ATR-N).

Dialectical Behavior Therapy (DBT)

Developed throughout the 1970s and 1980s, by psychologist Marsha M. Linehan (Linehan 1993), for the purpose of treating borderline personality disorder (BPD), DBT is a form of Cognitive Behavior Therapy (CBT) that emphasizes the therapeutic relationship and utilizes skills training in the context of validation and acceptance to provide a natural catalyst for change. DBT has grown into evidence-based practice that is widely used in a variety of mental health settings; those benefiting most from DBT are individuals whose emotional experience is intense and consuming in a way that makes return to baseline a difficult process.

DBT, in its intended form, is carried out through a combination of group and individual sessions; the process is didactic and experiential, with learning and practice taking place directly in the therapeutic environment. Skills are taught in the immediacy of the client–therapist relationship and through client–client interactions, and when natural conflicts occur, individuals are encouraged to practice their newly learned skills in real time and with the support of the therapist and the group.

Because the work of DBT is rooted in cognitive behavioral theories, first steps include identifying thoughts and beliefs about the self and others that are not conducive to coping and then learning and developing new ways of thinking and acting on thoughts. Coping skills are explored and integrated into social interactions that enable individuals to manage a sudden emotional change without it having a significant or lasting impact on the individual's day. Unlike traditional CBT, which focuses on challenging maladaptive cognitive processes, DBT places importance on validating and accepting thoughts and beliefs as they exist, however helpful or unhelpful. The "dialectical" descriptor implies cognitive work that is meant to allow for multiple paths of thinking simultaneously, acknowledging the elements of truth in and creating space for each of them without doing so at the expense of any other; for example, one might be putting maximum effort into something while also being open to the possibility of being capable of doing even more or doing differently.

This initial unconditional positive regard on the part of the therapist and the individual for the individual's current thinking creates room for and allows for belief in the possibility of change; challenging of thoughts can then happen naturally as the individual learns new skills and starts an organic process of change. Strengths are identified and built upon, and as new skills are learned and integrated, the need for unhelpful thinking decreases on its own. Rather than remaining as opposing forces, validation and acceptance exist in tension with change-oriented and didactic therapeutic work, and the navigation of that tension becomes the vehicle for change.

Linehan's early work was based on the biosocial theory, which explained emotional intensity and the accompanying delayed decrease to baseline as a dysfunction of emotional regulation brought on by an activating event in childhood or ongoing environmental factors in youth. The event or environment fostered emotional vulnerability, lowering the child's threshold for emotional arousal, impairing the ability to de-escalate, and encouraging quick but maladaptive coping mechanisms that enabled as rapid a decrease to baseline as possible but inhibited emotional learning and processing, and often caused harm. For this reason, DBT's skills education incorporates practice in identifying, naming, and processing emotions.

As a comprehensive treatment program, DBT includes concrete psychoeducation and immediate practice in mindfulness, interpersonal effectiveness, conflict resolution, crisis management and distress tolerance, reality acceptance, and emotion regulation. Individuals are given the tools to self-monitor and are supported in building for themselves an environment conducive to growth and change. Generalization of interpersonal and coping skills is encouraged through the use of assignments to be completed between therapy sessions.

Though developed initially by Linehan as a treatment for BPD—specifically for suicidal ideation or parasuicidality in BPD—DBT's success in active treatment and support in professional literature has encouraged use by clinicians working with individuals with similar needs. Acute and chronic mental health conditions in which maladaptive coping has developed or may develop, inhibiting growth and functioning, can be treated successfully with DBT. This includes substance use disorders, eating disorders, depression and anxiety, and grief and trauma work.

Expressive therapy modalities may be used in conjunction with DBT in a few combinations; the expressive work can itself be a coping skill, it can structure the learning of skills, or it can be a means of providing the context in which to practice the skills. In Part III of this text, you will find two protocols that involve the use of DBT interventions, in combination with creative arts therapy approaches.

ART THERAPY RELATIONAL NEUROSCIENCE (ATR-N)

King-West and Hass-Cohen (2008) believe understanding a person's traumatic story through the lens of interpersonal neurobiology (IPNB) is beneficial for the following reasons:

1. It explains problems inherent in the original trauma and secondary retraumatization.

2. It redefines the interpretation of the art images to include non-symbolic sensory representations of fragmented memories.

3. It amplifies the advantages of the visual motor activities associated with art making.

4. It highlights the significance of the here-and-now with a caring and empathic therapist.

5. It suggests an individual's attachment styles are experience dependent and can change throughout the lifespan.

The primary purpose of their ATR-N approach is to emphasize the dynamic and plastic nature of the human nervous system, and its potential for change. When change arises from positive experiences, such as engagement with "enriching and novel experiences" they contribute to resiliency. When change arises from positive experiences, such as engagement with "enriching and novel experiences," those changes most likely contribute to resiliency (Hass-Cohen and Findlay, 2015, p.5). This approach is comprised of six principles, which are summarized by the acronym: CREATE (Hass-Cohen and Findlay, 2015, p.10):

1. *Creative embodiment.* Highlights the therapeutic effects of kinesthetic art making, movement, play and touch, including freedom from constricting affect and the co-construction of safe interpersonal experiences.

2. *Relational resonating.* Emphasizes the importance of attuned therapeutic relationships; positive interactions and their mental representations have the potential to stabilize affect regulation, update autobiographical memories, and contribute to earned-secure attachment.

3. *Expressive communicating.* Reflects how motivation and emotion are stimulated by the vivid and sensory qualities of art media, presenting an opportunity to express, communicate, and regulate strong emotions that may be evoked.

4. *Adaptive responding.* Art therapists provide a dynamic balancing of arousal and avoidance—essential to creating a feeling of safety, control, acceptance, and resiliency—through the use of diverse materials and demonstrative therapeutic intervention.

5. *Transformative integrating.* Occurs over time with repeated association of secure affective experiences and sensory expression. Symbol making and talking about art making can reorganize and restructure implicit emotional memories into explicit conscious narratives, which is how a negative memory can be reinterpreted as a positive experience.

6. *Empathizing and compassion.* Involves the development of insight and compassion towards oneself and others, as well as towards the art product. Empathy and compassion are linked to the capacity for affect regulation, because they allow for the acceptance of one's own self and the selfhood of others.

The ATR-N approach is particularly useful to the creative arts therapist, because it rests at the crux of the "cross-fertilization" of neuroscience research and psychotherapy. To implement the ATR-N approach is to pay homage to three key efforts that have stemmed from this embryo: attachment and IPNB-based treatment, trauma-informed practice, and mindfulness-based practices. These efforts all have a focus on relational communication as a basis for therapeutic change, and have demonstrated the possibility for resiliency and an improved quality of life for those suffering with trauma, grief, and loss (Hass-Cohen and Findlay, 2015).

To illustrate mindfulness-based practices, first Romona Mukherjee and then Karen Gibbons offer examples from their work with grieving clients, in the next section.

The passage into rebirth

One of the greatest gifts of the Eastern traditions of spirituality is the complete acceptance that death is an inevitable and even important aspect of life that merely reflects a transition or passage into rebirth. This freedom from the *fear* around death is rooted in the recognition of the cyclical nature of life, of all beings. There is creation (birth), existence (life), and dissolution (death). All cells, all atoms, all beings, societies, countries, environments, galaxies go through this cycle. This fundamental acknowledgement of the cyclical nature of existence frames death as a necessary and even hallowed rite of passage. Death is not a finite end; it is a transition into the next evolution of the subtle or soulful body.

Now, relating to death with such plain and unwavering acceptance, identifying with it as a fluid transition (rather than a cold and rigid end), does not spare anyone the searing pain of grief. However, it does alleviate the tremendous fear associated with death and loss. One can access some thread in consciousness which recognizes the pain of grief to be part of the larger continuum—a larger cycle that will have its own birth, life, and death/rebirth. The feeling of grief is triggered (born) at the experience of loss, it lives through the cycle of bereavement and healing, and it is laid to rest after a certain point of healing. This cycle can continue for a few rounds until the wound of grief is completely healed. For example, it can be retriggered at a different point of life stressor, residual pain may surface and live with new nuances until the cycle completes, and once again, through the process of healing, it is laid to rest. Each time this happens, there are new levels of insight and wisdom to inform the process, and deepen the individual's awareness of themselves and the world around them.

Shifting pain

Ensuring that this process is not an endless cycle of pain, reliving pain, reliving more pain, and drowning in the suffering of relentless pain calls for *mindfulness*, one gathers information from each round of experience to deepen their understanding, to pay close attention to the nuances of the pain that is presenting itself, and witnesses his or her relationship to that pain as it shifts.

Mindfulness meditation has its roots in Eastern philosophy, primarily in Buddhist traditions. The practice of mindfulness is a practice of observing or paying close attention to, without judgment, what is *true* in the present moment. One begins to discern the debilitating, incessant, and often toxic additives that mind*less* thoughts impose onto the truth of any given moment. A mind*ful* lens allows for cultivation of a kind and curious observation of each moment, thus allowing for a particular kind of spaciousness in which pain or grief can run its course until it releases back into the creases of consciousness.

A therapist's responsibility

For me, as a therapist, without a doubt, the most provocative issue I have had to deal with has been providing support to a client who has suffered the death of a loved one, especially a parent. I know this is true because if I am honest with myself and you, the thing *I* fear most (at this moment) is the death of my parents. Working effectively with any issue in the field of therapy, whether it is grief, trauma—sexual/physical/emotional, injustice and oppression, relationship conflicts, identity and self-worth, requires first that You—*as the guide*—get very acquainted with your own relationship to those issues.

Each of us has our own stories when it comes to how we relate to death, and those stories evolve over time; maybe the fear of losing a parent shifts to the fear of losing a beloved, and then to the fear of losing a child. Perhaps we never think about death until we are sideswiped by the sudden loss of a friend, loss of a pet, or surprised when a tender chord is struck at the death of a distant friend, colleague, or relative who might as well have been a stranger. Death brings up a considerable amount of uncertainty and ambivalence for some and sheer terror for others, especially for those living in the West. Generally, in the West, it is treated as something to avoid discussing and almost superstitiously deny as a reality. It is as if doing so will make it a less plausible outcome. Invariably this approach results in a much deeper plunge into despair when the inevitable reality strikes. That said, we must acknowledge the increasing embrace (in Western consciousness) of Eastern or more ancient philosophies which recognize the cyclical nature of life and relate to death as a necessary and even glorious part of the soul's journey, the soul's return to Source.

And so, your process begins now. Take the next several moments for this short but illuminating exercise.

Shift your gaze away from this page. Let your eyes land on a plant or an image that is soothing. Take three deep breaths, each one longer than the one before, each exhalation twice as long as the inhalation. Close your eyes, and contemplate these questions (tip: you can record yourself asking the questions and then listen with your eyes closed):

- Where do I lie in the spectrum of relating to death?

- Do I see it as a finite reality?

- Do I see it as part of a greater cyclical process?

- Do I imagine it as something in between?

- Am I dissatisfied with the options for understanding given to me?

- Do I have wounds to be healed around death?

Make a note of your answers, and be curious to see how your answers change shape, tone, and timbre over time. This exercise is important because if you hope to provide guidance effectively, you must have a deep acquaintance with your own understanding of death. If you have not examined it for yourself, and any uneasiness you have with death is sensed, then despite your refined knowledge of tools and techniques, the impact of your interventions will be far less potent. If you wish to use mindfulness practices, first start by cultivating your own mindful awareness of how you relate to death. Having a gauge on your own understanding of it will help you assess where your client lies on the spectrum so that you can meet them there, and guide them from a place of recognition and resonance rather than a textbook knowledge of steps and stages.

The client's process

A client suffering the despair and depressive flat line of losing a loved one is naturally experiencing the deep pain of the void left in the absence of the lost one. But even more so, the experience is one of complete dissolution of a reality in which the loved one was a key character with a specific role in the design of the client's life, like a pillar upholding the structure of one part of a building. Suddenly the client is met with the possibility of that structure crumbling, the desperation of trying to hold it together, and an incredible feeling of smallness in the midst of a world that suddenly feels incomprehensible. This contraction in the sense of self, collapsing into a helpless and victimized sense of self, and tremendous feeling of alone-ness pervades almost everything in the client's experience.

As guide to a client who is looking for grounding in the midst of such transition, I invite you to start by first holding the space with a sense of warmth and safety, often using a grounding exercise with breath and feeling the feet root down into the earth. This is to land in the space and to anchor it into their mind and body, that the therapy space is safe, nurturing, and calm. I establish that therapy is not going to fix the problem or even take the pain away, but that the client can walk forward through this painful process knowing that they now have someone alongside them when it becomes unbearable. We also establish that there is no knowing when the pain will subside, but we do know that it will, it will. One day. And until that day, they are not alone in facing the fury of whatever comes up in the process.

Case example

When I first met Cleo she was 31 years old and her chief complaint was "mixed anxiety and depression." She reported feeling "victimized by the burden of fear, excessive worry, and guilt." She presented as anxious, weighted, she had a tremble in her voice, and a quality of dignity about her alongside a frightened sense of fragility, which she worked hard to mask. She explained that she grew up in a tumultuous household which she adapted to by becoming meticulous and perfectionistic about everything in her life, "taking control" in such a way as to ensure that she did not add to the fury of the home front. A year prior to starting therapy, both of her parents died within a few months of each other, quite suddenly and unexpectedly. She arrived at therapy finding herself grappling with the staggering pain of loss of her parents, but also of any sense of safety or home. She was also tossed in the convoluted legal process of dealing with her parents' estate. She choked up and grew tearful as she expressed guilt for not having been more present with her parents when they were alive and there for her.

In our very first session, after giving voice to the story and circumstance, we moved quickly into body awareness. The retelling of everything triggered emotion, anxiety, and shallowness of breath. So I gently interrupted her and asked her to pause for a moment and notice where she felt the most sensation in her body at that moment.

C: My chest and throat.

R: How would you describe that sensation?

C: Tight, hollow, empty.

R: Take in a breath right into that place where there is sensation. Let the breath out be twice as long. If it is hard to breathe, don't force it, just become aware that there is breath flowing through you right now. Good. With each breath in, become a little more deliberate. With each breath out, let it go for twice as long. On the next breath in, as you breathe it out, let the eyes close and feel yourself go inward, deep inside to the center of that place where there was a tight sensation before. Distracting thoughts, judgmental thoughts, and resistance to the practice of focusing on the breath and the "deep inside" are all a part of the practice itself. People who *try* to *stop* thinking, judging, or distracting themselves, because they think they need to do that *in order to* meditate "properly" only make it worse. You have to embrace it *all*, and let it move in and through you. Notice if you get sucked into the movie the mind is playing for you. If you do, it is normal. But as you notice it, come back to your breath, back to your body. Back to the rise and fall of the chest with each breath, like waves of an ocean. Take a moment to bring your awareness to that space where there was sensation before. What do you notice now?

She reported that the sensation had not dissipated completely, but the grip it had on her heart had loosened significantly. She was in fact shocked at "how quickly [she] went so deep" and she recognized with a new level of awareness *how* much fear she held in her body and a strong desire to be free of it. We closed the session agreeing to continue to work this way over the course of therapy, and that over the week until our next meeting, she would incorporate a daily practice of taking three to five long, deep breaths in with the breath out twice as long, paying close attention to the thoughts and sensations that arise without analyzing or judging but rather witnessing them.

In the following session, she stated that the practice illuminated her as to the conflict she had between her mind, which was racked by fearful thoughts, and her body, which was desperate to let it all go. The fear of being alone, the fear of crumbling under the immense pressure of her responsibilities, the fear of losing control, and in doing so failing to honor her parents' legacy all culminated into an unbearable and paralyzing plague. In her case, the pain of grieving her parents appeared to manifest as a tremendous emptiness, a loss of identity, but also an odd freedom from the role she played as "absorber of conflict" in the family constellation. She witnessed scathing self-condemnation for even considering that the tragedy of her parents' transition could possibly be connected with a feeling of freedom.

Over the course of our sessions, we used mindfulness practices of paying close attention to the thoughts and sensations in the body to become closely acquainted with the different emotions that were operating her system at any given moment. She became more adept at witnessing the quality of sensation, the thoughts associated with it, and identifying judgmental thoughts and actively letting them go, returning to her alignment with the witness.

She became acquainted with her fear as a mechanism for protection. She also witnessed the part of herself who could *choose* fear or something more resourceful such as trust in herself. Over time she came to accept that something of this severity of pain was necessary in order for her to discover her resilience, and more importantly, her Truth. She lamented that she had to endure such intense tragedy to tap into her Self, she observed feelings of victimization for "having to get hit so hard" to learn about herself. But even these thoughts soon became thoughts generated by the mind, which she could choose to lament, or decide against entertaining them because they served little purpose beyond perpetuating negativity.

Near the end of our work together, she came to accept that everything she had experienced was part of her journey, that she preferred to view it as something beyond her mind's comprehension, but still grounded in some form of universal wisdom that she sensed and had started to trust. She began to receive the idea that excruciating as it was, the pain was a great catalyst to bring her into knowing her Self and her life purpose. She had always been interested in the healing arts and began to pursue greater study of yoga, massage, and body wellness practices. In time, she was able to take ownership of her role as a healer in her own right, she began to derive strength from the vision of her mother as a powerful guide for her. She recognized that the pain she endured forced her to recognize her own as well as humanity's breathtaking capacity for resilience.

In our final sessions, we went into a guided visualization in which she imagined in the very depths of herself a fresh, fertile soil, beautiful, abundant earth. She saw herself planting a seed, and she took great pleasure in the process to come of nourishing that seed that it would grow beautifully into the next iteration of what this life would bring. She went on to pursue extensive study, knowledge, and wisdom in the healing arts and currently runs her own successful business as a practitioner of mind/body wellness. She continues to cycle through her own episodes with grief, each time growing more deeply nuanced and wise, but never without letting herself fall apart first. Now she does not fear becoming undone the same way she did before as she recognizes the cycle, and trusts the process.

CONCLUSION

During my work with Cleo, I observed my own fears and sorrow around loss surface many times. As I held the space for her process, I witnessed my own flashes of fear and desperation around losing my loved ones. There were moments in which I grew tearful with her because the situation was truly a devastating one and I felt helpless as to what I could possibly do to help. There were other moments when I felt clear that she would get through it, and my role in holding the space for her was exactly what I needed to be doing. I witnessed my own reactions without judgment or attachment, and actively practiced shifting my attention to her and her needs in the moment. As we worked together, I realized that (in the larger continuum), she chose me as a therapist in order for me to clarify my own relationship to death. During our therapeutic process, it became my discipline in mindfulness to experience the despair evoked in the session, witness it without fear, and transmute it into the endless well of compassion that mindfulness practices ask of us. Witnessing her resilience reinforced my own belief in the splendor of the human spirit. I also became deeply acquainted with my own capacity for compassion, a state in which I could state the truth, even if it was painful, while still holding the space of great love with strong tenderness.

It is wildly uncomfortable to deal with death, but when we sit through the process, one breath at a time, we see that grief becomes one of the fibers that makes us up, that cycles through us; nothing more, nothing less.

ADDENDUM

I recently received this message from Cleo. It had been three years since our final session of the round of more intensive work, though we have met intermittently since then. This is what she said:

> Five years ago today, I was a different person—an exhausted, confused 30-year-old with a family but no active connection to my heart or my purpose. My mother's death was the first domino to fall and five years later I've lost them all, but gained an immeasurable sense of self, empowerment and capacity for gratitude. I've felt an enormous amount of pain in the last five years, more than I would wish on anyone, but it mirrors the depth of the love for life I also feel now. The lessons embedded in the challenges that come our way are like gold if we can see them as opportunities. Days like today will always be hard, but I'm choosing to honor instead of mourn, to feel the beauty instead of weep, and to grow instead of shrink in the face of hardship.

Identifying and healing grief in an alcohol and drug treatment program through the use of mindful yoga and art therapy

Mindfulness, yoga, and art

To be mindful is to have full attention in the present moment, and to attend to this experience without judgment. Techniques that promote mindfulness are called practices because being mindful is not an achievement that is accomplished, but rather simply being, without the editorializing of the ego. To practice means to come back, again and again, to this state of being, free from a goal or value judgment (Kabot-Zinn, 2012).

Meditation, yoga and art can all be practiced in a non-judgmental manner and so the combined modalities of yoga and art therapy can be an excellent protocol for encouraging mindfulness (Gibbons, 2015). Helping people to find resolution of grief using mindful techniques has the advantage of meeting the grieving person where they are. Mental, emotional, and physical aspects of grief are addressed by yoga and art therapy. Also, yoga and art can both provide a means to make sense of unwelcome change by reconstructing stories, creating meaning, and facilitating growth (Neimeyer and Young-Eisendrath, 2015; Thompson and Neimeyer, 2014). There is no single way to experience or resolve grief. A mindful approach means that whatever stage or emotion is prominent at a particular moment in treatment can be fully experienced and readily integrated (Philbin, 2009).

In the presence of addiction, the mental, emotional, and physical aspects of grief can be intertwined with trauma, where individuals use substances to avoid the pain of grief as much as they do to avoid the pain of trauma. The grief may be so deeply embedded in the trauma that any attempt at processing will be frozen. Neither can be processed without gently attending to grief. In cases where the trauma is severe, due to witnessing or being involved in violent acts, the person may be aware of PTSD symptoms yet remain unaware of symptoms or sensations connected with grief. Particularly in this case, some form of mindfulness approach can bring physical and emotional awareness and begin to make treatment more accessible (Dayton, 2000).

Additionally, layers of cultural habit support avoidance. For people struggling with addiction, avoidance can become a lifestyle, and the fear of opening the can of worms that trauma may represent is strong. A healing environment for trauma complicated by grief is one which will allow the stories to be told in a mindful, safe setting with opportunity for nonverbal, non-threatening means of addressing trauma. Under these conditions grief can also be experienced, expressed and integrated in a titrated way. In other words, a safe facilitated setting is important in creating a means to manage uncontrollable feelings (Volpicelli *et al.*, 1999). The following case study describes a yoga and art therapy treatment approach for grief complicated by the presence of unresolved trauma.

Background

The men living in this residential alcohol and drug treatment center were not generally attuned to mindfulness and seemed to this observer also avoidant of recognizing grief. If they were committed to treatment, they were often concretely focused on the nuts and bolts of treatment, typically working the 12-steps or diligently focused on practical goals like job training. Both grief and trauma would often go unexpressed. When trauma is comorbid with addiction it can sometimes remain undiagnosed, particularly complex trauma that insidiously affects every aspect of addiction recovery and may be a prime cause of addiction (Caruth and Burke, 2006). It is possible that many of the residents in this treatment program were affected by trauma, but only those who had a PTSD diagnosis or had acknowledged that the effects of trauma were an issue in their recovery process were referred to the yoga and art therapy group.

Mindful yoga and art therapy groups

Grief constricted by trauma was often present for individuals taking part in an ongoing, weekly yoga and art therapy group specifically targeting trauma. The group was offered in an all-male residential drug treatment program in an urban setting. After several six-week cycles the group developed an exclusive tone of trust and mutual respect, and, over time, the confidential nature of the group allowed the presence of grief, as a paramount issue, to be uncovered. The group would never have been overtly characterized as a grief group, but separating the trauma from the grief and gently allowing group members' stories to be seen and heard allowed grief to be expressed and understood, and was the key to this group's success.

Group structure

Yoga and art groups were consistently structured, following the same format each week. Each group began with a "check-in" question. The question was designed to orient the group toward a certain theme, such as trust, security, managing stress, and so on. With feedback from the participants, the facilitator would help the group form an intention, a positive statement in the present tense, which would serve as the focus of that day's group. The intention would then be paired with a mudra (a hand gesture meant to direct the body's energy) (LePage and LePage, 2013), which would be held during a brief meditation. For the meditation, group members were encouraged to repeat the intention slowly, both aloud and silently. This meditation was the start of the group's yoga/mindfulness practice, continuing with participants being led through a series of simple yoga poses or breath practices, with the aim of directing focus on immediate physical and emotional experience. Focus on present experience helped the participants come into the room in mind, body, and spirit, putting aside whatever was preoccupying them as they entered the room.

Yoga poses or breath practices, as well as the mudras, were chosen for qualities that supported the original intention. Yoga practice was always optional, provided that those choosing not to participate remained respectful. Even those not fully following the verbal instructions were visibly calmed and brought into sync with rest of the group simply by witnessing the experience, and it should be noted that nearly all group members would participate in all aspects of the group after a few weeks of observation.

An art directive followed the yoga. Each intervention was meant to coincide with the theme or intention, as well as providing trauma-informed care, including psychoeducation, expressive activities and processing (Miller and Guidry, 2001). After each person had a chance to present their artwork and receive questions and observations from other participants, the group closed with a "check-out" question. This may have been a reframing of the original question or simply a word describing the experience.

Case study

The following is a composite case study, not meant to reflect a single client, but compiled to highlight the important aspects of treatment, particularly the role of grief and grief processing as a pivotal component of the client's ability to move forward in recovery and create a sober identity for themselves.

We will call our subject Melvin, a 40-year-old African–American male. He was a resident of an alcohol and drug treatment center in an urban setting, mandated for 12 months of treatment after being charged with a drug-related offense. Melvin attended the weekly yoga and art therapy group for those who have experienced trauma. The group's purpose was made clear to participants, but there was no requirement or pressure to verbally share specifics about the trauma. Group members were asked to make a six-week commitment to the group, which was a closed group of four to six members. Group members could repeat cycles as often as they wished.

Melvin had been attending the group for several cycles. After minimally participating in the mindfulness/yoga portion of the group for the first cycle, Melvin began to avidly participate and encourage others to participate as well. He typically entered the group room with a surly attitude, often preoccupied and uncommunicative. His mood and demeanor routinely shifted after meditating, and sometimes he would say, "Wow, I almost fell asleep!" indicating that his mind and body had become calm. His participation in the art directives followed a similar path. Early in treatment his artwork was typically sparse; he would often find an alternative to the art directive, or perhaps put in minimal effort. However, the nature of the product was not an issue in this group where the facilitator often remarked, "In art therapy you can't do it wrong."

The group was on week two of the theme "exploring strengths." The group members had created personal symbols and were now sewing felt on burlap to make their symbol into a banner. Although the act of sewing was new to some, they were all engaged and determined. On this day there was conversation while the men worked. Their discussion centered around conflicting feelings among group members, who were processing the loss of an admired resident and group member who had been recently discharged from the program due to relapse. Some were angry with him for concealing his struggle and not turning to them for support, others were sympathetic and viewed relapse as part of the recovery process. Differing views made the atmosphere uncomfortable at times, but the tone remained peaceful as the work continued. Melvin took the opportunity to express his view about relapse and his continuing support for the lost group member. Perhaps in response to heightened feelings of grief and loss, triggered in the safe environment of the group, Melvin then began to compare his own trauma history with that of the missing participant. This was actually a means of introducing, for the first time, a rough narrative description of Melvin's primary trauma: he had witnessed the murder of a close friend. At this point, he had little interest in detailing the incident; in fact he behaved as if it were already common knowledge, and instead he spoke of his love for his dead friend, and the self-respect he lost because his subsequent relationships were distorted through the lens of his own anger.

The experience of safety in the group, where it was recently demonstrated that conflicting emotions could be tolerated, was perhaps the catalyst for Melvin's ability to express his feelings of grief. The grief, which previously could only be expressed in numbness, anger, and suppression, was now a confusing jumble of sadness, fear, longing, anger, love, and regret. Melvin was comfortable expressing the confusion and seemed visibly relieved to focus on grief, simply accepting the trauma as a fact of his experience. At this point, he spontaneously added a heart shape to his banner. The group closed with the check-out question, "What is one word for an emotional strength that has been expressed in your banner?" Melvin replied, "Love."

As the group cycle continued, Melvin readily participated in all aspects of the group. He gradually was able to acknowledge the helpfulness of the mindfulness practice. He noted that sometimes he did not initially want to participate, because he knew he would be induced to shift his mood. Perhaps he was reluctant to move away from the protective sulking, complaining, or focusing on perceived transgressions by others that allowed him to cope with the environment outside the group. During future check-outs, however, he would consciously express his appreciation for the group process and his understanding that he was making choices to participate that allowed him to express vulnerable feelings that he could not expose elsewhere. In his artwork he became willing to create complete pieces and the heart symbol recurred regularly.

In subsequent groups Melvin was able to refer more freely to his trauma story and the group remained neutral witnesses to his evolving position in relation to it. He continued to express his grief, and began to allow the themes of the groups to be used as a tool to find voice for sadness, fear, regret, and so on, as he was ready. After four cycles, Melvin chose to leave the group. He was advancing in the recovery program and was interviewing for jobs and looking for an apartment. A new sense of confidence was evident, and his attitude and demeanor had become cheerful and positive. Melvin was moving forward with a clearer sense of himself. This self-awareness was demonstrated when he would sometimes stop in at the beginning of group sessions and offer words of encouragement to remaining group members.

CONCLUSION

Occasions for grief are frequent in the lives of the men at this site. In addition to grief associated with trauma, as the men develop a new sober identity there is grief over the loss of their previous identity, however flawed. There is also grief associated with the hurt or wrong they caused others while actively using addictive substances. The culture of the institution parallels a tendency in the larger culture to ignore or actively suppress grief. The group members who were angry with their relapsed friend were resisting the experience of loss. It is important that there was acceptance for all levels of readiness to process grief and trauma. In this yoga and art therapy group, the focus on the present moment contributed to the sense of acceptance as well as the group members' ability to move at their own pace and navigate their own path of healing. Symptoms of grief could easily become overwhelming for those in recovery, who are not accustomed to coping with feelings at all, having successfully avoided or masked feelings with alcohol or drugs. Treatment offering mindful yoga and art therapy provides an environment with tools for both processing grief and gaining the emotional literacy necessary to deal with grief and other emotions inevitably encountered in sobriety (Khanna and Greeson, 2013).

References

Arango, P., Houtrow, A.J., Kuhthau, K.A., Kuo, D.Z., Neff, J.M., and Simmons, J.M. (2011) 'Family-centered care: Current applications and future directions in pediatric health care.' *Maternal and Child Health Journal 16*, 297–305.

Bertman, S. (1999) 'Introduction.' In S.L. Bertman (ed.) *Grief and the Healing Arts: Creativity as Therapy*. Amityville, NY: Baywood Publishing Co.

Caruth, B. and Burke, P. (2006) 'Psychological trauma and addiction treatment.' *Journal of Chemical Dependency Treatment 8*, 2, 1–14.

Corr, C. (2015) 'Let's stop staging persons who are coping with loss.' *Illness, Crisis and Loss 23*, 3, 226–241.

Dayton, T. (2000) *Trauma and Addiction: Ending the Cycle of Pain through Emotional Literacy*. Deerfield Beach, FL: Health Communications.

Fonagy, P. and Target, M. (2006) 'The mentalization focused approach to self pathology.' *Journal of Personality Disorders 20*, 6, 544–576.

Forstmeier, S. and Maecker, A. (2007) 'Comparison of two diagnostic systems for complicated grief.' *Journal of Affective Disorders 99*, 1–3, 203–211.

Gibbons, K. (2015) *Integrating Art Therapy and Yoga Therapy: Yoga, Art, and the Use of Intention*. London: Jessica Kingsley Publishers.

Harvard Mental Health Letter (2011) 'Beyond the five stages of grief.' Harvard Health Publications. Available at www.health.harvard.edu/newsletter_article/beyond-the-five-stages-of-grief, accessed on December 15, 2016.

Hass-Cohen, N. and Findlay, J. (2015) *Art Therapy and the Neuroscience of Relationships, Creativity, and Resiliency: Skills and Practices*. New York: W.W. Norton.

Horowitz, M.J., Siegel, B., Holen, A., and Bonanno, G.A. (1997) 'Diagnostic criteria for complicated grief disorder.' *American Journal of Psychology 154*, 904–910.

Jacobs, S., Mazure, C., and Prigerson, H. (2000) 'Diagnostic criteria for traumatic grief.' *Death Studies 24*, 185–199.

Jones, B., Contro, N., and Koch, K.D. (2014) 'The duty of the physician to care for the family in pediatric palliative care: Context, communication and caring.' *Pediatrics 33*, S8–S15.

Kabot-Zinn, J. (2012) *Mindfulness for Beginners: Reclaiming the Present Moment and Your Life.* Boulder, CO: Sounds True.

Khanna, S. and Greeson, J. (2013) 'A narrative review of yoga and mindfulness as complimentary therapies for addiction.' *Complementary Therapies in Medicine* June 21, 3, 244–252.

King-West, E. and Hass-Cohen, N. (2008) 'Art therapy, neuroscience and complex PTSD.' In N. Hass-Cohen and R. Carr (eds) *Art Therapy and Clinical Neuroscience.* London: Jessica Kingsley Publishers.

Konisberg, R. (2011) *The Truth about Grief: The Myth of Its Five Stages and the New Science of Loss.* New York: Simon & Schuster.

Kübler-Ross, E. (1969) *On Death and Dying.* New York: Scribner.

Kübler-Ross, E. and Kessler, D. (2005) *On Grief and Grieving: Finding the Meaning of Grief through the Five Stages of Loss.* New York: Scribner.

LePage, J. and LePage, L. (2013) *Mudras for Healing and Transformation.* Sebastopol, CA: Integrative Yoga Therapy.

Lichtenthal, W.G., Cruess, D.G., and Prigerson, H.G. (2004) 'A case for establishing Complicated Grief as a distinct mental disorder in DSM-V.' *Clinical Psychology Review 24*, 637–662.

Linehan, M.M. (1993) *Cognitive-Behavioral Treatment of Borderline Personality Disorder.* New York: Guilford Press.

Miller, D. and Guidry, L. (2001) *Addictions and Trauma Recovery: Healing the Body, Mind and Spirit.* New York: W.W. Norton.

Neimeyer, R. and Young-Eisendrath, P. (2015) 'Assessing a Buddhist treatment for bereavement and loss: The mustard seed project.' *Death Studies 39*, 5, 263–273.

Philbin, K. (2009) 'Transpersonal integrative yoga therapy: A protocol for grief and bereavement.' *International Journal of Yoga Therapy 19*, 129–141.

Prigerson, H.G. and Jacobs, S.C. (2001) 'Traumatic grief as a distinct disorder: A rationale, consensus criteria, and a preliminary empirical test.' In M.S. Stroebe, R.O. Hansson, W. Stroebe, and H. Schut (eds) *Handbook of Bereavement Research.* Washington, DC: APA.

Prigerson, H.G., Shear, M.K., Jacobs, S.C., Reynolds, C.F., *et al.* (1999) 'Consensus criteria for traumatic grief: A preliminary empirical test.' *British Journal of Psychiatry 174*, 67–73.

Raphael, B. and Martinek, N. (1997) 'Assessing traumatic bereavement and PTSD.' In J.P. Wilson and T.M. Keane (eds) *Assessing Psychological Trauma and PTSD.* New York: Guilford.

Shear, K., Monk, T., Houck, P., Melhem, N., *et al.* (2007) 'An attachment-based model of complicated grief including the role of avoidance.' *European Archives of Psychiatry and Clinical Neurosciences 257*, 8, 453–461.

Sherebrin, H. (1999) 'The role of the visual image in psychodynamics of grief resolution (viewed through Jewish law and tradition).' In S.L. Bertman (ed.) *Grief and the Healing Arts: Creativity as Therapy.* Amityville, NY: Baywood Publishing.

Stroebe, M. and Schut, H. (1999) 'The dual process model of coping with bereavement: rationale and description.' *Death Studies 23*, 197–224.

Thompson, B. and Neimeyer, R. (eds) (2014) *Grief and the Expressive Arts.* New York: Routledge.

Umphrey, L.R. and Cacciatore, J. (2014) 'Love and death: Relational metaphors following the death of a child.' *Journal of Relationships Research 5*, e4, 1–8.

Viorst, J. (1986) *Necessary Losses.* New York: Ballantine Books.

Volpicelli, J., Balaraman, G., Hahn, J., Wallace, H. and Bux, D. (1999) 'The role of uncontrollable trauma in PTSD and alcohol addiction.' *Alcohol Research and Health 23*, 4, 256–262.

Wallin, D. (2007) *Attachment in Psychotherapy.* New York: Guilford.

Williams, M. and Penman, D. (2011) *Mindfulness: An Eight-Week Plan for Finding Peace in a Frantic World.* New York: Rodale.

PART II

Self-Studies

6

Imaginal Dialogues

Coping with Countertransference

Marisa Zarczynski

Overview

Since I reached my mid-20s, I have thought more about motherhood than I ever have in the past. Many old friends, acquaintances, classmates, and past colleagues are getting married or not getting married and are either having or thinking about having children. I knew this time in my life would eventually come where people I knew and know would start to settle down and go through this process. While I do not judge them I have known from my young adulthood that I do not want children, and for a long time I was convinced I never wanted to get married. I remember my grandfather asking me, a cousin, and my brother when he would have some grandchildren. We all looked at one another and responded with "Not yet," or in my case, "Never."

I remember feeling confident with my answer at the time, and reassured myself that it was better to be honest with my grandfather than give him false hope. However, I also remember how disappointed he looked when I had given him my answer. In addition, my brother had thrown me a glance, which I presumed to be surprise, as we had never discussed the topic before. I also thought that he too looked disappointed. It was after that point that I really started to look at mothers with their children everywhere I went, in a somewhat different light. I would see these pairings and sometimes wonder, "What would that really be like for me?"

On occasion, I would smile at the thought of what my child might look like or feel like in my arms. I would ponder what kind of person this child would grow up to be and the kind of dedication it takes to be a parent. This line of thinking always leads me to the same place: I do not want to have children of my own.

When pushed to explain why I do not want children I have a list of reasons. The first and foremost reason is my deep-seated feeling that I would not want any child of mine to go through the difficulties, misery, and pain I have gone through in my life. I do not want to bring a child into this world knowing it might have bipolar disorder or possibly schizophrenia, which I believe to be inherent in my family. This is not to say that I think others suffering with mental illness should not bring children into this world. This is simply my decision. In addition, my family on both sides have a long history of substance abuse, mainly alcoholism. Both of these factors influence my decision since they have both been shown to be genetic and often linked together.

I definitely look back at my life and remember plenty of times being nurtured both emotionally and physically by my family, friends, teachers, and later, mentors. However, I also remember many times where I felt ignored by my family or friends, not loved as I would have liked. I distinctly remember my father asking me what was wrong with me when I was a young teenager and I told him I was depressed, and he firmly stated, "It's all in your head."

Looking back, there is truth to his statement: my bipolar disorder is in my head, in my neurotransmitters, serotonin levels and over-activity (or lack thereof) in certain parts of my brain. However, my father meant this to be a dismissing comment, as if my depression was not real and I was just making it up and should not dwell on such things. As I grew up, I felt most of all that my father was not nurturing and for the most part felt no need to show his emotions to his children. While he was never diagnosed with a mental illness it seemed obvious to me that he suffered from depression and social anxiety, but now I will never know for sure. My father passed away while I was in my second year of college. I became closest to him in the last years before his passing. However, his death was unexpected and there was no saying "goodbye." I really grieved his passing after college. I suppose at the time I was in denial and threw myself into my schoolwork and jobs at college. It was not until after I graduated that I painted my first portrait of my father. Although I did not know it then, it was my way of coping and saying goodbye to him.

My mother, on the other hand, was nurturing but this changed over the years. While she has always been supportive of most of my recent life choices, she has a very hard time expressing her emotions towards me, unless I push them out of her. Outsiders might say she is even cold, but I know this is not true. She doesn't seem to have this difficulty when nurturing friends and other loved ones in her family; only my brother and I seemed to have been more difficult for her.

Since art therapy requires that we be aware not only of what is going on with our clients but in tune with what we ourselves are feeling and reacting to (both within and outside of sessions), it seems logical to pursue such a mode of self-inquiry to further understand the relationship between myself, my clients (who may struggle with similar illnesses and life-affecting decisions), and my work as both an artist and art therapist. This chapter includes an exploration of 1) auto-ethnography, as a starting point for examining self-stories and unsecure attachments, and 2) the utility of imaginal dialogues in therapy and in processing countertransference.

Auto-ethnography: The intentionality of self-story

Defining auto-ethnography for my purposes deals with intentionality. Intentionality refers to making our motives known for sharing a particular life event and then sharing our own insights from the experience, which can transform both our readers and us. Some authors have observed that we are not the "owners" of our personal stories when shared since the meaning of such an account only comes when there is an interaction between the writer and the reader of such a personal account. It has also been noted that reading such personal accounts forces a reader to critically reflect on their respective roles in current social structures. Despite being an underutilized and criticized form of inquiry, auto-ethnography can help us to understand personal actions within the context of society. While this does not address the narcissism some associate with this kind of approach, it does support my belief that our life experiences make us unique and can therefore help us to understand similar experiences, which we may not have been otherwise able to approach.

With this concept of auto-ethnography in mind, I approach broken or un-secure attachments, which are experiences that are felt and manifested both physiologically and psychologically. The ability or inability to be aware of such attachments is important. It is critical for both the individual and those who might interact with them. The ability to be aware of such interactions also plays an important role in the therapeutic process. The therapeutic process is not one-sided. Instead, it is a complex interplay between therapist and client.

This contributes to the art therapy community in an intimate way. As part of the therapeutic relationship, we must be responsible for investigating ourselves and our perceived realities and not just those of our clients. In addition, through the process of dialoguing with images and recording the dialogues, an art therapist can become more aware of potential countertransference issues.

With this concept of auto-ethnography in mind, I approach broken or un-secure attachments, which are experiences that are felt and manifested both physiologically and psychologically. The ability or inability to be aware of such attachments is important. It is not only critical for the individual and those who might interact with them, but this also plays an important role in the therapeutic process, which is not one sided but, rather, a complex interplay between therapist and client.

Identifying broken or un-secure attachments

In his book *Attachment in Psychotherapy*, David J. Wallin (2007) discusses John Bowlby's ideas about the "internal working model" that had been proposed by Kenneth Craik:

> Bowlby argued, the infant's repeated interactions with caregivers result in knowledge about the interpersonal world that registers internally as a working model—Bowlby theorized that from early infancy the individual's working model of attachment enables him or her to recognize patterns of interaction with the caregiver that already repeatedly occurred and thus to "know" what the caregiver will do next. Because the working model influences both expectations and the behavior that flows from them, it can shape interactions as well as being shaped by them. (pp.26–27)

If the idea of the internal working model could serve to help an individual by assisting them in essentially thinking, and thus reacting, to what they believe a caregiver might do, what happens when the internal working model is damaged? And how might this affect the therapeutic relationship? How does this impact the "intentionality" with which we select and relay our self-stories?

Bowlby's conclusion is that individuals develop "self-protective" or even "self-defeating" actions. We develop private and secretive stories with their own "intentionality," beyond the scope of our conscious awareness.

We see this as therapists, and like our clients, might use defenses in such a way as to damage the self. If this internal working model functions outside of awareness but can be "updated" or "revised" (albeit with resistance), how can we as therapists be more self-aware and in turn assist our clients in doing so through the therapeutic relationship?

Therapists can help bring such behavior into awareness, both for themselves and to help patients, through the use of play and imaginal dialoguing. This complex process allows an individual to become more self-aware, which ultimately aids in forming secure attachments, and allows for greater freedom of choice in selecting and/or creating a preferable "story of self."

Play and imaginal dialogues

In his book *Art as Medicine: Creating a Therapy of the Imagination*, McNiff (1992) states that "outside the realm of psychosis, image dialogues deepen the creative process" (p.109). He goes on to write about talking with images as being something that is not fixed or finite, but rather an experience that can be ongoing as long as the image speaks to us. He states, "Image dialogue is based on acceptance of the autonomous life of pictures within a world of interactions and multiple perspectives. The artist realizes that the process of expression is never finished. It is unending dialogue" (p.105).

McNiff based his ideas of imaginal dialogue on many existing psychoanalytic theories, psychology, and art therapy experiences in which he realized talking at the images only served the ego rather than the complete self (1992, p.105). He has worked extensively not only with the dreams of his clients and students but his own artwork, and often refers to art therapy as being a healing tool that lends itself to the soul, taking the word therapy from the Greek *therapeia*, roughly meaning "to heal," particularly in a "medical" sense.

Jung's practice of "active imagination" follows the artistic tradition of encouraging characters and images to reveal themselves, to speak for themselves, and influence the person who contemplates them (McNiff, 1992). McNiff links this idea to his own work with clients, stating that "[t]he discipline of formulating the specific qualities of an imaginal figure, as distinguished from the self, is a therapeutic and artistic objective. While articulating the characters of imaginal figures, we are sharpening our aesthetic and emotional sensibilities" (McNiff, 1992, pp.110–111). In other words, we talk to our images, and then imagine how our images would respond. We dialogue with our imagination.

Imaginal dialogues could be viewed as play (mainly narrative play) for the sake of emotional development, not unlike a child needs play and uses narrative to develop. Or it could also be similar to the way we use auto-ethnography to infuse our self-selected, playful narratives with both conscious and unconscious "intentionality." Tuber (2008) describes how play can build confidence, something necessary when starting out in any profession but especially one that deals with helping those in need as individuals who rely on us for secure attachment. Slade (1994) discusses the "functions of playing" and how this links to children's unconscious and conscious workings. Slade also writes about how symbolic play helps to create meaning for children, and discusses the differences between working with children and adults; adult clients "talk through" their issues, which can be "curative," while children play out such narratives when they are able (p.91).

My personal experience of using image dialogue as a way to cope with countertransference has been helpful in my work with populations often considered to be "difficult" and resistant to therapeutic work. For example, female forensic and inpatient populations (both child/adolescent and adult), as well as young adults who have aged out of the foster care system. Having image dialogue as one of the tools I use to help me with understanding my client's resistance not only to creating artwork but discussing their work, especially in group settings, has been very cathartic, meditative, and insightful for me as an art therapist. It has also allowed me to explore my own resistance to working with particular clients and personal frustrations when creating my private artwork.

Grief and countertansference

Working with and around grief feelings can put the art therapist at risk of merging with her clients and their symptoms. This self-study and the examples shared were utilized as a means of addressing my own merging with clients, who were diagnosed with bipolar disorder, and hospitalized on inpatient units. I started to realize that I was merging with clients when I started to create more meaningful artwork during group therapy sessions rather than just doodling alongside the clients. I started to enjoy the time to make art when I should have been more observant of what my clients were doing (watching how they were creating art, etc.). When I found the art-making time of my clients to be therapeutic for my own wellbeing, I knew I had to step back and work on my internalized notions of my self-story. I had to work on my countertransference issues and also with my personal grief revolving around my bipolar diagnosis.

Only through this type of investigation will art therapy manifest its psychological and artistic depth. We art therapists contribute something different and more intimate when we reflect upon our personal experience with art. Some might disregard this type of self-analysis because of its "subjectivity." I have found the self-analysis of art therapists to be more direct than their analysis of another person's art, which is equally subjective, and "once removed" from the process of working with materials. As helpful as the art therapist's interpretations of another person's experience may be in therapy, they do not bring us close to the phenomenon of art as the art therapist's self- interpretations do (McNiff, 1989, p.205).

Malchiodi (2006) advocates for using "Feeling Journals." She has used them not only with clients but also kept one for herself, for over 25 years, to explore her own thoughts and feelings, both in her own life and concerning her work with clients. She advises clients and therapists to "Write something about your drawing on the back of it or on another piece of paper," asking yourself later questions like, "Have your images evolved over time? Are there any regularly recurring emotions? How do you portray them?" She goes on to suggest that individuals "[t]ry to periodically write down some of the answers to these questions; this will help you discover patterns, forms, colors, and content that are part of your unique visual vocabulary for expressing feelings" (p.154).

In Figures 6.1, 6.2, and 6.3, I explore the interactions between my self-story, the countertransference reactions, and grief feelings I experienced while engaging with certain individuals, and the use of imaginal dialogues and art making, to navigate those muddy waters.

The artwork

When I created Figure 6.1, a painting of me as a young child, I was working as an art therapist intern at a major New York City hospital, on the adult inpatient psychiatric unit with mainly dual diagnosed patients. As my internship was coming to a close, I began experiencing anxiety and feelings of depression when working with these clients. It became obvious to my supervisor that something was going on; I had trouble expressing myself in supervision sessions, and became tearful at one point. I spoke to my supervisor about my bipolar disorder, as it appeared to be affecting the way in which I was interacting with clients as an art therapist intern. I became aware of my countertransference issues when I felt the therapeutic release of creating artwork in groups I was supposed to be running. I created this piece of artwork (Figure 6.1) in a general response to the populations I was working with; they made me acutely aware of my own mental illness and fears of one day being hospitalized myself.

Figure 6.1 Image from childhood

Figure 6.2 Fetus in womb of warmth

I had been thinking about my childhood for the last couple of days after completing "Image from childhood" (Figure 6.1) and the imaginal dialogue that went with it, which led me to think of motherhood. I painted an image of what is supposed to be a growing fetus surrounded by the warmth and nourishment of a womb (Figure 6.2). At the last minute, I added the "cuts" on the various colors of this womb dripping some kind of substance.

As I have reached my late 20s and will very soon be 30, I am constantly hearing about a woman's "biological ticking clock." In that phrase, there is a sense of pressure to be absolutely sure about this decision before it is biologically too late. While this is a decision I have contemplated thoroughly, there seem to be doubts lingering somewhere in my mind that maybe I am only making this decision based on fear. Maybe I have let the fear of having a child with a mental illness (who might go through the same difficulties as I have) get in the way of ever being able to even develop the desire to have children.

Whether it is my fears that have lead me to my current position about not having children or just my natural instinct not to want to reproduce, I know I cannot be alone in whatever fears and doubts I have. I am sure that many mothers and fathers that go through a similar process of fear and anxiety, but maybe they do not have to worry about the strong possibility of their child being mentally ill or what it would be like to raise a child while suffering from bipolar.

When I reflect on the "warmth and nourishment" of the womb in Figure 6.2, I look back at my life and remember plenty of times being nurtured both emotionally and physically by my family, friends, teachers, and later, mentors. This idea of nurturing reminds me a lot of working with clients at my two internships during my graduate program.

Therapists, by definition, nurture their clients emotionally. It often seemed that this new nurturing during therapy could be reparative as if it helps to heal a possible lack of nurturing they had or perceived to have as younger individuals. I have experienced this in my own therapy, where I sometimes come out of a session feeling more confident and reassured, like a child might feel after being attended to or positively rewarded by a parent. This exercise revealed to me how aware I must be of the nurturing nature of the work we do with clients both individually and in groups, and how fragile this sense of nurturing can be. It also revealed to me that while we have to be responsible and ethical in our work as art therapists, we must remember that the healing being done is inevitably up to the client, and being aware of my countertransference is important so that I do not metaphorically "carry" the weight of clients on my shoulders—or in the case of this painting, in my metaphorical "womb."

An imaginal dialogue

Figure 6.3 Skull and candles

Figure 6.3 and the related dialogue helped me to understand, on a deeper level, the kind of fear and anxiety one might feel being on an inpatient unit, in addition to one's own original diagnoses. Unfortunately, it can be easy to forget that for clients, in any circumstance, it takes courage to come to therapy—to reach out and ask for help. We, as therapists, are only part of a much larger and longer life process for clients with chronic mental illness. This impacted my "self-story" because it made me feel less alone. Knowing that there are so many other people that suffer from mental illness gives you a sense of belonging. It is a unique community and one that is filled with stigma and misunderstanding, but also a community of people who feel and have the ability to work and change their life circumstances like any other person in any other community. As a therapist this impacts me because it serves as a reminder that we are an important part of this process, that we can help to foster change, but it does not happen in a day and sometimes takes a team of professionals. Learning to work as part of a team (whether that be a medical team or the team dynamic of running a group or individual session) is essential. The following is a portion of the imaginal dialogue for Figure 6.3.

- *What is the first thing that comes to mind when you look at this painting?* The first thing that comes to my mind is lack of support, both literally and metaphorically. The skull rests on three vertebras, the bones that make up the neck and spine. They appear unstable, as if they might collapse at any moment, leaving the skull to fall off the table upon which its chin is resting.

- *What do you know about being unstable?* I have felt unstable since I was about 11 or 12 years old, right before I first started to see a therapist at 13 (albeit against my will). I was diagnosed with clinical depression, insomnia, and an unidentified personality disorder. I remember being very sad, lonely, and angry at the world during that time. I often felt confused about the feelings I was having and would have mildly violent outbursts towards family members and friends when provoked (at least when I felt threatened). In moments of clarity, I would wonder why I behaved the way I did and would have a great deal of guilt. I felt as though I was always apologizing for one thing or another. I can't remember now how long I stayed in therapy; it could not have been more than a few months.

The first therapist I ever saw specialized in children and young adults, and after two sessions she transferred me to another therapist at a well-known hospital in New York City. She called me one night and told me that she felt uncomfortable treating me as she was unable to sleep and was perpetually worried about me and whether or not I would harm myself. This is also around the time that I started to cut myself. They were superficial surface cuts to my arms but nonetheless a form of self-mutilation.

I remember hating my new therapist. She prescribed anti-depressants, which made me feel worse and which had terrible side effects. I remember having horrible gastro-intestinal problems, headaches, lightheadedness, and friends told me that I was "like a zombie" and did not seem like myself. After a few sessions with this new therapist, she handed me over to what I believe was a social worker, at the same hospital. She was convinced that I should go to a girls' home and be removed from my family. At that point, I refused to go back to any doctors.

When I turned 14 and started at a very competitive specialized high school for the arts, my insomnia got so bad that I was missing classes all the time. I was often sent to the nurse's office to "rest" and eventually failed one or two of my classes. By the time I was 15, it was obvious (to my mother, at least), that there was a serious problem. I saw at least three specialized sleep doctors and tried a variety of sleeping medications and methods. Eventually, when none of this worked, we sought out a holistic route and I received acupuncture and hypnotherapy. This too did nothing for me.

Around this time, my mother asked for a divorce from my father, which I had been encouraging her to do for years. When this happened, my mother moved out of the apartment I had grown up in, and I quickly followed. My brother stayed with my father. To make matters worse we lived in different apartments, but in the same building; it was very odd. Soon to follow was my brother's arrest. He was eventually cleared, but that and another physical altercation between him and me left us not speaking for almost two years. I felt I had unstable sleeping, unstable school, unstable home environment, and an unstable social life. I remember feeling like my entire world was crashing down around me.

- *What else comes to mind when you look at this painting?* It is very morbid, which for me is not very strange. I started writing poetry when I was very young, after my first encounter with a special course in elementary school. I received some silly award for my work but at the time I was very pleased with myself and ever since then I have kept journals, which mainly contain my poetry. Around the time I started middle school, I began writing very morbid poetry, making many references to death and dying and the occasional mention of suicide. I wrote of friendships that ended badly and true love I wish I had, how I cursed other people and God. I did not grow up in a very religious family, but my mother did start going to church around this time and my father grew up Orthodox Catholic. I was very determined for so young a person that God did not exist and somewhere deep down inside I resented my mother for believing or even being spiritual. Even to this day, while I am not a believer, I sometimes wish that I had faith and religion in my life. I wonder if I might find comfort in this as so many others do.

I have always been intrigued by death and what happens to us when we are gone, and in the greater scope of things whether this really matters, that we are just such a small part of the universe's infinitude. But after working with very young children with cancer in an outpatient setting of a hospital, at my first graduate school internship, I realized that this attitude I have carried for so long allowed me to work with these children without becoming heartbroken and upset every day. While there was nothing insignificant about their situations it did strike me as strange that I was able to handle that environment as well as I did. And ironically, I did not handle the death of my father the summer before my sophomore year in college well at all. In fact, I still have many unresolved issues around my father's passing and the effects of our relationship on my everyday life.

I would say that I am much less morbid now than I was as a middle-school student. When I first started my training in graduate school, I came across an old poem and a fictional short story that I wrote for a class from that time period, and remember thinking to myself, "Why didn't any of my teachers talk to my parents? Why did no one think that I might need help?"

- *What is going on inside the open skull in this painting?* There is a snake with no head or tail, a kind of endless creature that infinitely wraps around itself. This is sometimes how I visualize my diagnosis of bipolar disorder, a never-ending cycle. A disorder that even when treated properly, in my case with medications and consistent talk therapy, is never cured—a part of me that I might never be rid of unless health workers, doctors, and scientists find a "cure." I think of it as slimy and slithering in this endless heavy knot that longs to be undone. I sometimes imagine slaying this creature as if it were some dragon in a fairy tale and that all would be right in the kingdom of my mind once it was gone. However, over the years I have also come to imagine the other parts of me as ever learning and growing, leaning hopefully every day closer to the light which metaphorically represents a sense of hope. The roses represent these other parts, the pieces of myself that I have come to appreciate over the years.

Like roses or any flower, I must be cared for and looked after; I need water, sun, and nutrients to thrive, like any other creature. But my roses are jagged and thorny, sometimes betraying me. I begin to hope sometimes that I have finally found my balance between these two parts of me and then I will have an episode. It takes me a while to believe again that I will be okay and that I will get through the difficulties that life throws my way, or even the difficulties I have created.

I am just learning to fully accept and own this duality, in the way that one might own up to an addiction. It was not until my junior year of college that I was correctly diagnosed with bipolar disorder, thanks to the keen observation of a college counselor and his wife who was studying to be a clinical social worker. It has since taken me six years to be able to talk about my diagnosis with my immediate family and even some of my friends. In addition, my training in my graduate program helped me to "own" this part of me, that mental health is a matter of degree. While I believed and witnessed that everyone has their own problems and issues, it was not until I started to think about my illness as a matter of degree, and less of a curse and more of a disease, that I was able to speak freely among my professors, supervisors, and peers about my diagnosis. This has helped me to work with clients who suffer from a range of issues and from a different perspective (one that is more empathetic and less angry and not dominated by fear). I am, however, a work in progress (not unlike my past) as I am sure future clients will be too. I am finally starting to accept that this is okay, that this duality makes me who I am and if I hate myself for something I did not choose I will always be miserable, as I cannot change the fact that I am bipolar.

- *What about the candles in the painting?* Right now, as I look at the candles, I am reminded that we all burn out at some point and life will end. I do not want to spend my whole life in fear of my mental illness. In this moment, in a week that has been good and productive, I feel like there are so many things I still want to do and accomplish and believe that I can. I am not manic but closer to my baseline. I am aware that I have recently been taking a new medication and therapy has been going well. I know that I might not feel this way tomorrow, or a week from now, but I am allowing myself to enjoy the moment while it lasts, instead of dwelling on the fact that I know it will not.

Protocol: Imaginal dialogues and coping with countertransference

Objective

To explore countertransferential material for the purposes of improving treatment and the therapeutic alliance.

Material goal

The therapist will complete as many artworks as is necessary in service of the objective, and in facilitation of the following measurable goals:

- The therapist will be able to identify how countertransferential material may be significantly impacting the therapeutic relationship, as evidenced by verbal statement and/or visual depiction.

- The therapist will be able to identify one or two ways in which the processing of countertransferential material may be used to improve treatment outcomes, as evidenced by verbal statement and/or visual depiction.

Duration

As is appropriate to the individual's schedule.

Curriculum

STEP 1 FILTERING THE FEELINGS

Create a mandala that represents how you feel in this moment, with respect to your therapeutic work with clients. You may use any material that speaks to you. After you have completed your work, dialogue with the piece, focusing out how much of your feeling states and/or mental and emotional preoccupations feel like they authentically originate from you, or from your clients. Sample questions might include:

- Where is your eye drawn on the page? Why do you think that is? Where does your eye go next?

- How does your attention move through the piece?

- What does it feel like in your body to examine this image? If this image were in your body, where would it be? How would it feel? How would it move?

- What words come to mind?

- What thoughts or memories float into your consciousness?

- What feels as if it relates to your client? What feels as if it relates to you, personally? Where and how does this material become blended?

- What aspect of your client's story feels too close to your own? Where and how are they different? How might you create space around these "crossroads" of insight?

STEP 2 MATERIAL EXPLORATION

Play and experiment with a variety of materials until you find which ones resonate the most. This may involve creating multiple sketches and/or artworks, or only one. The intent is to explore until you have an affective response to the visceral qualities of the medium of choice, and if it feels like a good "fit" for exploring your identified topic. Try tuning your thoughts out and allow your physical and emotional responses to speak to you.

STEP 3 DIVE IN

Reflect on your initial mandala and its dialogue. Free write, circle, or otherwise note some of the themes or topics you notice frequently popping up. Select one to three topics/themes that you would like to explore more in depth. Begin working on a piece to address whichever topic you have selected to tackle first. As your work progresses, you may decide to work on multiple pieces and topics at one time, or perhaps you prefer to address them one by one. In whatever manner you decide to proceed, remember to dialogue with your artwork and allow the answers to authentically emerge from the stillness of your mind and inner space, without criticism or judgement. As you begin to respond to them, more specific questions may come to mind, and I would invite you to write those down and address them as well.

STEP 4 REFLECTION

Examine your artworks as a gestalt. Review what themes came up in your dialogues and construct a narrative that tells the story of this exploration. Questions to ask yourself might include:

- What have you learned about yourself?

- How has this informed your experience of grief?

- How has this informed your understanding of your client's grief?

- What gift has your countertransference granted you?

- How might this inform new directions in treatment?

References

Malchiodi, C.A. (2006) *The Art Therapy Sourcebook*. Second edition. New York: McGraw-Hill Professional Publishing.

McNiff, S. (1989) *Depth Psychology of Art*. Springfield, IL: Charles C. Thomas.

McNiff, S. (1992) *Art as Medicine: Creating a Therapy of the Imagination*. Boston, MA: Shambhala.

Slade, A. (1994) 'Making meaning and making believe: Their role in the clinical process.' In A. Slade and D.P. Wolf (eds) *Children at Play: Clinical and Developmental Approaches to Meaning and Representation*. New York: Oxford University Press.

Tuber, S. (2008) *Attachment, Play, and Authenticity: A Winnicott Primer*. Lanham, MD: Rowman & Littlefield.

Wallin, D.J. (2007) *Attachment in Psychotherapy*. New York: Guilford Press.

7

Mandala Making through Crochet to Navigate Grief

Julie Day

Crochet as a therapeutic vehicle
The differences between art and craft

When one thinks of the field of art therapy, handcrafts such as knitting, crochet, needlepoint, quilting, etc., do not typically come to mind. In fact, the word "craft" has a somewhat negative connotation due to the limitations commonly associated with its potential for expression. Crafts are usually functional, follow a specific pattern, and do not attempt to express feeling or metaphor in the finished product. However, while following a pattern does impose certain expressive limitations, one can still find personal symbolism and therapeutic benefit in choice of materials, desired outcome, and through the process of creation.

Therapeutic qualities

It is important to note the therapeutic benefits of crochet's repetitive quality. Crandall-Frazier (2008) has called crochet "hands-on meditation" that helps to align our hearts, nurture the spirit, quiet the mind, and center the soul (p.8). When we take time to hone our craft by practicing with the hook and thread, our skills will improve and so will our ability to cope with stress. Crochet then becomes a practice, with a corresponding increase in mindfulness and intention (Crandall-Frazier, 2008, pp.88–89). There is a "meditative effect of working with our hands…the effect of repetition that takes us to a place where our bodies are relaxed and our minds become still" (p.99). With practice, crochet can provide a space for contemplation where we can ponder questions and solutions and process difficult feelings.

Mandalas: A journey to wholeness

Like the grounding qualities found in the order and patterns of crochet, "this urge for orientation apparently inspires the creation of mandalas as well" (Fincher, 2010, p.21). During times of transition, the need and desire to "center ourselves" by focusing inward can help us orient ourselves to whatever the new reality might be. "The mandala helps us draw on unconscious reservoirs of strength that make possible a reorientation to the external world" (Kellogg as cited in Fincher, 2010, p.24). Whether through the death of a loved one, trauma from a disaster, or a wounded ego, everyone, at some point, will have the need and desire for meaning and finding a way to feel whole again. Fincher claims that in order to do this, we must "establish a relationship with this mysterious center within us (the Self)" (p.21). Mandalas can either hold those broken, chaotic parts for us or be a refuge from them.

My history of loss
Paternal loss in childhood

My journey with patriarchal loss began long before my grandfather died in March of 2014. I lost my biological father and his entire family by the time I turned two years old. My parents' short-lived and ill-matched marriage dissipated after my young mother's harsh realization that the mental illness and addiction manifested by her new husband was not what she had expected. Contact was completely severed and my mother quickly remarried to escape the embarrassment of living back home with her disapproving parents and a toddler.

It wasn't long before it began to be clear that husband number two was yet another strikeout. Emotionally unavailable, though financially responsible, my mother's hope for a receptive, engaged father for her children quickly began to dim. I was 19 when they divorced, which was a relief. No longer in fear of my stepfather's consternation and short temper, the loss brought a sort of peace. Despite his physical presence, the pain of his emotional absence had worn us down. Anxiety had ruled our household for years.

Soon after the divorce, I set off to New York City to start afresh, away from the crumbled heap of my family. Within three years, I had gotten married and completed my undergraduate degree. Immediately after graduation, I had my first child—my son. I threw myself into my new role as wife and mother, determined to create a strong, healthy family and not to perpetuate the patterns of my past. My husband is a gentle, family-focused man. In an indirect way (as I have watched him be emotionally engaged as father over the years), I have felt some personal reparations for a lifetime of let down and hurt by the absent fathers in my life. At least going forward, I could provide my children with the missing piece that I never had.

Hospice internship: Client J

Eleven years and three children later, I enrolled in the master's program at Pratt Institute. In September of my second year, I began my second internship at hospice. The first patient I began to work with was "J," a man who had lived on the inpatient unit for three years. He was an avid crocheter who literally worked all day on his craft, making afghans and prayer shawls as gifts for other residents and staff. He had very few family visitors, but developed friendships with the hospice staff and volunteers. Until his admittance, J was estranged from his entire family. Here was a man who I did not know until the last six months of his life, but he had been just like my fathers to his children—absent and aloof. Perhaps it was because

I did not have an emotional attachment to him, or perhaps because I spoke a similar artistic language, but we connected.

J had learned to crochet as a child at his grandmother's knee and had worked many years on fishing boats, making and repairing nets. At this point in his life, crochet became his way to reach out to others, and metaphorically mend some of the mistakes from his past. Crochet seemed to help pass the endless hours of waiting for death, and also became his voice. J was dying of throat cancer and had a large tumor on his neck that grew rapidly until it was difficult for him to talk at all.

Loss of normalcy: Beginning to crochet

Consequently, when I began to learn to crochet a year earlier, my 11-year-old son (who had always struggled with anxiety and mild obsessive thoughts) had suffered a psychotic break. My life goals came to a screeching halt. I reluctantly took a leave of absence from graduate school to begin searching for answers and help for my son. He would eventually be diagnosed with obsessive compulsive disorder. The strain on our family was immense. We were all trying to keep our home as stress free as possible, but inside I was unraveling— full of anxiety for the wellbeing of my family. I was scared to breathe or relax, always searching my son's face for his withdrawal inside himself and the relentless, obsessive thoughts that plagued his young mind.

7.1 Front side stone mandala

The small stones I began to crochet night after night became a literal lifesaver (Figure 7.1). I needed to focus on something other than my loss of normalcy, and the rhythmic hooking became a calming meditation. I was drawn to simple, neutral thread using one of the smallest crochet needles available. I enjoyed following a pattern and not having to think about my life—just to count the stitches and focus on the movement of my hands. I may not have been able to make immediate sense of what was happening in my family, but I could follow the directions and produce something I could hold on to, something beautiful that gave me satisfaction and a sense of accomplishment. When it came time to stretch the doily around the stone, it felt good to pull it as tightly as possible until it was snug and secure. It stayed in place when I let go, and I felt grounded as I held the stone in my hand. I even made a small one for my son to take to school to keep in his pocket and to hold whenever the anxiety kicked in. My hopes were that it would ground him too.

Building bridges

Connecting with J

J was quite suspicious of my motives during our first visit. Most hospice staff or volunteers wanted something from him, whether it was an afghan he had made or his time. What he really wanted was to be able keep working on his various crochet projects and keep his hands and mind busy. I had decided to bring my own crochet as a way to connect with him. Once I pulled it out and showed him what I was working on, he began to relax and get back to his current project. By working beside J, I gave him the liberty to stay focused and some relief from the expectations of his typical visitors.

To further ease his concern about my motives, I left the stone I made that first day in an effort to create a bond through our shared medium. For once, J was on the receiving end rather than being the one who gave. He was touched by my gesture. Safrai (2013) stated that, in hospice, the therapist's intention should be to bond quickly and to connect with the patient. When a person "find[s] supportive relationships, [it can] enable him to gain confidence and equanimity even in the face of death" (p.128). Our work together continued until the end of J's life, providing connection and consistency, and hopefully giving him courage to face the unknown.

Our styles were very different at first. J's small hospice room was packed with skeins of thick crochet yarn in every color of the rainbow. He worked on large linear or square projects that often took weeks to finish. I worked in one neutral color using thin crochet thread in a circular manner on small circular stones. Each piece took me an hour or two to make. After a few visits, I realized that although we both crocheted, I was still missing a chance for a deeper connection with J as my process and materials were so different from his. Next to J's vibrant, plush, large, embracing projects, my small, tightly crocheted stones appeared closed, tense, and anemic. I recognized the irony in this—the dying man embracing life in his art making process and the young student not fully living through hers.

Using crochet as an artistic medium and emotional metaphor can teach us to change our perspective on how we look at things. At that point in time, I was clearly only seeing life from one, tightly controlled and limited angle. My interaction with J gave me permission and safety to work in a bigger, more expressive way. If he could create embracing textile work full of color and life despite his grim future, what was my excuse?

I went out and bought several skeins of thick, soft yarn in bright, appealing, rich colors. Recognizing that my previous, small projects spoke to my need to feel accomplished by seeing quick progress and completion, I decided upon a throw blanket composed of many smaller squares rather than a large, linear afghan. Our relationship changed the day I brought in my new yarn. J became more of a mentor as he helped me learn to use the new materials and to calculate the finished dimensions. I found a pattern which spoke to me, and as I began making my squares, I realized I was beginning a tactile mandala meditative practice.

Revisiting loss

I began to measure the length of the sessions with J by how many crochet mandalas I made. It felt more natural to stop once I had completed a square rather than watch the clock and leave in the middle of a mandala. After all, time is measured differently in hospice. It felt absurd to rigidly structure my sessions by the clock, which spoke only to my schedule, and took me out of J's reality, which was free from the typical responsibilities of independent living out in the world. The only thing that mattered was the here and now in his small room, surrounded by hundreds of skeins of yarn. That is the language he spoke and the only structure that mattered to him.

At first, I could only make one mandala in our 90 or so minutes, but as my skills developed, I could finish two. Sometimes, J and I would talk about the things that were on his mind while we worked, and sometimes we worked quietly side by side. Our sessions became a time of quiet companionship for him and a refuge for me, a place for me to escape my life that was becoming increasingly complicated.

WORLDS COLLIDE

In October, my own grandfather was admitted to that very same hospice. My grandfather had always been a distant presence, which fit the pattern of patriarchal figures in my life. Occasionally, he would come into town and take us out to dinner, but he was never able to provide more emotional interaction than that. Roughly six months before my grandfather entered hospice, his second wife had suddenly passed away. Within that time, he went from having very little contact with his extended family and living independently, to full dependence on them, and then finally to hospice.

When my grandfather arrived at hospice, so did my family. Although I often longed for positive familial connection, the reality was that we are a large, diverse family spread across the country with only occasional contact, so this transition was quite a shock. Living in a somewhat remote location without many options for an art therapy internship, I debated seriously with my supervisor as to whether or not I should continue at this site with this highly unorthodox situation. I resolved to stay and be aware of the issues that might arise relating to my relationships with my grandfather and extended family. However, nothing could fully prepare me for the immersive experience I went on to have as both a student intern at a hospice and the family member of a loved one who was dying there.

Most days, I would finish seeing my patients, then dutifully head to my grandfather's room. Sometimes he was alone and other times one of his six children (my mother among them) would be with him. I dreaded these visits because my grandfather never wanted me there and would often tell me to leave. I, however, felt obligated by my family to stay. I would try to work on my crochet, but my grandfather would find my work distracting and angrily tell me to put it away. I found myself so tightly wound when I left at the end of the day that I would go home and feverishly crochet mandalas late into the evening until I felt relief.

I never told J about my grandfather. During the weeks that were more stressful and emotionally overwhelming, J's small room became a peaceful haven for me. When I walked in his room, I left my personal life and worries at the door. The sessions gave me an opportunity to focus on someone else and to observe J's process of slowly working towards his goals through his work. I also focused on my own goal of completing the afghan. It helped to have this project requiring me to make the squares, piece by piece. It reminded me to take one step at a time, one day at a time. J would always keep me on track with his questions and expectations of my progress, but also in the change of perspective I would gain from being in a dying man's room. All that mattered was the here and now, not what was going on outside, in the hospital, in my family, or in the world. J gave me a gift.

ENDINGS

As time went by, J could no longer focus for long stretches on his work. He tired more easily and his thoughts became foggy. He would fall asleep sitting up. Soon, he simply sat in bed and watched me crochet. Eventually, the tumor on his throat made it impossible to talk. He then began to sleep through most of our visits, but still wanted me to be there. He would briefly open his eyes and give me a small nod and go back to sleep. Every week I went, and every week I worked on my two mandalas. I felt it provided a sense of normalcy for him while his body was shutting down.

J passed away quietly one evening in February. Having seen the steady decline in his health, I felt somewhat prepared for this news. Although I was relieved he wasn't in pain anymore, I selfishly mourned the loss of our visits together, his companionship, and steadying influence in my life. My own grandfather lay just a few doors down, yet J was the one who had allowed me in. J permitted me to share in and witness the last, most sacred moments of his life. We connected in a way I never had with my grandfather.

After six excruciatingly long months on the inpatient unit at hospice, my grandfather passed away from Parkinson's disease, one month before my internship was to end. As his health had declined, visits from extended family increased. I felt like my day-to-day life had been hijacked. The focus was constantly around the family drama between the six siblings and everyone's opinion as to how best to care for my grandfather. Many feelings began to surface around my place in my mother's family, the only extended family I have. I felt resentful, lonely, and misunderstood as my experience was different than everyone else's. Yes, I was a family member, but I also worked at the hospice as an intern. It was a constant effort to try and maintain professional boundaries that no one else in my family had to worry about, while managing the very complex and personal feelings I was having.

As demanding as my grandfather's care was on his children, I was resentful that they *had* a father that wanted them there. It dawned on me one day, while watching my mother interact with my grandfather, that I will never have the experience of sitting by my father's bedside. Neither my biological father, nor my stepfather would ever make that request, and my grandfather did not want me near him either. It hurt.

THE MEMORIAL

It's been said that "You cannot grieve only one loss... the grief brings into your awareness all the losses that have occurred in your life, past and present" (Kübler-Ross and Kessler, 2005, p.73). At the memorial two weeks after my grandfather's passing, what could have been a unifying experience turned into a flagrant display of the recurring feelings of loss that I have struggled with my entire life. Somehow, my husband and children and I were forgotten about in the seating arrangement for the service, and rather than be with the rest of the 30 members of the family, we were seated in makeshift seating in the very back corner of the room. I felt grief rise up in this lost opportunity to connect and be recognized as an integral part of a family. I now understood the truth of Kübler-Ross and

Kessler's (2005) statement that "the time after a significant loss is full of the feelings that we usually have spent a lifetime trying not to feel. Sadness, anger, and emotional pain sit on our doorstep with a deeper range than we have ever felt" (p.230). I felt all of these things as I sat apart from my family and observed the service as an outsider.

The situation at the memorial touched a nerve so deep inside me that I could no longer hold my emotions in check. My mother's family is the only family I have, and I desperately desired to belong and to share fully in this experience of mourning. However, the lines had been clearly drawn and I began to unravel. I was unable to clearly and effectively convey this to my mother who was angry at me for expressing my sadness at such an inopportune time. She had her own grief to process. She could not be there in the way that I needed her to, which was simply to be remembered and included. I felt hurt, deeply betrayed, and resentful, and mourned not only the loss of another father figure (in both my grandfather and in J) but in the loss of another opportunity for connection within a family.

Reshaping grief: Putting the pieces back together

Because grief is subjective, the only way we can comprehend and process it is through our personal experience. "Initially it captures us, but we can capture it back and reshape it… Ultimately, the potential for healing in the midst of suffering exists because grief is about creating and transforming bonds of attachment, not severing them irrevocably" (Bertman, 1999, p.15). I knew that I needed to acknowledge the complex feelings of loss around attachment brought up by my grandfather's death and somehow give myself time to reflect and process them.

THE AFGHAN

My crocheted mandala squares from the last seven months were collected in a large bag in the corner of my living room. At this point, they were a mess from transporting them to and from hospice and their recent neglect after J's death. Perhaps it was the disconnection that I felt internally, but looking at those pieces sloppily stacked on top of each other, I finally had the urge to complete the afghan.

The skeins were no longer neatly contained in their paper wrappers, but were unraveled and tangled up in my bag. Each night was a tedious process of untangling and straightening yarn before I could make any progress. I felt that the physical work with my hands intricately mirrored the emotional work I was doing—examining and untangling the relationships and attachments that felt so broken, chaotic, and messy.

I needed to re-establish order and connection in my own life and with my family. As I rebuilt and reshaped these vibrant colors into new circular patterns and connections, I started to feel a sense of control and purpose. As I started to bring each mandala square together into a larger whole, I began to recognize deep personal symbolism in the process. In my own way, I was picking up the pieces and putting them back together again. I was then able to move into acceptance and eventually a desire to forge new connections, beginning first within my crochet practice, and later within my family.

Grief and the resurgence of past hurts serve an important purpose. "As the pain emerges, we find new ways of healing ourselves that may not have existed before. Return visits to old hurts are an exercise in completion, as we return to wholeness and reintegration" (Kübler-Ross and Kessler, 2005, p.76). I was the only person who could provide healing for myself. Through my crochet, I began to heal by literally making thousands of small connections and in the completion of each mandala. It was an exercise, a practice that started small and manageable in my hands, and grew until it covered me. It wasn't until that point that I could safely look outward and apply my practice to my relationships.

SQUARING THE CIRCLE

The process of bringing together and joining the many mandala squares provided yet another opportunity to look differently and more deeply at my process. I laid them all out on the floor so that I could see them clearly and arrange them. It became difficult to keep all the rows in order. Although I stacked and labeled them, I still made some mistakes, but rather than undo my progress, I tried to be flexible and continue to move forward.

I joined the squares with black yarn, which created a grid-like border that reinforced every square. From the front, the black was only seen in the corners and around the outer edge, but on the back, the grid was prominent and bold. I realized I had not only squared the circles individually for the second time, but also the project as a whole (Figure 7.2). The symbolism of squaring the circle is complex and layered. The square, a firm, four-sided figure, "suggests balance, wholeness, and completion. Four sets boundaries, defines limits, and organizes spaces" (Fincher, 2010, p.98). This further confirmed I was on the right track with my materials and process. With the squaring of each border, I reinforced the wholeness of my Self and began to make sense of my experience and recognize my truth. This long-term crochet piece began simply as a way to connect with a dying patient. Ultimately, it became a container and visual metaphor for my emotional journey of that year.

7.2 Adding the black yarn, front

Afterthoughts

Fox poignantly stated, "Chaos is a prelude to creativity. Artists wrestle with chaos, take it apart, deconstruct and reconstruct from it" (2002, pp.7–8). I believe grief and chaos are interchangeable. Grief was transformed and reconstructed through the therapeutic medium of crochet and I was able to heal and move forward, finding support and insight in the multifaceted therapeutic process. When we create something with our hands, "in meeting the demands of the craft, we develop strength to meet the demands of life" (Kapitan, 2011, p.95). We can come to achieve balance between our internal and external experiences.

The afghan is a tangible, enduring reminder of one of the most personally significant and soul-shaking years of my life. The recurring theme of feeling alone and needing comfort as my grief surfaced were evident in my subconscious work of creating a literal embrace in the form of an afghan. I not only survived the process of working through my loss, but was also able to grow and expand emotionally, just as my piece grew from small, manageable connections into a large embracing whole. Rather than needing to be held, like the small crocheted stones, my process brought me to create a piece that can hold myself as well as others.

Protocol: Creating mandalas as a therapeutic crochet practice to process grief and loss

Objective

To explore and process complex feelings of loss by creating a regular, mindful crochet practice.

Material goal

One crochet mandala square completed per session until the goal of a specified number of squares is accomplished.

Duration

As is appropriate to the individual's schedule and skill level. Ideally, a daily practice of one crochet mandala square per session, approximately 45 minutes to an hour. This, of course, is dependent upon the participant's skill level with the medium. This exercise is intended for intermediate level crocheters with some knowledge and previous experience with the craft.

Curriculum

Take a trip to the yarn store and allow the type of yarn to choose you. Feel the different textures and weight. Once you have selected the yarn and at least four colors, look on the label to see what size of crochet hook you will need.

STEP 1 ESTABLISH A SPACE AND LEARN A PATTERN FOR YOUR PRACTICE

Decide upon an uninterrupted time of day and find a quiet, comfortable space. Prepare your materials and have them within reach so that you can practice undisturbed. A sunburst pattern is recommended for beginners.

These are the materials you will need:

- four+ skeins of various colors of yarn

- crochet hook

- scissors

- embroidery needle

- container for your finished squares (box, bag, etc.) as well as for your supplies

- sunburst pattern.[1]

STEP 2 PRACTICE UNTIL YOUR CRAFT BECOMES A PRACTICE

Expect it will take a couple of sessions to master the pattern, if not more. Take as much time as you need without putting pressure on yourself to do it perfectly from the start. Once you have mastered the pattern, begin your practice by sitting quietly for a moment and noticing any negative, chaotic emotions residing in your body. Take a few deep breaths and begin the simple steps of the first round. As you continue, visualize the feelings moving out of your body, down your arms and into the stitches where they begin to take form and are held in an organized, controlled piece. Focus on steadying your breathing, noticing each connection, as you create a piece that literally grows from a simple chain into a strong, capable mandala.

You may have a project in mind, and you may not, which is perfectly fine and not a reason to put off your practice. You will eventually be led to what your squares will become based on your needs at the time. Do you need to be held? An afghan or throw. Do you need to

---

[1]   Tutorial at http://nittybits.blogspot.nl/2013/01/sunburst-granny-square-blanket-tutorial.html

hold or contain? A bag. Do you need comfort? A pillow. There are so many options!

This directive is only to get you started in your practice and help create a safe space and container to discharge loaded and often confusing emotions that accompany loss. It is also an exercise in completion. Where you go from there is up to you.

References

Bertman, S. (1999) 'Introduction.' In Sandra L. Bertman (ed.) *Grief and the Healing Arts: Creativity as Therapy.* Amityville, NY: Baywood Publishing.

Crandall-Frazier, C. (2008) *Contemplative Crochet: A Hands-On Guide for Interlocking Faith and Craft.* Woodstock, VT: SkyLight Paths Publishing.

Fincher, S. (2010) *Creating Mandalas: For Insight, Healing, and Self-Expression.* Boston, MA: Shambhala Publications.

Fox, M. (2002) *Creativity: Where the Divine and the Human Meet.* New York: Penguin Putnam.

Kapitan, L. (2011) 'Close to the heart: Art therapy's link to craft and art production.' *Art Therapy: Journal of the American Art Therapy Association 28,* 3, 94–95.

Kübler-Ross, E. and Kessler, D. (2005) *On Grief and Grieving: Finding the Meaning of Grief through the Five Stages of Loss.* New York: Scribner.

Safrai, M. (2013) 'Art therapy in hospice: A catalyst for insight and healing.' *Art Therapy: Journal of the American Art Therapy Association 30,* 3, 122–129.

8

The Tree of Life

A Transpersonal Heuristic Journey

Susan Leopold

I had always been drawn to tree imagery, so when I saw the Dulwich Centre's "The Tree of Life: An Approach to Working with Vulnerable Children" I became really curious about the therapeutic potential of using the tree image in art therapy. The Dulwich approach is a workshop designed to help people of all ages who have experienced environmental or developmental trauma. Group members create a tree comprising roots (heritage), ground (present life), trunk (values and skills), branches (hopes and dreams), leaves (important people), fruits (gifts received), and flowers/seeds (gifts passed on). Participants create and discuss individual trees and then group them in a forest. These Tree of Life workshops have proven very popular internationally in individual and group sessions in schools, private practice, hospitals, and in community settings.

My curiosity piqued, I decided to find out more about trees' diverse cultural symbolic meanings. Why were people the world over so drawn to this symbol? The more I read about the tree, the more mysterious the symbol became. But what a beautiful forest to get lost in!

Art and shamanism

Creativity is part of what it means to be human—Aristotle defined art as an innate human capacity (Dutton, 2009, pp.32–33). What's more, the creative act of art making acts as a mediator between the individual and the group; it is thus an integral part of spirituality and myth. When the brain's cerebellum, limbic system, and orbital frontal cortex are synchronized, connections between procedural, emotional, and more propositional kinds of information are enabled. Functionally integrated emotions, words, and actions make for a more powerful brain and a consciousness that creates new insight and awareness, ready for the language of spirituality and its related component: art (Winkleman and Baker, 2015). Powerfully charismatic religious leaders in human prehistory, *shamans*, were perhaps the first artists:

> Charged with the responsibility of maintaining the health of the tribe, the prehistoric shaman remains the archetype of all artists… The shaman epitomizes the human need to fly…beyond the everyday realm…in order to conjure worlds of visionary presence and power. (Tucker, 1992, pp.21–22)

In universal shamanic practices such as induced altered states of consciousness, various brain processes were integrated, resulting in the production of visual symbols, analogical thought processes, and social cohesion through ritual. Shamanism may have performed a significant role in human cognitive and social evolution (Winkleman and Baker, 2015).

The creative arts therapist fits the archetype of the shaman: she brings clients beyond the everyday world into the world of imagination, possibility, hope, and health, and her work takes place in the safety of a bounded sacred space. Here, the imaginal arrives, inspires, and connects us to something larger than ourselves. Research into the shamanic roots of art may be greatly significant to my research question.

Tree of Life: archetypal image in relation to symbols, metaphor, religion, and myth

The transpersonal archetypal image of the Tree of Life serves as a template for all creative and transformational processes. A dynamic, mandala-like image, the Tree of Life weaves together many elements into a cyclical story. It holds life energy and reveals a path to transformation, removing blockages that keep energy from flowing. It is said to hold all other archetypes within it.

CREATION MYTHS AND ANALYTICAL PSYCHOLOGY

Archetypes are fundamental basic patterns—templates for behavior—present in the unconscious of all human beings. Archetypes are verbs, not nouns; they point the way to something beyond themselves, something that can never be fully known (Hollis, 2000). Perhaps this sense of a mystery beyond, a feeling of almost finding connection to something larger, is what is meant by *awe*. Carl Jung often referred to the tree archetype in dream imagery as an indicator of psychic growth. He published paintings of trees created by people who had no previous knowledge of the symbolism (Cook, 1974). For him, the tree archetype in these creations was a shared image emerging from the collective unconscious.

The Tree of Life is an amalgam of repeating patterns—including serpent, tree, river, fruit of everlasting life, and other variants—found in world creation myths (Haynes, 2009). Multiple symbolic incarnations of archetypal symbols reverberate through time and culture and, underneath historical specificity, the fundamental archetypal patterns remain the same. And since the archetypes are universal, they are all present in the unconscious of each person. But they combine in infinite variations to create individual human psyches (Johnson, 1986, p.11).

TREE OF LIFE IN EGYPT

The Egyptian Tree of Life was both celestial and terrestrial. It played a prominent role in Egypt's religious belief system (Haynes, 2009).

Many Egyptian goddesses were shown as important parts of the Tree, and the god Osiris was himself imprisoned in a tree.

TREE OF LIFE IN THE KABBALAH

The Tree of Life is a central image in the Jewish Kabbalah. The Tree describes the conduits (the Ten Sefirot) bridging the space between the finite (man) and the infinite (God). To acquire knowledge, we must separate or differentiate ourselves from an undifferentiated potential state of being, or what may be seen as a state of perfection, or God. The light of God's revelation enters the Sefirot but is so intense that they shatter. Humanity's task is to put them back together again. In their repaired state, they become a unified organism reflecting the soul of man. Total integration is achieved through practicing good deeds (*mitzvoth*) and pursuing teachings (*Torah*).

TREE OF LIFE IN THE BOOK OF GENESIS

There were two trees in the Garden of Eden—the Tree of Life and the Tree of Knowledge of Good and Evil. In some Jewish teachings, the Tree of Life grew within the Tree of Knowledge (Shore, 1989). Adam and Eve are forbidden by God to eat the fruit from the Tree of Knowledge. Tempted by the serpent to eat from the Tree of Knowledge, they disobey; their eyes are opened and they realize their nakedness. They are punished and must leave the Garden, never to return. As a result, they become aware of their mortality and are forced to work all the days of their now limited lives. "Like Adam, man grasps the fruit of finite freedom and experience, accepting the fear and guilt that accompany any act of independent self-realization" (Cook, 1974, p.25).

TREE OF LIFE IN NORSE MYTH

In Norse mythology, *Yggdrasil*, or the Great World Tree, stands at the center of three cosmic realms—heaven, earth, and underworld (Cook, 1974). A giant ash tree, it had three roots: one extending among the gods; one into the void; and one over hell, under which was a well and an Ouroboros-type serpent, chewing on the root (Haynes, 2009). The roots linked all three worlds, and the well was the source of the world's rivers. The goddesses of fate were said to live near the tree, and the water that moistened the tree was so sacred that it transformed all to whiteness. Two birds were said to live in the branches of the tree (Haynes, 2009). Odin, a major Nordic deity, suffered for nine days and nights as he hung from the tree. In doing so he conquered death. Odin's power to bind, symbolized by knots and weaving motifs in Yggdrasil's image, could inspire a warrior's courage or freeze him with fear and induce panic (Cook, 1974). These symbols—tree, serpent, rivers, water, whiteness, and birds— are common transcultural symbols found in the Tree of Life image (Haynes, 2009).

TREE OF LIFE IN ANCIENT AMERICA

In pre-Columbian Native American art, such as Navajo sand paintings and Aztec tree images, the world was divided into four regions of religious significance. A Tree of the Middle Place emerged from the navel of the earth goddess at the centre of the cosmos. Surrounded by the gods of the four cardinal directions and containing the symbols of a bifurcated Tree of Life, a bird was at the midpoint, from where the tree branched out into a circular form symbolizing the world sea. Lying below was an alligator, a symbolic variant of the serpent (Haynes, 2009).

Transpersonal inquiry and grief

Transpersonal inquiry is a method of obtaining knowledge by deeply engaging in experiences using an open-ended process comprising intuition, creative processes, and altered states of consciousness. One sits in the middle ground between right and wrong, black and white. A nonjudgmental, empathic stance, it aids in contextualizing loss and grief in the narrative of one's life. In ritual engagement with art making, one sits with the art in similar fashion. The plan is to have no real plan, but simply to hold the image in mind and begin, staying open to whatever might come. Rituals are containers. In their bounded, safe space, difficult feelings can be worked through and transformed, lessening anxiety. Ritualistic dialoguing with imagery allows loss, whether experienced in the past or anticipated in the future, to surface. Dialoguing and writing provide additional containment for overwhelming feelings, deepening the artistic process further. Writing and dialoguing deepens understanding of symbols such as the tree, since words integrate right and left brain processes, bringing unconscious symbols into ego consciousness, thereby reducing anxiety and tension and increasing emotional health and wellbeing.

The tree, containing the dualities of absence/presence, growth/decay, empty/full, transformation/stillness, inner/outer, is a template for this process.

My story

I have made art ever since childhood, but I began to understand the meaning of my work only when I embarked on a personal therapeutic journey through spaces of grief and loss. I played with images relating to the tree and let them simmer before I began any art making in my studio. I looked at trees on my bike rides and walks, and picked up materials that called out to me, unaware of any conscious decision-making process: rocks, wood, feathers, string, rusted metals, wire, transparent beads, crystals. I reflected upon, sat with, and ritually engaged with each one, and playfully experimented with combinations of these materials in various ways to find new meanings. My instinctual choices of natural objects and rusted or clear transparent beads and crystals represented the tree as both growing and decaying, a background to my own process of letting go and opening to the new.

Assembling the assemblages

I lay out all the elements on the floor and begin to assemble my creations separately, working on them as a series rather than focusing on each piece individually, a trick I use to quiet my inner critic. I also play music as I work.

After laying out all pieces for the tree assemblages and reflecting on the series as a whole, I became aware that my unconscious choices of natural objects and rusted or clear transparent beads and crystals represented the tree as both growing and decaying, a wonderful surprise for me—these feathers, stones, and winglike objects turned out to be abstractions of "treeness." The early assemblages in the series were like abstract variations leading to the final image in the series, the "green-hearted tree," the most literal tree. Working in a series like this, I stay very loose and open and when I work in multiples, I am free to move quickly from piece to piece, not getting stuck along the way. If something isn't working I am free to put it aside, move on and come back to it later with fresh eyes. Figure 8.2 is the culminating tree.

I was drawn to anchor each piece with spiral wire mandalas. In my process, finding myself drawn to the soothing repetitive hand movements of wrapping and binding, I methodically connected each small element to another element with wire. Wire, a resistive material, seemed to absorb my anxious energy, regulating my overwhelming sadness. I also used wire cutters and scissors to cut large metal pieces, which felt simultaneously destructive and soothing. I was working with destructive aggression and anger, transforming these overwhelming emotions into a softer although still painful sadness of melancholy and loss.

I used a way of working from my Pratt supervisor, Josie Abbenante, involving three phases—dialogue, reflection, and integration—after the creation of each assemblage. I sat with the creations, dialogued with them, and then allowed a poem for each assemblage to emerge, along with fresh insight. This play-filled, improvisatory process took place within a framed, bounded space that involved no intended goal other than engagement in the creative process. By using both tangible (assemblages) and intangible art (writing), I was able to achieve a deeper connection to Sacred Tree of Life imagery, one of my intended goals for this self-study. I had entered the process without a road map. The only prerequisite was to keep my eyes and heart open to whatever emerged.

Dialogue, reflection, and poetic integration

The dialogue, reflection, and integration process for each assemblage took roughly one day. The poetry came from sifting through the words that had emerged from the dialogue with the art. I discovered that through this process I was able to gain access to unconscious feelings towards my client as well as to connect to my client's emotional experience. Simply making the art or talking about the session with my supervisor did not bring as deep an understanding of our therapeutic relationship. Incorporating writing into my art making allowed me to explore and further emotionally process all seven assemblages on a deeper level.

Assemblage A

Although this assemblage (Figure 8.1) does not look literally like a tree, several tree elements in it called to me. For example, feathers represent birds, spirituality, and the shaman's journey; books are made of paper, paper comes from trees, and birds line nests with paper. The title, "All about earthquakes," came from a book with that title. I altered the structure of the book by taking it apart, incorporating various elements (such as parts of the cover and pages) into the assemblage. I incorporated the actual word "earthquake" into the art by rolling and binding a torn page with that word. When I work with traumatized children in play therapy, sometimes their grief, loss, or traumatic experiences seem to lie just beneath the surface, like a dormant earthquake. Through my own creative process and work as an art psychotherapist, I have learned to attune to the energy of these children, to sense and help contain any potential seismic shifts of emotion.

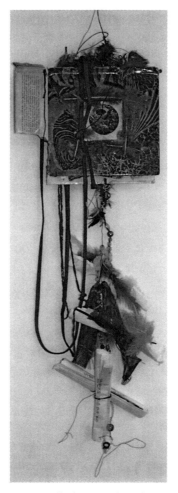

8.1 All about earthquakes

PORTION OF IMAGINAL DIALOGUE FROM ASSEMBLAGE A

I am top heavy, I am a book, I am two-sided, I am hanging, I am a circle, I am within a frame, I am deep, I am in the ocean, I am looking at shells, I am looking at sea creatures. I feel curious, I feel beautiful, I feel complete, I need to be seen, I need to be open. I am writing, I am holding secrets, I am holding stories inside, I am growing, I am looking, I am made from a tree.

POETIC INTEGRATION FOR ASSEMBLAGE A

Top-heavy sea creatures/Circularly framed and looking at shells/Growing curiously, a beautiful story/Seeing the need to completely open/And writing secret books/From inside trees

I circled the words "I am...I feel" that stood out in any way. The emergent words that had an effect on me were: "top-heavy," "book," "two-sided," "sea creatures," "circle," "frame," "shells," "stories," "inside," "tree," "looking," "growing," "curious," "seeing," "need," "open," and "complete." I reorganized them until their implicit meaning emerged, resonating with my own inner experiences of grief and loss. As an artist, I was learning to follow and trust my own healing process. "Circularly framed" showed me how I am learning to stay grounded as an art therapist. I work with traumatized children using play. Often, they share their overwhelming experiences of trauma. Holding the therapeutic frame, both I and they can find ourselves "growing curiously a beautiful story" together, sometimes transforming the unsayable through art making, and creating words for preverbal or unformulated experience.

Assemblage B

This assemblage (Figure 8.2) is an abstract representation of the Tree of Life Symbol as the cross, or the axis mundi, or the center of the earth, the feathers our representations of heaven, birds, and the shamanic. The ball of threads feels nest-like. The crystal represents light, healing, inner knowledge—all references to the Tree of Life. The title of this assemblage, "A green-hearted tree," speaks to my feeling of being at a crossroads. If I can stay on this path through my grief process, allowing myself the necessary time and space, I may then emerge and, on the other side of this painful place, find what the future holds.

8.2 A green-hearted tree

PORTION OF IMAGINAL DIALOGUE FOR ASSEMBLAGE B

I am symmetrical, I am made of many materials, I am spiraling, I am strong in the center, I am centered, I am wrapped, I am grounded, I am the crossroads, I am an open mandala, I am clear as a crystal, I am faceted, I feel full of the earth, I feel strong, I feel coiled, I feel energy, I feel heavy, I need to protect, I need to bind, I need to hold, I need to hang, I am a signal, I am a symbol,

I am shells, feathers and bark, I am alive, I am a signpost, I am a memory, I am fascinating.

POETIC INTEGRATION FOR ASSEMBLAGE B

Gold wondered climbing/Growing up and down process/ Curiosity's water wings/Bounded center holding/Earth's wooden shadows/Enter through climbing golden leaves/Along curiosity's water wings/Rootingly connected/Containing two-sided shadows

Emergent words having an effect on me were: "symmetrical," "material," "wrapped," "centered," "grounded," "spiraling," "strong," "crossroads," "open," "mandala," "clear as a crystal," "faceted," "full," "earth," "shells," "feathers," "bark," "hang," "need," "memory," "signpost," and "fascinating." I played with these words until their meaning resonated with me: they speak to my present transition into the empty nest stage of life. I am suddenly more aware of the inevitable loss of what I have so carefully nurtured as well as the possibility of impending future losses. My grief seems to contain many earlier life losses, a nest of losses, a sense of losing what never was and what now can never be. I find great healing potential in the strength of these words. They tell me that great gifts and strength come with transition and that I can weather earth's storm by staying open and grounded.

Reflection and discussion

I was able to identify themes and patterns in the artwork. First, I shifted to working with different earth materials, such as driftwood, clay, shells, feathers, crystals, nest-like materials, stones, and already rusted metal. I also found that I was repeatedly creating mandalas, spiral shapes, and crosses in these assemblages. On further reflection, themes of the center, the shadow, binding, holding, nests, energy, verticality, luminosity, heaviness, and weightlessness emerged in my art. Many artists have described a feeling of inner connectedness resulting from the creative process; for example: "Art can serve the alignment of soul and 'smaller' self through creative expression and thereby play a role in the healing process" (Grey and Wilber, 1998, p.189). I became aware of the way I face transitions—face loss and fear, as well as growth—along the path of individuation. Through my art making, I was connecting back to my own artistic core.

I experienced an embodied connection to my art—a positive healing experience—when I followed my instinct to bring the work home and sit underneath it every morning as a form of ritual engagement. Making these works gave me deep satisfaction, but what was different for me when I was sitting with them at home was the sense of being protected, of safety. I discovered that I could trust the way I implicitly connect to tactile materials arranged in my assemblage art, which allow me to communicate my deepest emotions and connect to both myself and others. The rocks, wood, feathers, crystals, birds, bark, wire, mandala shapes, shells, and translucent, luminous beads spoke to me and allowed me to connect with and free up my creative energy.

As a longtime professional artist, I had trained myself not to get attached to my work, since it would usually be sold. But the theme of longing for connection surfaced in my poems. The most illuminating and healing message that my art reflected back to me was that within loss lies growth and even hope. While loss is inevitable, I still felt encouraged to dive into life.

Creating, dialoguing with, and reflecting on tree images revealed that my strength as both an artist and a therapist lies in knowing and trusting the healing potential of the creative process. When I remain grounded in my own healing, I can be a better container for my clients as they strengthen their own sense of agency and learn to trust their own inner guidance.

Protocol: Using found objects, collage, writing, and dialoguing with the creations to process and transform grief

Objective

To facilitate the grief process, to promote healing.

Active engagement in art making regulates feelings of anxiety, depression, and hopelessness via an intermodal use of visual art and writing, transforming and giving words to previously unformulated experiences in relation to grief.

Material goal

Complete four assemblage creations with the stated objective.

Duration

A daily ritual, taking a minimum of an hour and a half to two hours per session, weekly, for six weeks.

Curriculum

SESSION 1 PLAYING WITH THE IMAGINAL

Spend time collecting tree images and absorbing the tree symbol through literature, film, and simply looking at trees in your environment. Be playful in your approach. Let yourself be drawn to whatever calls to you. You are on a gathering mission—there is no right or wrong, and now is not the time to edit. Keep a journal. Try sketching some of the trees that you see or that come to mind. Create fantasy trees. Examine how others have created tree images. You are creating a "stew" of treeness. Allow your stew to simmer and percolate. This is a brainstorming phase. Let your findings surprise you.

Author's note: Even before entering the studio, the creative process begins in the mind/body, with a focus on an idea that begins to percolate in the imagination.

SESSION 2 ASSEMBLING THE ASSEMBLAGES

Find a space big enough for you to lay out your findings so that you can see them all in front of you. Sit with them. Pick up the objects and notice how they feel in your hand. What are their textures? Journal your thoughts, sketch. Try playing some soft background music as you sit with them. Use deep breathing to promote relaxation and help quiet the inner critic. Allow whatever needs to emerge, and let the art elements come together as they will. Once all eight pieces are laid out side by side, ask the following questions and pay close attention to any sensations arising in your body, such as any increase or decrease of energy. Use your journal if you wish.

- What do you see? Describe exactly what you see and stay on the surface: "I see a red line intersecting with a yellow diagonal circle." Do not interpret.

- What surprises you?

- What stands out?

- What dominates?

- What needs attention?

- What needs to be moved or joined elsewhere?

- What feels right?

- What needs reworking?

- What needs to be let go of?

- What pieces draw you in more, that you want to stay with? That you feel attached to?

Keep asking questions until you feel you are at a place of rest, where you can pause and reflect. Remember you can always rework your creations in this process.

SESSIONS 3, 4, AND 5 DIALOGUE, REFLECTION, AND INTEGRATION WITH EACH ASSEMBLAGE

Now that you have finished your assemblages, it is time for ritual dialoguing, reflection, and integration of all you have learned by creating a poem. Allow at least one session, roughly an hour and a half to two hours (longer if need be) for this three-part process. Begin with your first assemblage. Once you have completed the three-part process, move to the next assemblage, one per session until done.

SESSION 6 INTEGRATION

Lay out all the artworks, and spend time walking around them, looking at them from different angles. Return to your journal and ask yourself these questions about the series as a whole:

- What do I see? (Describe what you see and do not interpret. Stay on the surface.)

- What surprises me?

- What needs changing?

- How do the pieces connect to each other?

When you are done, circle the words that stand out to you. Then ask:

- Are there any surprises now?

- Can you fit the words together in a new order?

- Do the words lead to further image making? (If so, create new images.)

- Are you still in the place where you initially started this process? Or has there been a shift? What do you notice now?

- Do you feel lighter? If not, what is in the way?

References

Cook, R. (1974) *The Tree of Life: Image for the Cosmos.* New York: Thames & Hudson.

Dutton, D. (2009) *The Art Instinct: Beauty, Pleasure, and Human Evolution.* New York: Bloomsbury Press.

Grey, A. and Wilber, K. (1998) *The Mission of Art.* Boston, MA: Shambhala.

Haynes, G. (2009) *Tree of Life, Mythical Archetype: Revelations from the Symbols of Ancient Troy.* San Francisco, CA: Symbolon.

Hollis, J. (2000) *The Archetypal Imagination.* College Station, TX: Texas A&M University Press.

Johnson, R.A. (1986) *Inner Work: Using Dreams and Active Imagination for Personal Growth.* New York: Dell.

Shore, E. (1989) 'The tree at the heart of the garden.' *Parabola: Myth and the Quest for Meaning 14*, 3, 38–43.

Tucker, M. (1992) *Dreaming with Open Eyes: The Shamanic Spirit in Twentieth Century Art and Culture.* San Francisco, CA: Aquarian/HarperSanFrancisco.

Winkleman, M. and Baker, J.R. (2015) *Supernatural as Natural: A Biocultural Approach to Religion.* New York: Routledge.

9

Interpersonal Knots

An Art-Based Exploration of Tying and Untying

Juliana Thrall

Overview

Tying myself into the story

I began exploring themes of connection and loss using tying and untying of knots. I found knot tying to be a cyclical and restorative process. Untying leads to tying again; disconnecting and reconnecting make better, stronger, and clearer connections. Additionally, one movement continually leads to the next. Our past indicates our present and our present conveys our past. In studying the present, "you must inevitably include the past, to the extent that it has determined the present" (Klineberg, 1967, p.218). Personal connections and relationships are relevant to our continual movement forward and growth as a person. But, at what moment does a connection happen? And when are we aware of connecting to others?

Connecting to people is a universal and primary dynamic of relationships, both in personal and professional settings. Gordon (2011) states that connecting "begins with a look at how textiles tie us together in our most intimate relationships" (p.116). Considering interpersonal relationships, I was hoping to discover the dynamics of how I relate to others by considering ways I connect, remain connected, and how I feel in those connections. This process also directed me to recognize when these connections stopped, were broken, and how I went about repairing them.

When relationships break, we are often cut off from the connections and are searching for a new way to tie ourselves back into the tapestry we spent our lives creating. At times, I feel like an expert joiner of communities, bringing my threads into a new place. Other times, I feel like the thread that does not belong and I become desperate for connection. Two years ago, I left my expertly crafted community in New York City to work my dream job in central Minnesota. This change was drastic and imposing. Logically, I knew I would have to surrender my connections, as they would no longer be a part of my daily existence. Yet those connections would always be with me; they helped me create the person I am today. Emotionally, I took a huge hit. I felt a massive block in my knot tying, connecting process. I had to grieve the loss of one way of life in order to be open to making a new way of life.

Moving around: Adjustment and loss

Satir and Baldwin (1983) explain that we often forget the facts of our past, but our minds "are amazingly reliable about emotional learnings" (p.181) we acquire, beginning in our first relationships. If we encounter extremely stressful experiences in our family life at a young age, "those stress patterns learned in childhood will affect the person throughout his life, unless they are replaced by new learnings" (Satir and Baldwin, 1983, p.181). The patterns of moving from one place to another affected choices I made as a child and choices I continued to make throughout my adult life.

Being uprooted several times positioned me to remain flexible and constantly modify my environment and rediscover how I saw myself. Abandonment became more powerful, creating a gulf between the people who invested in me and the people I invested in. It also generated expectations about living in one place for short spurts.

I internalized these expectations to move dramatic distances every few years. Thus my connections to community needed to also remain flexible.

I sublimated my fears about being uprooted into play, fantasy, and art making. I would search my house for items like empty shoeboxes, doilies, fabric, strings, and the like to create elaborate houses for my Barbie dolls. It took several hours to perfect my scenes, paying attention to every detail and adjusting the space until I felt satisfied. In the end, I spent maybe ten minutes playing with the doll before I became bored. These play sessions allowed me to work through the trauma of being relocated to faraway places where I had no connections. I practiced being in a new environment in the safety of play and fantasy. Evans (1996) states that "Once a person discusses, or even anticipates discussing an 'internal' experience, it is no longer private or internal, but becomes an interpersonal event" (p.57). By creating make-believe scenes for the fantasies of relationships and safety, I explored my internal experiences of abandonment, fear of the unknown, and loss of rootedness.

Knots

Why use knot tying to explore connection and disconnection? Collier (2012) defines knots as a process of "fastening or securing… by tying or interweaving" (p.26). Barber (1994) describes the process of weaving in two parts—first the "lengthy task of making, organizing, and mounting onto the loom the foundation set of threads," then second, knotting two strands of fiber together known as "laying the weft" (p.18). The effort, exploration, movement, and literal connections taking place make this fiber art practice ideal for exploring connectivity. Chevalier and Gheerbrand (1994) reference knots as an "agent, which links all states of being to one another" (p.991), acting as links to the here and now as well as imagined worlds and beings. If these knots connect one piece to the next, then each knot has a predetermined position.

Conversely, knots also tangle, implying that knots can be messy or clumped in an undirected fashion. Personality formation can be seen through the process of both unknotting and knotting (Archive for Research in Archetypal Symbolism (ARAS), 2010). "Knots are constraints, complications, complexities, and entanglements" (Chevalier and Gheerbrand, 1994, p.575), all suggesting characteristics found in personalities. The tangled and constrained nature of knots implies knots also need to be returned to their original form through the process of untying, unknotting, or unwinding.

In practice

Breaking connections and repairing relationships

When I reached the end of my weaving, I could not fully articulate my experience. I began engaging with the metaphors of tying and untying, relating them to my internal dialogue. These insights led me to integrate my art process with the data. I utilized a concept map to help me verbalize and integrate the emerging patterns of untangling the past, tying new knots, breaking and repairing, integrating into community and metaphor of the net. See Figures 9.1 and 9.2 for images from my art process.

Figure 9.1 Final weaving

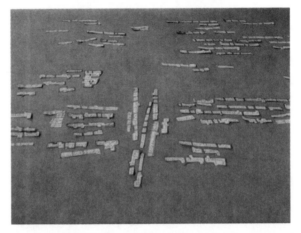

Figure 9.2 Small piece of the mind map from my journal

I spent countless hours untangling groups of knots, repeatedly freeing tangles. I felt I was untangling the chaos, or making form out of formlessness. I noticed every act of disconnecting had a meaningful effect on the next planned interaction. I described my process of untangling as "I am unlocking, untying, unwinding, uncoiling; I am exhausting [sic]." Knot tying challenged me to push through exhaustion and tension. Each time I unclogged one set, I had to solve the next set. Untying easily became annoying, consistently finding myself frustrated and tired. As the weaving progressed, I became more impatient, causing preemptive untangling of more strands of yarn. In turn, this process helped me increase the ability to make faster connections. Eventually, I surrendered. These tangles were a necessary part of the overall process. By letting go, I came to realize I needed to untangle my past before I could create anything new.

Untangling my past meant undoing patterns of enmeshed boundaries to make healthy boundaries. The chaos and confusion created by these tangles prevented effective productivity. Metzner (1985) argues that relational obstructions "may actually exist in the body as tensed and contracted muscles, or congealed and congested connective tissue or vascular tissue" (p.41). Once the strands were free, I transformed the blocked energy to create intentional knots, weaving a new structure and relieving the tension in my body. Each knot inched me closer to overcoming fears of vulnerability and fragility because strong and secure connections were now holding me together.

By engaging intentionally and reinforcing healthy boundaries, I internalized each experience, creating a memory of that connection. Making knots allowed me to explore the feelings associated with establishing and reinforcing healthy boundaries as well as sublimating my negative experiences into positive practice. The repetitive nature of my weaving integrated my practice into my still developing peer relationships (Gordon, 2011). This groundwork will remain in my body as a felt memory, as well as an internalized conscious understanding of the positive and freeing nature of healthy boundaries.

I chose yarn, knowing that this material would break as I stretched, pulled, and knotted it together. I wanted to experience breakages because relationships can lose connection, have conflict, and bring anxiety. Collier (2012) explains, "Knots invariably weaken the rope in which they are made" (p.26). Due to the weakening, knotted ropes can become strained. At the breaking point, the rope "almost always fails at the knot or close to it" (Collier, 2012, p.26). Just as I desired, the yarn broke, yet I entered into an immediate panic, feeling as though I was falling apart at the seams. My first thoughts were "Oh no, how do I fix this?!" These thoughts instantly brought me back to past anxiety in relationships. I experienced a sense of dread about what I did to cause the break, worried about why I could not prevent the break, and had an urgent desire to repair it.

I previously avoided confrontation to prevent anxious feelings. The weaving process forced me to confront my anxiety in the moment. In my journal I noted, "I am soft and vulnerable, gentle and sweet, yet, I am needing repair after repair." My patterns of fearing confrontation in relationships were reactivated through the breakages in the yarn. I felt I could not leave the broken strands on the floor or allow the pieces to fall away; I had a strong impulse to allow myself to feel the anxiety of these detachments and find ways to repair the breaks. These reconnections were necessary to complete the greater story of my weaving and continue forward.

Changing my treatment of the yarn strands, I continued working until the strain became too great, in effect, hanging by a thread. Instead of panicking, I found making repairs to broken and frayed strands offered relief from the anxiety. I wrote, "I am breaking, but then repairing; I am cohesive; I am beginning to see a shift" and "I have been breaking many more parts and repairing them still; I have not lost anyone today." During these sessions, I felt a transformation, first letting go of frustration, then relief after repairing a severed connection. In both cases the yarn was stretched to the limit, but resolved in a mended connection.

Joining the network

The process of connecting through knots felt constructive, providing me with new ways to engage in life and to find meaning in connections. In order for relationships to develop, I had to connect and reach out towards others. Lee and Robbins (2000) explain that people engage in social experiences, such as maintaining and building relationships and joining group activities, to "satisfy and sustain one of the most fundamental psychological needs—the need for belonging" (p.484). The need to belong is measured through the level of motivation needed "to be accepted by others and avoid being shunned" (Malone, Pillow, and Osman, 2012, p.311).

I hesitated in my attempts to connect during the beginning stages because I was unsure if the connection would stay in place when it broke and needed repair. When I became vulnerable and extended myself toward others, I began to feel a sense of belonging. The more peer contact I engaged in, the more integrated I felt within my network of peers. I feared that moving into the group too hastily would prevent strong relationships and I worried I would make fleeting connections that could easily unravel. As an adult, I continued the pattern of moving large distances, which in turn caused me to continue engaging with these fears. After moving, the desire to rebuild what I had in the previous location permeated my way of relating. Finding a new rhythm of connecting is just as important as the connections themselves.

Evans (1996) explains that integration involves reciprocal processes, where corresponding needs can be resolved, mutual patterns of relating developed, and satisfaction of needs to belong can be facilitated. Satir and Baldwin (1983) suggest that integration happens once resolution "has been made on the issue that created the turmoil" (p.220). In my case, I had to overcome fear of abandonment and experiences with poor boundaries to trust that I could make consistent connections with others. Through networking knots in various arrangements, I was able to make conscious decisions about how and when to make connections so I could create healthy pathways to improve communication within the network of peer relationships.

Protocol: Knot tying through the lens of a grief recovery model

Objective

To form and strengthen inner resources through practicing new patterns of connecting and disconnecting using art therapy interventions focusing on a grief recovery model.

Material goal

To complete nine sessions relating to the objective.

Duration

Ideally, as a minimum, one and a half hours per session, once a week for nine weeks. Adjustments can be made to accommodate the individual's schedule and needs.

Curriculum

These are the materials you will need:

- soft and flexible yarn, natural preferred

- an anchor: a wooden dowel or branch, at least half an inch thick, between 6 and 12 inches long

- a ruler

- fabric scissors

- a journal

- a drawing board with clips or legal-size clipboard.

SESSION 1 PREPARING THE WORK STATION
AND PRACTICING KNOTS

The purpose of this session is to prepare the workspace and set up the anchor.

1. Attach the anchor to a flat surface such as a drawing board with clips or legal-size clipboard. Use a piece of yarn 2–3 inches longer than your dowel and tie it to both ends. This creates a loop to secure the anchor to the board using the clip.

2. Once the dowel has been stabilized, measure each yarn strand to be four times the measurement of your intended project— e.g. your goal is to make a 12-inch weaving, so each strand needs to be 48 inches long.

3. Using the larks head knot, attach each strand to the dowel. Fold your strand in half, then use the fold in the middle to hang off the dowel to create a loop. Wrap the strands around the dowel and pull the ends through the loop. Keep adding strands in multiples of four.

4. Try some of the knots you are planning on using during the program. For knot tying directions, see the International Guild of Knot Tyers' charts.[1]

5. For about ten minutes, write in your journal exploring themes and metaphors relating to your art process.

SESSION 2 MEETING OF OPPOSITES: WHAT IS
THE WORST POSSIBLE OUTCOME?

The purpose of this session is to begin to explore the knot-tying process in relation to perception of mistakes in connecting to others.

1. Spend about an hour tying and untying knots. Notice how your body responds to the actions and where your thoughts lead you.

2. For 10–15 minutes write about your knot-tying process, focusing on your personal reflections from the art making relating to how you approach "mistakes" with others. Were you able to give

---

1   www.surreyknots.org.uk/igkt-knot-charts.htm

yourself permission to make mistakes? In what areas of your life do you struggle with mistake making?

SESSION 3 STRENGTHENING CONNECTIONS

The purpose of this session is to explore how the knot tying tells the story of your intersections of connection.

1. Spend about an hour continuing tying and untying knots. Notice how your body responds to the actions and where your thoughts lead you.

2. For 10–15 minutes write about your knot-tying process, focusing on your personal reflections relating to how making connections strengthens your sense of self. What helps you strengthen your connections? What weakens the connections?

SESSION 4 ASSEMBLING MOMENTS

The purpose of this session is to explore how each specific knot makes or breaks a connection to a larger story through slowing down the tying process.

1. Spend about an hour continuing tying and untying knots. Notice how your body responds to the actions and where your thoughts lead you.

2. For 10–15 minutes write about your knot-tying process, focusing on your personal reflections about the physical and emotional work put into your process. How did the knots tie you to the past and reflect on your present? What part of the art process takes the most effort physically, emotionally? Are there any areas that bring more emotion to the surface?

SESSION 5 TESTING THE LIMITS

The purpose of this session is to allow the material qualities of the yarn to lead your knot-tying process.

1. Spend about an hour continuing tying and untying knots. Notice how your body responds to the actions and where your thoughts and emotions lead you.

2. For 10–15 minutes write about your knot-tying process, focusing on your personal reflections relating to how making connections strengthens your sense of self. Does allowing the material qualities to lead your decision making change the way you approach developing connections? Did you notice any changes when you tried something different?

SESSION 6 LETTING GO

The purpose of this session is to consider the breaks, tears, rips, and stretches that cause disconnection and consider if and how those broken parts can be repaired.

1. Spend about an hour continuing tying and untying knots. Notice how your body responds to the actions and where your thoughts lead you.

2. For 10–15 minutes write about your knot-tying process, focusing on your personal reflections about how repairs and disconnection affects the way you relate to others. What was the hardest part of letting go? Were you able to let go? What feelings did you associate with repairing the knot? How might this process relate to the session about making mistakes?

SESSION 7 REPAIRING THE LOSS

The purpose of this session is to explore how the weaving becomes a safe place to explore emotions about grief and loss.

1. Spend about an hour continuing tying and untying knots. Notice how your body responds to the actions and where your thoughts lead you.

2. For 10–15 minutes write about your knot-tying process, focusing on your personal reflections on how making connections strengthens your sense of self. What types of spaces did you create with the knots and do they have meaning? What types of scars are represented in your weaving? Can you see them easily? How does your weaving create a ritual of moving through loss? How does it create the space for something new?

SESSION 8 PROCESSING THE STORY

The purpose of this session is to explore how the layering of knots becomes your story and the rituals that make up the different ways of relating to the people in your life.

1. Spend about an hour continuing tying and untying knots. Notice how your body responds to the actions and where your thoughts lead you.

2. For 10–15 minutes write about your knot-tying process, focusing on your personal reflections from the art making. What types of rituals and rhythms did you notice in your knot tying? How do rituals reflect your feelings during the making of the knots? In what ways does your art process require ritual to help move through loss?

SESSION 9 REFLECTING

The purpose of this session is to complete the weaving, then reflect upon the symbols and themes that became part of your woven story.

1. Finish the ends of your weaving. Complete any knots that feel left undone and decide how you want to "end" your art piece. Some options are to leave the ends loose, tie off each end with a final knot cutting off excess yarn, or roll up the ends and use extra yarn or another material to tie off the remaining yarn.

2. Review your previous journal entries. Pick out repeating words, themes, symbols, and stories that jump out at you. Create a mind map with your narrative/vision at the center and work outwards using each of the themes you noticed.

3. For 10–15 minutes write about your mapping process. What themes appeared throughout the sessions? Did any specific moments stick out to you as a stage of growth? In what ways did letting go and giving yourself permission to make mistakes inform the rest of your knot-tying process? What was the most difficult session for you emotionally? What helped you process those feelings? What are your thoughts and feelings on ending the art process?

References

Archive for Research in Archetypal Symbolism (ARAS) (2010) *The Book of Symbols.* Cologne, Germany: Taschen.

Barber, E.W. (1994) *Woman's Work: The First 20,000 years.* New York: W.W. Norton.

Chevalier, J. and Gheerbrand, A. (1994) *Dictionary of Symbols.* Cambridge, MA: Basil Blackwell.

Collier, A.F. (2012) *Using Textile Arts and Handcrafts in Therapy with Women: Weaving Lives Back Together.* Philadelphia, PA: Jessica Kingsley Publishers.

Evans, F.B. (1996) *Harry Stack Sullivan: Interpersonal Theory and Psychotherapy.* New York: Routledge.

Gordon, B. (2011) *Textiles: The Whole Story.* London: Thames & Hudson.

Klineberg, O. (1967) 'Discussion.' In P. Mullahy (ed.) *The Contributions of Harry Stack Sullivan: A Symposium on Interpersonal Theory in Psychiatry and Social Science.* New York: Science House.

Lee, R.M. and Robbins, S.B. (2000) 'Understanding social connectedness in college women and men.' *Journal of Counseling and Development 78,* 4, 484–491.

Malone, G.P., Pillow, D.R., and Osman, A. (2012) 'The general belongingness scale (GBS): Assessing achieved belongingness.' *Personality and Individual Differences 52,* 3, 311–316.

Metzner, R. (1985) 'Knots, ties, nets, and bonds in relationships.' *The Journal of Transpersonal Psychology 17,* 1, 41–45.

Satir, V. and Baldwin, M. (1983) *Satir Step by Step: A Guide to Creating Change in Families.* Palo Alto, CA: Science & Behavior Books.

10

The Memory Box

Laurel Larson

Living with the dying

On a warm day in early September of 2012, I trudged up to my Grandma Jean's apartment with a trash-picked desk drawer and a large bin of art supplies in tow. We sat out on her small balcony in the sunshine with two diet cokes on ice and started painting. It would be one of the last times that I would find her lucid enough to create with me. She died the following March.

But let me start at the beginning. You see, I'm an art therapist. I have always been an art therapist, ever since I knew what one was. I can't imagine another career that would be so personally fulfilling and creative, with a constant ebb and flow of the creative process, an outpouring of the self, changing perspectives, and its ability to keep me present. I currently work with hospice patients at a long-term care facility and it has transformed how I view the end-of-life process, the blessing and the curse of living a long life, and the grieving process that begins when someone is sick, long before they die. But more importantly it has made me aware of the gift and privilege that it is to be present for someone's end-of-life care, and to use the creative process to define and enhance this tragically beautiful, painful, and unique moment in time.

This brings me back to my Grandma Jean. In order to understand the magnitude of the loss I experienced when she died, you must know that I was very close to her and she was a strong presence through my childhood and into my adult life.

The body box

While I was home on a break from college, I noticed a marked change in my grandma, although I couldn't really pinpoint what it was. Her behavior was increasingly anxious in situations that would not normally be anxiety provoking and she also appeared to fixate on things that had no meaning.

On the official website for the Alzheimer's Association[1] they explain, "The main cause of behavioral symptoms in Alzheimer's (AD) and other progressive dementias is the deterioration of brain cells which causes a decline in the individual's ability to make sense of the world" (Alzheimer's Association, 2016). Because my visits with Grandma Jean at this point were sporadic, her decline was always more apparent to me. In all of the books, articles, journals, and websites that I've delved into through the years, one thing that has been consistent across the board is the feelings of helplessness upon witnessing initial signs of memory loss and confusion in a loved one, and uncertainty in how to proceed.

I find that as a society we've become focused on studying the disease, what causes it and why, and new research is promising. However, in one of my favorite books on death and dying, entitled *How We Die*, Sherwin B. Nuland discusses the "emotional carnage" (1993, p.92) and how it hits families and friends of the afflicted, and those who are left behind in its wake, an imperative aspect of this devastating disease, and what I found helpful in my own process.

The mystery of memory

I knew I had a small window of time to try to create a memory box with my Grandma Jean. I took advantage of the opportunity to learn more about who she was and what was important to her, as a way

---

[1]   www.alz.org

to somehow capture her essence in this box and seal it up, safe and sound, for no one else to touch but only to see.

I find it most interesting to create a memory box specifically with my AD patients when they are in this moment of flux; where they still have awareness of who they are and what is important to them, but the level of confusion is increasing and their cognitive ability is decreasing. I personally find this phase intriguing because when cognition breaks down, so can many barriers that were once held up by ego strength. The patient can almost take on a child-like wonder that is uninhibited, making for interesting art making and verbal processing. When I choose a drawer, we then transform it, filling it with images, collage cutouts, family photographs, colors, and design that reflect the life that this particular person has led. The box becomes a metaphor for the body and it leaves a tangible piece of art that represents this one, sweet life from an incredibly specific angle. It allows the patient to have the gift of choice in how they view their life and what they would like to leave behind.

I have found it imperative to create when one is still able to be a dynamic participant in this particular art directive. I found myself sitting with my Grandma Jean in this exact window. So, on a warm day in September, I sat with my grandmother bound and determined to create a memory box with her, but also open to the possibility that she wouldn't understand the concept or want to do it. I unlocked the door and found her napping on her small couch in the living room, looking so small. She turned to look at me smiled, "Hi Laur." I breathed a sigh of relief. Today, she still knew who I was.

We went out onto the balcony to take advantage of the weather. The hostess in her still existed and she poured me a Diet Coke on ice and brought it outside so we could paint. She chose her favorite "dusty rose" color, and started painting the drawer (Figure 10.1). The repetition of moving the brush back and forth seemed soothing for her and was simple enough for her to do. When she became warm we went inside to sort through magazines and boxes of family photos. She carefully chose photos of importance to her, all of which sparked memories and drew upon emotions from a lifetime ago. I assisted in choosing words for her, giving her verbal cues as we went through each magazine. When she had had enough, I packed everything up and tucked her in to bed to rest before dinner. This was the last time we were ever able to work on the box together.

Figure 10.1 Prepping the box with Grandma

Over the course of the next few months there was much change, including moving her into a specialized facility for memory care, which all took precedence over working on the box. And then, on the evening of March 10, 2013 she was found unresponsive on the floor of her bedroom. I couldn't bring myself to look at her body in the small emergency room where she was taken, not wanting it to be my last memory of her. My mom said she looked peaceful, as if she were asleep, cheeks still rosy. She would be cremated the next day.

The box showed up at my house and I remember my mom asking if she should pitch it, to which I replied, "Oh no…I'll keep it. I'll do something with it." And so it has sat in my living room bureau. The resistance I have felt in looking at it or completing it was real. It was raw emotion, feeling guilty for never finishing it with her and also not knowing how exactly to piece these images together to represent her—her body, her essence, her truth—inside of this box.

So it's been nearly three years since her death, the loss of our family matriarch, where I was given a real opportunity to finish the memory box, and had a purpose for doing it, if you will. My hope is to assemble the box in a way that makes sense to me, to honor her, and as a way to further grieve her death and bring a deeper sense of peace within myself over this loss.

Creative survival: Learning to let go

I spread all of the images out one by one and examined each, remembering why she chose each photo and each word. I recall verbally prompting her at times to think about her memories, the good and the bad, and to choose photographs accordingly. I worked my way around the perimeter of the box, knowing that I wanted the picture of my grandparents together in the center. I put images where I wanted them and I made the call to omit some photos, which I didn't take lightly. I think I was finally able to discern this *current* process from the *past* process. This project was for me now, in her memory.

As I started to glue the images in, there were feelings of finality and relief. I finished gluing the photographs in by placing the final image of my grandparents in the center of the box. Towards the end I layered in some of the words she chose and most of them made me smile.

When I was grappling with being finished, I scoured the table to make sure I didn't leave anything out and found one final collage image tucked under the folder that I knew I must include in the box. As I recall, it was one that Grandma Jean was drawn to right when she saw it in a magazine. It's a large shot of a beach, with seagulls flying overhead. I started painting a blue sky background, with white fluffy clouds that sloped down the interior walls of the box (Figure 10.2). As I painted and blended, I thought of the connection from my childhood spent on the lake, to my grandmother, to this image that now appeared heavenly to me, and it seemed only right to glue it to the ceiling of the box. My personal spiritual beliefs are complicated and mostly unknown, and I'm not completely sure what hers were either, but it felt right to finish the box by gluing in this last picture and to finally let go.

Figure 10.2 The finished memory box

Discussion

Kenneth J. Doka, a contributor and editor of the book *The Longest Loss: Alzheimer's Disease and Dementia*, describes grief as the "constant yet hidden companion of Alzheimer's Disease" (Doka and Tucci, 2015, p.1). When we are close with someone who begins to display symptoms that turn out to be atypical to the aging process, grief can start to present itself in the earliest of these stages. The grief continues to evolve as a new version of our loved one emerges, and will transform over time as the physical and mental state deteriorate. Feelings of uncertainty in not knowing if you did enough for that person during the illness and notions of guilt in feeling relieved and emancipated at the time of death can be present during the illness and well after the loss (Doka and Tucci, 2015). Doka also coined the term *disenfranchised grief* that is defined by these feelings of emancipation that many caregivers may feel when a loved one dies. Its basis is rooted in the feelings of relief, more specifically what one may not miss about caring for their recently lost loved one (Elison and McGonigle, 2015, p.58). The day-to-day grind and stress a caregiver feels can be overwhelming, as well as the constant repetition and patience needed (and sometimes lost). I can concur that these themes which were present for me at the time of my grandma's illness were brought up again for me while completing this memory box, and even further while writing this chapter.

These complex and polarized emotions were confusing for me. How could I be buried in such grief over this loss but also feel relieved that she is no longer in the throes of this illness? How can I selfishly grapple with feelings of reprieve that I no longer have to witness her decline? How can I be thankful that her death occurred while she still knew who I was and when she still had her sense of self? I think by recognizing these contrasting feelings I was able to fully realize how intense the grieving process has actually been for me. Being honest with myself about these feelings (and the resistance regarding these feelings) has clearly taken some time. I truly thought that I had closure after Grandma Jean's death by writing and presenting her eulogy, but now it's clear that this was merely a single stage of my complex grieving process, and that finishing the box is yet another.

When I gave birth to my son, one of my first thoughts was of my grandparents and how their presence would be missing in this new phase of my life. In a moment so full of joy and raw emotion, I found a sense of emptiness in the loss of their presence. Again, those polarizing emotions rearing their ugly heads.

Doka also touches on the idea of *anticipatory grief* or *anticipatory mourning.* He shares that Therese Rando (2000) redefines the idea that as an illness progresses there is "grief generated by losses experienced *within* the illness, rather than simply grief generated by an anticipation of future death" (cited by Doka and Tucci, 2015, p.1). The family or caregiver witness the gradual decompensation of their person before their eyes and will grieve through the entire process, bit by bit. The grief is ongoing and many caregivers experience loss as a continual process throughout the decline (and eventual death) of their person with Alzheimer's or Dementia (Doka and Tucci, 2015, p.2). Reading about this concept after the fact makes so much sense to me. Each time I would visit my Grandma Jean I would notice a little bit of her gone. Each time I noticed a change in her, I would recall my own sadness and awareness in things going only in one direction, no turning back.

A well-known art therapist Arthur Robbins, whom I studied under, wrote an important book that I continue to reference ten years into my art therapy practice. To me, the essence of the book *Therapeutic Presence* is the notion that being an effective art therapist is a delicate dance of maintaining a safe and objective emotional distance from our patients, while also allowing them to use us as holding "containers" for possible intense emotions, life experiences, and raw emotional nerves (Robbins, 1998, p.10). Also, the importance of being mindful of this throughout our clinical practice by engaging in our own therapeutic process and self-care. I have struggled with this at times, and have been able to hone in on his ideas when I'm experiencing a "merge" or some type of countertransference with a patient, and know when it's no longer therapeutic (Robbins, 1998, p.12). Throughout my practice I have kept this concept at my core, hopeful that it's kept me aware. Looking back on this entire process, it was most definitely a challenge to let go of this concept as I finished the memory box, being not the therapist but the granddaughter who was processing a major loss. Being not the "container," but literally filling a container up with tangible, personal memories. And, in further examination of this, being mindful of countertransference occurring in my practice.

The elephant in the room that I'm sure any reader has thought about by this point is how and if countertransference has come into play in my professional practice. The concept of this self-study running parallel with the work I'm doing with hospice patients was and is not lost on me, and I did a lot of processing with other clinicians to ensure that I continued to maintain integrity and awareness of any countertransference, especially with my Alzheimer's/dementia (AD) patients. Can I be honest and say that I've had some countertransference in my practice? Absolutely. But, according to *Issues and Ethics in the Helping Profession*, "Countertransference can be either a constructive or a destructive element in the therapeutic relationship" (Corey, Corey, and Callanan, 2003, p.48). And, "Destructive countertransference occurs when a counselor's own needs or unresolved personal conflicts become entangled in the therapeutic relationship, obstructing or destroying a sense of objectivity" (Corey, Corey, and Callanan, 2003, p.49).

It was important for me to separate my personal experience with my grandmother, including my grief, from the work I was doing in hospice. This meant continual processing with other clinicians, pushing through my own grieving process, and knowing my limitations as an art therapist. A metaphor for the patient–therapist relationship that I've kept in my mind through the years is the image of an ocean, the view head on, including the ocean floor and also the surface. The patient may be stuck at the bottom of the ocean, minimal air, drowning, and it is our job to stay afloat at the top of the water and cast a line down to the patient so that there is a connection to the surface. The patient can grab at the line, even pulling themselves up. But, we cannot be at the bottom of the ocean with our patients, for then we are trapped, just like they are. Nor can we physically do the work to single-handedly pull them to the surface, as it might compromise our own ability to effectively stay afloat. Art therapist Peta Thompson describes her personal experience of grief shrouding her like a mist, until she didn't know what it was like not to be without grief (2016). When we are in that space as clinicians, "veiled in grief," it can be difficult to see through the mist, and in turn difficult to be an effective therapist. Thus, I truly believe that through established boundaries and a strong professional support network

I was able to continue to be an authentic and effective art therapist during this difficult time in my personal life.

The final theme to discuss, and perhaps the most relevant, was how the art-making process truly allowed me a strong integration of grief feelings. I knew that ultimately this was my personal hope and goal of conducting this self-study in its entirety, but I was surprised in the extent that this process allowed me to gain insight into my own grief feelings and to further process these feelings in a constructive and tangible way, and to finally say goodbye.

While going through the small folder of images that my grandma and I collected together, I continued to be angered at photographs of family members who turned out to be deceitful or non-present in her life, especially towards the end. When a simple picture brought up the mistreatment of my grandparents something inside of me stirred that I didn't realize had been sitting in my gut this whole time. And I really didn't like the obligation that I would have to include those photos in the memory box. In the end, I think I found the true balance of setting aside some of my own feelings and including just a single photograph as a homage to her and what she wanted at the time. I knew there was a chance these feelings would emerge in assembling the memory box, But who was I to choose which memories she could include in *her* memory box, and who was I to hold onto feelings of betrayal by someone who probably never gave me a second thought? Years ago, someone once told me that holding a grudge is much like swallowing poison and expecting the other guy to get sick; it's not productive and there is no positive outcome. I think in the end I was finally able to let go of an underlying identification with my grandmother, which in turn loosened my perspective and over-identification with her, allowing for a deeper healing process. Thus, the true integration of grief.

Unfinished business

Something that may seem obvious to consider, but needs to be discussed, is the possibility of the patient declining to the point where they are unable to finish the box or dying before the completion. This is something that I speak openly about with the patient if they are cognitively able to understand. I directly ask the patient what their wishes might be if they should die before they finish the box. I have had patients ask me to leave it as-is and gift it to the family for them. At this time, I might ask them to write or dictate a note to be included in the presenting of the box.

If the patient has low cognition or is someone with short-term memory loss, their hospice status may not be something that is openly discussed with them. In those moments I do my best to trust the process and communicate well with the family so that they feel included as part of the process, even if it's presenting them with the unfinished memory box in the end.

Possible populations to work with might include, but are not limited to, hospice, adult psychiatric, geriatric, alcohol and other drug treatment, homeless, and veteran populations. I have assisted in creating memory boxes with each of these populations at some point, although the primary focus in my personal practice is with hospice patients.

Conclusion

In closing, this art therapy directive was ultimately a venue for me to process my grief in the loss of my Grandma Jean through a therapeutic process that I started with her, and then ended alone. It's a directive that can be translated well in working with the hospice population. By giving a hospice patient the tools and an opportunity to have freedom of choice, while oftentimes stuck in a world where choice is fleeting, we are fostering a meaningful gift filled with significant memories for both the patient and the family.

Specifically with AD patients, this intervention draws on long-term memory that is commonly intact amidst the day-to-day confusion. Maybe this directive isn't just limited to death and dying, but could also be interpreted as a way to process the end of a relationship or friendship, a capstone on a particular phase of life, or any experience that very much can harbor strong feelings of grief or loss. No matter the type of loss, this protocol lends itself to be an authentic and tangible way for an art therapist or individual to examine the many facets of a relationship or personal story, and for an individual to remark on what and who have been the key and significant factors in their life, choosing what and how they will leave them behind. Even in the center of despair and grief itself, we can assemble that story in a box to suspend those memories in time, safely kept and sealed inside.

Protocol: The memory box

Objective

This protocol may be used between therapist and client, for the therapist to process their own grief feelings, or for the client seeking to process his or her own grief feelings. My personal self-study in completing this memory box is completely unique because it started and finished with two different people, which should be taken into consideration.

Material goal

To complete a memory box and ritual, in order to integrate grief feelings and facilitate a positive experience of legacy.

Author's note: I use the memory box directive in my practice in an atypical way, in that I am allowing the dying person to process his or her own life prior to their own death, including grief, and giving them the power of choice in how they view their life (looking back on it) and what significant memories they want to canonize through this process. When I use this protocol with hospice patients in long-term care, I am not limited to any diagnosis, although Alzheimer's/dementia tends to be dominant with this particular population and setting.

That being said, someone who still has a high cognitive function and is independent (i.e. still their own power of attorney) can have a powerful experience in creating a memory box and being extremely deliberate with the inclusion of certain items, words, and images, with the intention of leaving it to someone when they die. It opens up an important conversation about mortality, wishes for their family, what they found to be most relevant in their lives, and how it all fits together like a puzzle. I've created memory boxes with Holocaust survivors who are able to parallel the trauma of the Holocaust with a life of freedom and love once they sought refuge in the United States. It can be a powerful way for patients to share memories of the past that continued to be a thread throughout their lives and into old age, a perspective that isn't always shared openly with family members, even their own children.

Duration

This protocol could last anywhere from seven sessions to upwards of ten sessions, depending on variables such as the patient's cognition, the number of photographs and information gathered for the collage in the box, which dictates how large a box to use and how long each session lasts. Some patients are able to work for a full hour while other patients are exhausted after just 20 minutes, whether it be emotionally or physically.

Curriculum

These are the materials you will need:

- scissors
- clear medium (matte or glossy) for gluing; epoxy glue for larger items
- photographs, photocopies, magazines
- acrylic paint
- wooden drawer or box from a chest of drawers, desk, or vintage sewing machine.

Author's note: The size of the box should be taken into consideration when assessing the patient. Someone with a high cognition and big ideas will need a nice-sized container. Someone with limited cognition might be overwhelmed by a drawer or box that is too big, so try to keep it small and simple.

I would suggest the sessions below. Time constraints, image availability, and physical ability will be variables throughout this process, so please keep that in mind.

SESSIONS 1 AND 2 (MORE IF NEEDED) CHOOSING A BOX AND COLLECTING WORDS AND IMAGES TO BE PUT IN THE BOX

This can be a tedious process for the geriatric population or someone with low cognition and short-term memory loss. Some may hit thresholds sooner than others. Verbal prompts will be necessary for someone with worsening eyesight, especially with smaller fonts. With the geriatric and hospice population I usually do the cutting out of images. Sometimes I have families bring in old photographs for the patient to choose from to include in the box. This is also another way to make the family aware of the project, and can open up much-needed dialogue between the therapist, patient, and family.

SESSION 3 BEGIN PREPARING THE BOX FOR COLLAGE

Choose paint/stain for the inside and outside, and formulate a plan with the patient on color and design. *Suggested prompts*: What color might best represent your essence? Would it be light, would it be dark, would it be more than one color?

SESSION 4 BEGIN THE COLLAGING PROCESS

When beginning the collaging process, use Mod Podge or another clear (matte or glossy) medium, good for gluing. *Suggested prompts*: Which words and images would you like to be central in the collage, as representing the most vital or important facets of your life? What images do you want to include but maybe not be highlighted? Please note, this can open up a dialogue about the memory box not necessarily having to be centralized around "happy times" but can include hardships, struggles, and trauma.

SESSION 5 CONTINUE THE COLLAGE PROCESS AND FINISH ASSEMBLING THE BOX

At this time, the therapist can give the patient verbal prompts to make sure that there isn't any aspect of the patient's life that has been left out that they may want to include. Personal items such as small trinkets, significant coins, love letters, jewelry—really anything the patient finds pertinent to include in the box can be added. Aside from the collage process, I have had a small piece of plexi-glass cut to match the shape and size of the box. This can be a good way to keep the insides safe, and if anything three-dimentional was included inside the box the plexi-glass can be nailed around the exterior and items inside can be kept safe from falling out.

SESSION 6 PROCESS THE BOX

This is an opportunity for the patient to dictate a letter to the therapist or verbalize their feelings regarding the box, and possibly have an open and honest conversation about their positive memories and/or regrets in life. I've had patients share that they felt sad they never found true love, or that they never had children. This is an objective and non-judgmental therapeutic space for the patient to verbalize their feelings in reflection on their own life. The box represents a tangible item for them to look at and identify with during this processing, and is the focal point of the discussion.

Author's note: For someone with AD the verbal processing may not be as in-depth, so as not to agitate the patient or bring up feelings they may not be able to adequately process or understand. This is why it's imperative that a clinical art therapist is present for this process.

SESSION 7 CLOSING RITUAL AND GIFTING OF THE BOX
TO FAMILY MEMBERS AND/OR CLOSE FRIENDS

This can be a powerful moment for both patient and family/friends in which the patient is able to experience and discuss the memory box openly. If you have created the box for your own personal process, maybe find a way to have a small ceremony or process its significance with a clinician so that you continue to benefit from the experience in a healthy way. I not only processed finishing my grandmother's box through writing this chapter, but also consulting various hospice clinicians so that I could more clearly see what themes were coming up for me and how to adequately address them.

References

Alzheimer's Association (2016) 'What is Alzheimer's?' Available at www.alz.org/alzheimers_disease_what_is_alzheimers.asp, accessed on December 15, 2016.

Corey, G., Corey, M., and Callanan, P. (2003) *Issues and Ethics in the Helping Professions*. Sixth edition. Pacific Grove, CA : Brookes/Cole & Thomson Learning.

Elison, J. and McGonigle, C. (2015) 'Birds sing after a storm: When dementia caregiving ends.' In K. Doka and A. Tucci (eds) *The Longest Loss: Alzheimer's Disease and Dementia*. Washington, DC: Hospice Foundation of America.

Doka, K. and Tucci, A. (2015) *The Longest Loss: Alzheimer's Disease and Dementia*. Washington, DC: Hospice Foundation of America.

Nuland, S.B. (1993) *How We Die: Reflection of Life's Final Chapter*. New York: Alfred A. Knopf.

Rando, T.A. (2000) *Clinical Dimensions of Anticipatory Mourning: Theory and Practice in Working with the Dying, Their Loved Ones and Their Caregivers*. Champaign, IL: Research Press.

Robbins, A. (1998) *Therapeutic Presence: Bridging Expression and Form*. London: Jessica Kingsley Publishers.

Thompson, P. (2016) *Working through grief.* (Blog, July 15). Available at https://petathompsonarttherapy.com/2016/07/08/working-through-grief, accessed on November 21, 2016.

11

Phototherapy Techniques and Grief

Kateleen Foy

Overview

My experience

Reality versus fiction. What is the difference between the two? When I was quite young, I frequently pondered these questions. My father lived with schizophrenia. He was diagnosed when I was two years old. During periods of intense psychosis, he would make statements such as, "That light across the street, do you see it? It's shooting a laser beam at me." As I turned to look at the light, I saw once again the same old street lamp that stood in the neighbor's yard. The neighbors had it turned on every night and with every sundown my dad would glare at that light convinced that it was causing his skin to sprout bruises all over his body. Reality for one is not the reality for all. My father's reality was different from mine, and I so badly wanted to be able to see what he saw, so I could understand him.

Growing up with a parent suffering from mental illness was extremely difficult for me and placed a great amount of stress on my mother. She became caregiver for a child and for an adult. My father quickly developed an alcohol addiction as a self-medicating method of coping with his daily anxieties. My mother looked high and low for different treatment options and for rehabs for him to try, but nothing stuck and nothing worked. As with many people who have schizophrenia, he did not trust doctors and medications and therefore refused to continue any type of treatment or to attempt to cut back on his alcohol consumption.

When I was about nine years old, my father suffered an intense decomposition phase. The delusion of the lamp with the laser beam took over his consciousness and bothered him at all times of the day. He was convinced that the neighbors were "out to get him" and this is why they kept the laser beam on at all times. One night, overwhelmed by the hallucinations in his mind, he attempted to act upon homicidal ideations. He left the house wielding a large knife and my mother called the police. With this escalation in violent behavior, he was hospitalized. Once released from the hospital, my mother put him on a plane to Ireland, where he would remain for the rest of his life.

We as a family planned visits to see him in Ireland. We visited him about four times in ten years. He was gone but yet not gone. He called as often as he could and we wrote letters. When I entered college, I visited him by myself when I was 19 and then again when I was 21. He left but then always returned. I do not think I ever prepared myself for the day he would not ever return. He had felt like a ghost calling me on the phone or writing letters to me. The man that I remembered as my father was not only struggling with his mental illness but struggling to live. He found no true relief from his reality. His reality was a constant nightmare of untrustworthy characters following him and harassing him every single day of his life. No one else could see this reality but I wanted to.

I pushed memories and feelings towards my father deep down inside of me and only allowed them to resurface when a planned visit was coming up. As I grew older and had separation from him and his symptoms, I wondered what it was that made him that way. I wanted to know what was going on inside his head and where that laser beam came from. I decided in college that I would major in Psychology and Fine Art Photography. I wanted this dual major because I needed to know all I could. I wanted to help other people with my father's condition and I also wanted to reduce the mounting feelings of resentment and blame I placed upon him. It seemed to me that the alcohol always made the schizophrenia worse, and I placed blame on him for resorting to this method of coping. I did not have enough understanding of why he was the way he was and why he was always followed by unseen people. I hoped that once I was out of school, I would have enough knowledge that I could approach my father with compassion instead of resentment. I wanted to study photography because I loved taking pictures.

A fork in the road

Before I could fulfill my dream of becoming a creative arts therapist my father passed away the June before my final year of study. He had developed fatal ulcers because he drank excess amounts of alcohol while taking anti-psychotic medications. His death was a shock. I had lost him ambiguously many times before when he would slip in and out of psychosis and then lost him again when he moved to Ireland. I felt the loss of him every time we went to visit and then left again without knowing the next time we would meet again. This loss, the final the loss I was not prepared for. With this loss came the horrid realization that all of my hopes and dreams for the future, for our possible future relationship were gone. No longer could I imagine growing older and wiser and meeting him with the compassion I have now gained through studying art therapy. No longer could I dream that all the studying and work I had been doing could help him. No longer did I have a father. Due to this loss and rush of complex emotions, I chose to explore my feelings of grief with photography therapy.

Phototherapy

Photography, like painting or sewing, requires a tool to be utilized in order to complete the art-making process. A camera is the medium needed for this art form. Cameras, like pencils or paintbrushes, are not all the same. Different cameras can have different functions and produce different types or pictures and images. And each of those tools has a varied ability to render details minutely and precisely, through which objectivity and authenticity achieve a unique power and fascination. A photograph tells us what "really" happened, or what we "really" look like, in a way that no verbal description can, and with pure objectivity (Hunsberger, 1984). Photography has the power to truly see what is there. This channel allows one to see and to be seen in the most authentic way possible. The camera provides a separate eye for the photographer, while also providing a barrier. The outside world can be seen through a square frame where one can selectively include or exclude elements of their environment from what is in their line of sight.

The use of a camera allows for space to be provided between the patient and the world and in the therapeutic relationship. Art making can be a stressful endeavor for some, conjuring feelings of performance anxiety and inadequacy when it comes to craft. For the art therapist, collage is often useful in working with hesitant clients who may be intimidated by the idea of making their own representational drawings or paintings (Chilton and Scotti, 2014). Phototherapy can operate under the same principle; clients may select an image from the tableau of the outside world, except with a greater sense of mastery and choice.

This technique can be used to connect the past with the present, connecting the physical world with the mystic one, showing us patterns in our lives, while assuming a holistic perspective on treatment practices (Briggs, 2014). Phototherapy techniques use visual stimulus to help a client remember things that they have forgotten or buried, bring these feelings into the present, allowing the client to make associations or connections that only become visible in retrospect. Phototherapy is not only about the photos themselves, but also about how a therapist can use these to help a client discover more about themselves (Weiser, 2001).

Giving structure to grief

Grief is the emotional and psychological response to the loss of someone who has died. Grief is an emotional phenomenon that can be seen in people universally. The response to grief varies from culture to culture but overall is felt similarly by all humans. Grief is an important feeling to feel. Many different coping strategies emerge when one is attempting to avoid grief feelings. Grief is essential to moving on past the loss that has occurred. The process of grieving and mourning are necessary to incorporate the loss into one's life. The intense emotions that develop after the loss can manifest through physical, cognitive, behavioral, and social dimensions. Some emotions typically experienced in the grieving process are sadness, sorrow, depression, melancholy, and dejection. Grieving is a highly individualized process but five distinct stages of grief have been identified by Kübler-Ross (2005). These stages are denial, anger, bargaining, depression, and acceptance. These stages are concrete in definition but are felt fluidly. One can move in and out of these stages without even noticing or move through them in a different order.

I gravitated to the Kübler-Ross model because it provides extremely concrete and structural scaffolding for understanding grief. I was deep in the grieving process while exploring this self-study, and the constant fluctuation of emotions I experienced made it difficult to describe my state of mind. Many research articles and books portrayed grief as complex and a confusing feeling to define. While sifting through this research, I became extremely frustrated and distraught that no one article could clearly tell me what was happening to me. Research on grief provides too many options for what could or could not be happening to one person. I did not need options. I did not need conflicting opinions on the subject. I needed a clear, concise explanation. I craved structure for the ambiguous assemblage of quarreling feelings going on inside me. Kübler-Ross explains a universal feeling in the simplest way possible:

1. *Denial.* The first stage of denial includes feelings of shock and disbelief.

2. *Anger.* Anger and rage are felt during this time; this anger can be directed at the outside world, oneself, and anything, depending on the circumstances surrounding the loss.

3. *Bargaining.* This is the negotiation stage. It is the idea that by entering into some sort of an agreement we may be able to postpone the inevitable happening.

4. *Depression.* It is common for one in this state to refuse visitors, spend much time alone and isolated, and to focus on the mathematical probability of death.

5. *Acceptance.* In this stage one moves through depression and comes to a resolution and integrates the loss into their lives.

The next section of this chapter will further guide you through my process of using phototherapy to process feelings of grief. The subsequent protocol outlines a map to follow, if my story should resonate with you.

In practice

I chose a very specific location to shoot the images that I knew would allow emotions to be stirred up and processed through the photography. My father moved from Ireland to New York City when he was about 21 years old. He ended up working as a bartender in the Bronx. After some time, he became close with the owner of the bar; the owner offered my father a position at another location he owned in upstate New York. This bar is called The Carriage House. In this bar, my father met my mother. They spent the first years of their relationship together in this area. My grandmother also lived in this area, and growing up we spent a lot of time as a family in this town. My father talked quite often about the beauty of the mountains and forest surrounding this place. He frequently said it was his favorite place in the world. This area is where I shot my images. Behind my grandmother's house, there is a vast forest, lake, and small ponds. This lush scenic site drew me in, and I knew this was where I needed to shoot this important work: a location outside Port Jervis, New York, along New York State Route 97. Its name is derived from the birds of prey that nest in the area. The location is also known for its winding roads.

I believe the combination of beautiful scenery and dangerous, snaking roads was what attracted my father to this spot. He always had a flair for danger. Kübler-Ross's last stage of grief is acceptance, and I believe that my own acceptance will look like this: wide open, free, beautiful, and dangerous.

The final stage of grief is scary. It means that the loss is so real that it will exist quietly in the back of your mind just like any other thought, sitting quietly, waiting for a time when you need it to reappear and join you for a brief moment and then sink back into silence. I so badly desired to be in this place but was also the most scared of this unreached stage.

The photographs

While I took many photographs on this journey, for the purposes of this chapter, I will examine four in particular. I call the first photograph on this journey "Acceptance on the river" (Figure 11.1). The winding road and curving river made me think of two separate pathways. My dad was now following the calm river and I was following the twisting road. After photographing this open space, I looked closer at the area around me and focused on an area of rocks full of cracks and distinct textures with rainwater gently dripping off them. The raindrops rolling off the rocks reminded me of tears. The glistening water reminded me of how wet eyes look glassy for a while once the tears have stopped falling.

Figure 11.1 Acceptance on the river

I then continued the drive to my grandmother's house. The Hawk's Nest is about 30 minutes from her house. Once there, I took my equipment into the house to check the setting and grab a towel to cover the camera and protect it from possible water damage. I felt resistant to start photographing here. I knew that the next stages I would be exploring were ones that I had experienced only a short time ago and I wanted to move away from those painful feelings. I allowed myself to take a quick break and sat inside the house for a few moments focusing on my breathing. I then looked out the window of the front room and saw a beautiful sight.

Through the window covered with mist, this tree's silhouette could be seen so clearly. I thought it was so beautiful to see through the window. This image (Figure 11.2) felt like my goal for the day. I wanted to move through the misty fog to get to a solid, grounded place like this oak tree.

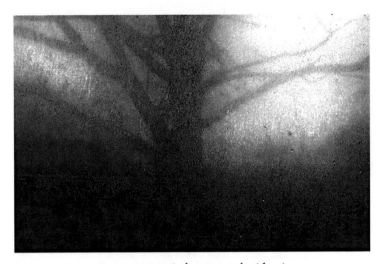

Figure 11.2 Window covered with mist

After this image, I was ready to continue photographing outside. I carried my heavy equipment with me into the forest. When standing on the back porch of my grandmother's house, the doors open to reveal a valley of long yellow grass. Behind the valley sits a quiet lake. I traveled along a path, reflecting on how I had been feeling over the past months since my father's death. I immediately felt sad. This feeling drew me close to water. I walked towards the lake.

I thought of the moment when my mother told me that my father died. I remembered the horrible, sinking feeling that took over my whole body. I remembered looking into her eyes and seeing the words form before she said them. I remembered the first thing I said, "No, but I start camp tomorrow." I remember feeling like a rock had fallen into my stomach and I could not move.

Once the initial shock started to wear off, the immense sadness began to move in. I carried my camera and tripod closer to the water. I aimed the lens down at the water's surface to try to capture the ripples of the falling raindrops.

The ripples reminded me of being at my father's wake when I cried uncontrollably for hours and hours. They reminded me of how my eyes hurt the day of the funeral. I had cried so much that my eyes were too dry to keep my contact lenses in and I had to wear my glasses to be able to see. I then thought of how overwhelming my thoughts were during this time. I was overwhelmed with thinking about every moment I had spent with my dad, things I could remember and things I could not remember. I was bogged down with these intrusive thoughts. I could not put them aside.

This frustration reminded me of how angry I was in the months after the funeral. I was enraged all the time at everyone and everything. I was clouded by it. The anger just walked side by side with me for a long time, encouraging me to act out on people who cared about me, to push others away and to keep to myself, which, in turn, made me more upset that I was constantly alone. I was angry with friends for not asking me how I was doing even though I had told them not to ask. So, I moved myself toward a group of trees. I purposefully threw the front trees out of focus to show how irksome my anger was and how unhelpful it was for me (Figure 11.3). I had no control over this self-sabotaging mechanism.

Figure 11.3 Front trees out of focus

Figure 11.4 The reeds stand in tranquility

The out-of-focus and dark trees in the foreground represent the anger that sat in the front of my mind during this stage of grief. They blocked my view of what was actually in front of me and caused me not to see reality clearly. The anger made me want to lash out at others because I could not contain the immensity of the feeling. The feeling needed to escape from my body.

The final photo I shot was symbolic of the state I was in (Figure 11.4). The reeds stand in tranquility while the light mist falls over. Raindrops sit frozen on tree branches. Fog lingers in the background. I felt sad at times but the anger had faded substantially. During early December, I had been excited for the upcoming winter break from graduate school. My father's ashes were still sitting in the house along with a small shrine of photographs. Going home that winter allowed me to feel closer to him. It felt like his spirit was around to hang out with his family for the holiday season. These more positive thoughts pushed the sadness away for a short time. These thoughts were most likely a product of my mind and body being too tired to produce negative emotions any longer, and were necessary for me. I believe it was important for the grieving process to be able to hope and imagine that the loved ones we have lost are around in whatever way they can be.

After taking this image, I felt finished. I felt that I had successfully moved through all my stages of my grief and represented them authentically. In total, I shot 142 images during the allotted time. I gave myself some space from the images and did not look at them for a week. Then I went and downloaded them onto my laptop and looked at them in Photoshop.

When I typically retouch images, I take a lot of time looking at details of the images to make adjustments. For these images, I did not want to take anything away from the emotional process that created them and, therefore, I did not manipulate them. I only used the Photoshop program to view and zoom in on images in order to make selections.

Discussion

Grief is a complex human experience. Through this process, I discovered information about myself and the methods I employ when faced with challenging emotions. Through my photographs, I was able to see into my emotional state clearly, as if looking through a window. The camera provided grounding and a protective barrier from my internal world of chaotic feelings, fostering a connection between outside and inside. The camera witnessed my process without judgment.

I would recommend, with the supervision of an art therapist, a client could use this procedure to process their grief within any setting. The camera equipment could be changed to a throw-away camera, a digital point-and-shoot camera, or even a cell phone camera. The art therapist would be a witness to the process and could act as the non-judgmental viewer. The procedural time could be shortened for convenience of working within a facility. The directive of this study could be adapted to involve a client creating his or her own environment to photograph.

In conclusion, photography can be used to connect the external world with one's internal world; the physicality of the medium creates a bridge between mind and body. This bridge can be used to anchor a grieving person, enabling one to connect with the present moment while experiencing intense, conflicting emotions of grief. More research needs to be conducted to further explore how this medium can be used to aid in cathartic experiences. The creative arts therapy field incorporates many types of art forms from painting, drawing, to puppet making, to ceramics. Likewise, phototherapy needs to be investigated in order to discover this medium's immense benefits to the creative arts therapy community.

Protocol: Phototherapy techniques and grief

Objective

Using phototherapy techniques, the client will explore and process unresolved feelings of grief.

Material goal

The client will take a specified number of pictures pertaining to relevant topics, and write a personal narrative about their grief experience.

Duration

As long as is needed to complete the Objective and Material goals.

Curriculum

These are the materials you will need:

- a camera (digital or film)

- writing utensils

- paper.

STEP 1 LETTER WRITING

Write at least one letter to your lost attachment figure (you may do more, if it feels right), and/or to the part of yourself that grieves, whatever your loss may be. Read this letter aloud and notice any themes, resentments, denials, guilt, or future fantasies you may be clinging to, and/or that have been left unresolved.

STEP 2 PLAN A PICTURE DAY

Decide where and how you would like to explore your grief and memorialize this loss, through the process of picture taking. *Consider:* Are there any special locations associated with this loss? Any meaningful activities or traditions that you would like to photograph? When you reflect on your loss, what images come to mind and how might that translate to the camera?

STEP 3 BEGIN THE JOURNEY

Once you have decided upon your subject matter and location, it is time to dive in. Your "picture day" may take only one day, or many. Make sure you provide for yourself the necessary space, time, and support, as you begin to engage in this process of capturing images and bridging your inner world with outer reality.

STEP 4 WRITE YOUR STORY

Reflect on the images you have taken and narrow down the selection to a handful of photographs that resonate on a deeper level. What is so special about these images? What do they remind you of? How do they express your grief? Assemble your thoughts into a personal narrative. This might be a poem, or a fairy tale, or fictional story. It might also simply be a chronological account of your process, overall. Whatever feels natural and authentic, allow the words and images to become integrated, and communicate the essence of your story.

STEP 5 EXPOSITION

Decide how you would like to memorialize and/or share your narrative. Will you assemble it into a scrapbook? Host a small, intimate memorial for your loved one and share it with family members? Maybe you decide to light a candle, say a prayer, burn the written narrative, and then scatter the ashes—or dump them in a potted plant. Perhaps this process inspires your next gallery series. Whatever you do, create some kind of ritualized memorial to encourage the exposition of your process to promote a sense of integration and resolution.

References

Briggs, M. M. (2014) 'Picturing self empowerment: A phenomenological study of adolescent girls that self injure involved in phototherapy group work.' Doctoral thesis, Kansas State University. Available at http://krex.k-state.edu/dspace/bitstream/handle/2097/15553/MelissaBriggs2013.pdf?sequence=3&isAllowed=y, accessed on December 16, 2016.

Chilton, G. and Scotti, V. (2014) 'Snipping, gluing, writing: The properties of collage as an arts-based research practice.' *Art Therapy: Journal of the American Art Therapy Association 31*, 4, 163–171.

Hunsberger, P. (1984) 'Uses of instant-print photography in psychotherapy.' *Professional Psychology: Research and Practice 15*, 6, 884–890.

Kübler-Ross, E. (2005) *On Death and Dying*. New York: Scribner.

Weiser, J. (2001) 'Phototherapy techniques: Using clients' personal snapshots and family photos as counseling and therapy tools.' *Afterimage 29*, 3, 10.

12

A Woman Who Dreams

The Shadow Box

Kimberly Bush

Overview

In my office, I have a shadow box that sits on the mantle behind the couch where my patients usually sit. I made it six years after my mother died, as I was coming out of mourning and starting to imagine new life. Shades of green and blue are painted inside the interior. A black wax figure lies in the foreground on a lavender pillow, a voodoo candle in the shape of a woman that I found on a trip to Mexico. From her head rises a strand of turquoise yarn that twists into a nest and holds a small egg. The thread then moves upwards and onto a spindle where a starfish sits. Part of a sunflower looks in from the left and brings a bit of daylight to this nocturnal place. Two pairs of colorful birds surround this scene and hold bits of the yarn in their beaks. Above the box is a shoe form painted sky blue, weighing the entire image down (Figure 12.1).

Figure 12.1 Woman who dreams

There is a world in this box. And in my world, death is a woman who dreams. And the bird spirits build a new nest to hold the egg created from this dream. This is my dream: my image of hope for resurrection, for the dying into life, for the healing after death, and for the end of grief and mourning. It was my dream of new life after great loss. Even now, I often place small stones before the box as a form of offering.

A woman who dreams

In the summer of 1989, my mother died. Ovarian cancer is a sneaky disease. It creeps up on you and before you are able to feel it, the cancer has spread to deadly proportions. This was my mother's situation. She was 55 years old. The day after Mother's Day, she went into the hospital for surgery. She died two months later. This is what I wrote shortly after her death:

Saturday, July 15, 1989

In a white room
She died and flew
Leaving behind flesh
And bones and us
Where is she?
With what angel?
Lost deep in my memory
You swim like a fish
Show me more than
Your bones and flesh
Show me your wings
I cried rivers of tears
Everything poured out of me
WATER STAYED INSIDE YOU
And you drowned in a white bed.

Death was not new for me. Two years earlier, I had sat with my maternal grandmother in a nursing home as she slowly stopped breathing. I felt her soul hover around her body until it let go. I saw for the first time that the body was only a mere shell, binding us to the earth, and allowing our soul a temporary home.

After my mother died, I embarked on a journey. I asked questions and looked for answers. Why do we die? Where do we go? What is the meaning of life? I meditated with a guru but ended up in a Native American sweat lodge, sitting on the mud earthen floor and asking for my prayers to be heard as the steam rose from the sacrificial rocks. I prayed and sang. I cried for a vision on a mountaintop for four days and four nights with only a blanket, 405 prayer ties, and a white dress. Later, I danced all night for four days at Ghost Dance in California, around a fire, and shared visions of the ancestors with the rocks and the wind and the flames. I wished to sacrifice a part of myself to find meaning. But in the end, I didn't get my questions answered because I was looking outside of myself and thinking that God was above me, beyond me, and unreachable.

An alchemical process

After my vision quest, I decided to go back to school to study art therapy. I interned and then received a job at a hospital, working with children as a child life/art therapist in the pediatric medical surgical unit. I was drawn to the difficult cases: children with cancer, AIDS, and terminal illnesses. Assigned to the Pediatric Intensive Care Unit, many of the children on my caseload seemed to float between life and death. I often would sit with the parents because the children were intubated on respirators and these parents were waiting—waiting for the moment to re-engage in the life of their child. I brought art supplies in boxes, clay and tissue paper, colors, and paint.

One autumn day, four waiting mothers made a large tree out of paper. They hung it on the wall and wrote "Tree of Life" in three languages on the trunk: "Tree of Life," "Arbol de Vida," and the same words in Chinese characters. They cut out leaf shapes and wrote messages on them for their children. These were prayers, offerings, and pleas for life.

Others—strangers—also with sick children came to the tree. This tree filled up with leaves and became heavy with the fruit of many prayers. Somewhere in myself, I must have known that these mothers were evoking the presence of God in the Pediatric Intensive Care Unit waiting room, but I continued to search for the meaning in this. I still did not have answers to my questions. I did not understand what the waiting mothers were giving me. When I offered them art materials and a safe place to work, they had engaged in an alchemical process to make gold from raw materials yet they did it with such simplicity and humility. I continued to think that the answers were bigger and out of my reach.

The dying child inside

There was a baby admitted at two months old with a respiratory condition. His mother only spoke Spanish but we often sat together. She made tissue paper collages for him and hung them in the windows of the room. When the sun came through them and the room lights were dimmed, her baby's noisy, beeping room felt like a small church. I visited her every day. We played music for him and touched his little arms and legs. Sometimes she was afraid to hold him so the nurses helped us to position him in her arms. Two months went by; the baby's father visited in the evenings. I offered them herbal tea, books of poetry, and tried to imagine how they must feel and what they might need.

One evening as I was in my office and getting ready to leave, the baby's father came by and asked for some tea for his wife. He asked me in broken English and Spanish if I could come to the room. I arrived with the tea and hot water to find the curtains drawn. I knew from the somber feeling that this child had died. His mother stood in the dark at his bedside. She seemed afraid to approach his tiny body even though the nurses had unhooked the machines and taken all the tubes away. She wanted to place his small arms across his chest in the position of eternal rest, like a little angel. She asked for my help. I made little rolls with blankets and propped up his arms so that they would fold across his tiny body. Then I made some tea.

I recall that he looked peaceful for the first time since I had met him. This was the image his parents and I would take home with us that night and bring to our dreams. We sat together with him for a while longer.

Other children died, but many got better and came back later in party dresses and little suits to visit us. I learned that some children die when their parents finally take a break, leave to take a shower, or get a decent night's sleep on a real mattress. Really sick children sometimes try to stay in this world longer than it seems possible so as not to abandon their parents. But they seem to accept death in ways that the adults often cannot. I remember how a ten-year-old girl with end-stage cancer drew a picture of a black heart just days before she died. She had written a date in the center of the heart. It was not the date of the day she drew it; it was the day she would die, two days later.

I wanted to make meaning from these stories. I wanted to get so close to death that I could see the other side: breathe it, hold it, and drink tea with it. I wanted to know the answers to why we die, where we go, and what it means to be alive. I was faced with the individual stories of souls crossing over and I grieved the child who was dying inside me too.

Rainer Maria Rilke wrote about loss, grief, and the growth that comes from embracing the fullness of life. In one of the poems that I love most, he said, "I am circling around God, around the ancient tower, / and I have been circling for a thousand years, / and I still don't know if I am a falcon, or a storm, / or a great song" (Rilke, 1981). This poem has always given me hope. I read it at my wedding, six months before my mother died, and then again at a ceremony to honor the life of a 16-year-old poet, my friend's son, who died of a brain tumor.

Ultimately, I believe that this young man was my truest spiritual teacher, not a guru or a medicine man, but a boy who wrestled with the angels, asked questions, wrote poetry, and left eighth grade to fight for his life. He wrote about his intense pain and sadness, and about opening to love. He wrote about his cancer, transforming his bedroom into a temple of words and pictures, hidden messages and secrets that he would share with people when they visited. He taught me about the meaning of death, living every day as if it was possibly the last, and love. He showed me time and again that God resides within us and one does not need to seek a spiritual life but remain receptive to the world inside and outside us. He taught me about stillness and solitude, waiting, and the power of words and images in healing.

In practice

An inward process

As my mother lay dying in a hospital bed, I instinctively began making drawings as a way to connect to and express my experience of shock, grief, and loss. Drawing offered a way to suspend time and to connect to my heart through my body. My earlier art school training had not focused on using the creative process to respond to the internal world, yet intuitively I understood the necessity of using art to contain my feelings. Two years later, during my training as an art therapist, I learned to embrace making art as a process of moving inward. I developed a deeper consciousness and language for working from the inside out. I found that art could be a form of meditation and internal dialogue.

After my mother's death, I began to understand that my imagination listened and responded whether I was painting a still life or constructing a collage. By experiencing death at a time when I was actively seeking my path in life, I found that I could embrace art therapy for my own personal growth as well as a way to help others. I read all sorts of books about death. I devoured essays about how we die, explanations about what happens to the body, and poetry about what happens to the spirit. My mother had died in a hospital and my first job as an art therapist was working with medically fragile children and their families in a pediatric setting.

Although death is an integral part of life, it is also one of our biggest cultural taboos. Through history, human beings have continuously tried to make meaning from the cycle of life and death, and one way that we have done this is by making art. As I embarked on a journey to try to understand death. I used art making intentionally to focus on this process. My practice began when I started my first job as an art therapist. Each morning before going to my job at the hospital, I would sit down to work at my studio table for a couple hours. Each day, I set an intention for my practice and expectedly suspended space and time for a while. My intention was to explore loss while continuing to embrace life. In this way, I began to integrate what

I was learning from different perspectives: from the poetry I was reading, from my experiences working in the hospital, and from my reflections on my own loss. I often worked with watercolors, and incorporating collage and found objects. The shadow box sculpture came out of this practice as a way to contain my experiences as a therapist and explore the loss and grief of others as well as my own.

The shadow box

A box is a container. It has an inside and an outside like a body. When I worked inside this contained space, I used the form to hold me together and provide my inner thoughts and feelings a place to exist. I could feel safe inside the space of the box to explore myself more deeply. This particular box was found on the street of my inner-city neighborhood. I took it home and lived with it for a while. I had been collecting boxes and this one was especially beautiful to me. The carving of the edges offered extra layers of visual holding and protection. The box needed to be cleaned and painted. Over several days and weeks, I set the box out and allowed myself time to look at it and imagine its interior. In a way, I had to dream the imagery into being. I had to wait and allow the process to unfold.

My process

Being open to the world around me and the world inside me is inherent to my studio approach. Before I sit down to work, I gather materials that speak to me in some way. Images evoke memories and guide the process. Textures and colors can speak to emotional states of being. I collect fragments of paper and fabric. Images from magazines, books, and printed material are selected and stored until they are needed. I find natural objects when hiking like feathers, eggs, bones, shells, and stones. I buy objects when traveling like charms, candles, toys, and cards. These, along with paint, clay, glue, and yarn, are my art materials. This is how I worked as I created my shadow box piece. It is exemplary of my approach in art therapy practice and in my own personal work, to this day.

Reflections

At some point, I realized that I was making an altar. I was arranging found objects in a meaningful way to tell a story about my mother's death. Birds have always represented her and their flight was symbolic of the way her spirit flew out of her body. The egg symbolized the potential of rebirth and the continuous cycle of life.

There is a world in this box. And in my world, death is a woman who dreams. And the bird spirits build a new nest to hold the egg created from this dream. This is my dream: my image of hope for resurrection, for the dying into life, for the healing after death, and for the end of grief and mourning. It was my dream of new life after great loss.

Protocol: The shadow box

Objective

To process and hold feelings of loss and find grief support in symbolically representing one's inner world.

Material goal

To create a shadow box and/or a personal altar.

Duration

This art-making process could be done spontaneously in a single session or workshop, particularly if the materials were gathered ahead of time. While the process would still be personal, the artistic investment of the participating individual would be limited to materials provided rather than those that were gathered or found over time. Either way, constructing a shadow box is a process of arrangement and commemoration. Commemoration is remembrance expressed through ceremony.

Curriculum

STEP I COLLECT YOUR ART MATERIALS AND FIND A BOX THAT WILL SERVE TO CONTAIN YOUR FEELINGS

It can be paper, cardboard, wood, plastic, ceramic, and be round, square, rectangular, or oval. The kind of box that you use will represent the way that you hold the loss and process the grief, so take time to choose the container that feels right. Give yourself time to sit with your materials. Take in the colors, shapes, and textures of what you have collected. Create a space to work where you can set out your container and all of your collage materials to simply look at them. The size and permanency of your art-making space will determine how large you can work. Arrange your found objects with traditional art materials such as glue, paint, clay, and yarn.

STEP 2 SET AN INTENTION FOR YOUR ART MAKING PROCESS

Write down your intention in first person language and make an "I" statement. Rather than hoping or wishing, write as if your intention is happening right now. Embrace the present moment and release your intention into the process of using materials.

STEP 3 BEGIN ASSEMBLAGE AND COLLAGE WORK

Assemblage and collage work begins as a process of arrangement. Like setting a table, objects are placed in relationship to others to construct a composition. Through the arrangement of which objects touch each other and which ones do not, a story begins to emerge. Use your imagination and play. You do not need to glue anything down or make permanent choices. The process of arranging will offer you space to consider the relationships between two or more things so a narrative can emerge. Give yourself permission to create a world that only makes sense to you. Give yourself time to live with your composition before you decide to make it permanent. It is not necessary to use all your materials.

STEP 4 WHEN YOU HAVE COME TO A STOPPING POINT, TAKE TIME TO WRITE ABOUT YOUR ARTWORK

Sit in front of the piece and write anything that comes to your mind: a story, a description, a dialogue, anything. This will allow you to explore the experience through another lens and provide a way for you to record your internal thoughts and feelings. Additionally, if at any time during the process of arranging, assembling, or gluing you feel stuck, you can stop and write about how you feel. Being responsive through writing while sitting before your artwork provides an additional lens for connecting to your inner story.

Bringing internal imagery into consciousness is powerful. Using words to commemorate the loss offers opportunities for additional reflection and remembrance. These are important elements in healing the wounds of a loss.

STEP 5 FINALLY, FIND A PLACE IN YOUR LIVING ENVIRONMENT FOR YOUR FINISHED PIECE

This may be on a table or on a shelf, or in a private or public space; it is your choice. Giving your shadow box an intentional place to exist acknowledges that loss continues to live alongside the daily routines of your life. You may find yourself placing stones, shells, or photos around your box as offerings for your memories. In this way, you create a personal altar where loss is held, continues to be remembered, and is commemorated through personal ceremony.

Reference

Rilke, M.R. (1981) *Selected Poems of Rainer Maria Rilke.* New York: Harper Perennial.

PART III

Applications

13

Vicarious Trauma

Supporting Bereavement and Self-Care Practice through Art Therapy for Healthcare Providers

Sarah Yazdian Rubin and Lauren D. Smith

Overview

Art therapists and other psychosocial professionals engage with traumatic material in their work with patients. Art therapists in inpatient hospital settings encounter unique environmental challenges as well as various losses, including death. Coping with these losses is essential to the health and wellbeing of the therapist, and work sustainability. This chapter describes an art therapist's experience with loss and how community art experiences may address vicarious trauma and bolster self-care within the work environment.

Introduction

Working in pediatrics and palliative care as an art therapist affords me (Sarah) the tremendous privilege and opportunity to serve those in need in a way that I feel I can be most impactful in this world— through art and creative experience. The concept that vocation is the intersected point where the world's greatest need and one's passion meet resonates with me. More personally, I am guided by the Jewish concept of *tikkun olam*, which literally translates to mean "repair the world," or alternatively, "construction for eternity." I interpret tikkun olam to symbolize responsibility for my own moral, spiritual, and material welfare, as well the welfare of society at large, and realizing this responsibility through acts of loving kindness. The bravery, selflessness, resilience, and poignancy that mark many of my professional encounters are what motivate me to continue to serve some of the most medically fragile people and their families, to create meaning out of my experiences, and provide me with the kind of perspective that many people search the world for.

One cannot deny the amount of loss that is a part of this work— loss of patients, their vitality, their function, their faith. Many people ask me, "How do you do it? How are you not consumed by the sadness, the stress, the loss?" These are questions that professionals in helping professions must answer, to others and for themselves. Learning to prioritize self-care is a skill that I continue to develop, and as such, have developed an interest for caring for the caregiver.

As a seasoned colleague once shared with me: to work with illness is to work with death. When I walk into each patient room, I remind myself that I am entering an entire world, and sometimes, a home. There are moments when the art and creative experiences create and hold space—to mend, to heal, to engage, to connect. There are also moments when no words will do, no art intervention will do. There is just loss, emptiness, raw emotion, grief. Many have described grief simply and accurately: it's like a hole, but with weight. The cement-like weight of loss can occupy an entire space, leaving little room for much more. All one can do, sometimes, is to be there, be present with the human being sitting across from you, and bear witness. Of course, the consequence of remaining fully present in these moments is that you notice and absorb a lot more than you would otherwise, including things that one may prefer to unsee.

Bearing witness: Privilege, responsibility, and cost

Bearing witness is an active ingredient in healing for people who are suffering or traumatized. At its core, the presence of a witness allows an individual to be seen and heard. Through the act of sharing, and in its containment by the witness, the vitality of the story transcends the bounds of the storyteller and is entrusted in another. It is a unique privilege to be trusted with a human story. Bearing witness within the context of a professional relationship comes with responsibility. We join our patients in their most challenging moments and hold them in their suffering. There are ways that we engage, listen, respond, and hold even when there are no words exchanged. What does it mean for us to carry someone's story, and can we let these stories go? How do we carry these stories while maintaining capacity and strength to carry ourselves? Cultivating meaning out of our experiences of another's loss, grief, or trauma becomes paramount.

Clinicians who serve clients encountering trauma, grief, and loss often hear—and sometimes witness firsthand—disturbing and triggering experiences that can make the act of bearing witness fraught with challenges. Those working with vulnerable populations within a healthcare environment have an additional proximity to suffering and trauma, as the psychotherapeutic work is facilitated at the bedside, concurrent with medical care. As such, these clinicians are frequently and chronically exposed to acute and chronic illness, crisis, medical trauma, pain and painful medical procedures, life-threatening events, death, and acute distress/bereavement that create intense emotions (Barnsteiner and Gillis-Donovan, 1990).

The healthcare environment

The inpatient healthcare environment, with its own culture, language, and sensory challenges can destabilize and over-stimulate even the most vigilant or seasoned worker. In a typical hospital room, I will frequently see multiple IV lines with chemo or blood being administered, patients intubated and sedated, on ventilation support or receiving dialysis. I will see people with disfigured body parts, extreme swelling, cachexia, or with weeping skin. Monitors beep. Bodily smells infiltrate the space. "Codes" are amplified on the loudspeaker. Doctors frantically and violently attempt to resuscitate patients with their hands. The care and relationships we form with our patients make all of these environmental stressors and events all the more disturbing. In addition to the environmental stressors, there are patients and scenarios that are out of the ordinary and traumatic—sometimes experienced firsthand, and other times, shared through a story.

When caring hurts: Vicarious traumatization and burnout

Both singular and regular exposure to trauma can affect the healthcare provider both personally and professionally. Avoidance, numbing, increased arousal, role inefficacy, and relational difficulties are possible reactions to medical trauma (Alexander and Klein, 2001; Collins and Long, 2003; Figley, 1995; Sabin-Farrell and Turpin, 2003). Constant exposure to stress, the need to "carry on as usual" following a death or traumatizing event, and feelings of depression, grief, and guilt in response to loss is thought to have a cumulative effect on the provider over time and may increase the risk of vicarious trauma, compassion fatigue, or secondary traumatic stress and burnout (Weiss et al., 1995).

Vicarious traumatization is defined as the cumulative process "through which the therapist's inner experience is negatively transformed through empathic engagement with client's traumatic material" or imagery (Pearlman and Saakvitne, 1995, p.151). It is believed that individuals who work with traumatized people or trauma survivors may experience vicarious trauma. Hatfield, Cacioppo and Rapson (1994) describe the effect of emotional contagion from client to therapist/provider, supporting the idea of clinicians absorbing toxic emotional residue from witnessing or being exposed to trauma. Vicarious trauma is characterized by changes in the therapist's cognitive schemas and core beliefs, and may impact a clinician's worldview (Bober and Regehr, 2005).

There are individual and institutional consequences of vicarious traumatization such as decreased empathy, engagement in unprofessional conduct, relationship/family discord, and mental health issues. Negative effects on the organization include increased absenteeism and job turnover, reducing hours to part time, reduced job satisfaction and commitment, and financial strain as a result of turnover and new staff training. While there is limited literature on art therapists' levels of vicarious trauma and burnout in the hospital setting, in a study by Robins, Meltzer, and Zelikovsky (2009), the level of compassion fatigue in staff working in a children's hospital was similar to a trauma worker.

Self-care practice: Engagement, resilience, and post-traumatic growth

To support ethical and safe treatment outcomes, and clinician health and wellbeing, the therapist must prioritize and actively cultivate appropriate therapeutic boundaries and self-care. *Self-care—self-initiated, necessary and regulatory functions, actions or attitudes for oneself that renew energy, are life-giving, nurturing, or sustaining—*encompasses mental, physical, psychological, emotional, spiritual, and relational realms.

Self-care strategies that may be cultivated in the work environment include the use of mindfulness-based stress reduction and constructive engagement approaches, such as R.E.N.E.W. (*R*ecognize helplessness; *E*mbrace your first reaction; *N*ourish yourself; *E*mbody constructive engagement; *W*eave a new response). Such strategies emphasize mindful-engagement, awareness, and rewiring clinical experiences to promote resilience (Christopher and Maris, 2010; Back *et al.*, 2015). Clinicians and experts in this field use different terms to help identify, define, and validate the experiences, role, and identity of the professional helper to promote awareness of moral distress, vicarious trauma, and self-care. Van Dernoot Lipsky and Burk (2009, p.6) offer the concept of trauma stewardship:

> When we talk about trauma in terms of stewardship, we remember that we are being entrusted with people's stories and their very lives, animals' wellbeing, and our planet's health…We know that as stewards, we create a space for and honor others' hardship

and suffering, and yet we do not assume their pain as our own. We care for others to the best of our ability without taking on their paths as our paths... We develop and maintain a long-term strategy that enables us to remain whole and helpful to others and our surroundings even amid great challenges. To participate in trauma stewardship is to always remember the privilege and sacredness of being called to help. It means maintaining our highest ethics, integrity, and responsibility every step of the way.

Van der Kolk (as cited in van Dernoot Lipsky and Burk, 2009), explains that a "stress-resistant model of self-care" is fostered through a sense of personal control, or a sense of connection between inner feeling and external actions, and the belief "in their own capacity to influence the course of their lives" (p.121); the pursuit of personally meaningful tasks; healthy lifestyle choices; and social supports.

Resilience refers to a person's ability to adapt successfully to acute stress, trauma, or more chronic forms of adversity. We now know through variable-focused and person-focused investigations related to resilience that resilience is common and arises from normative functions of human adaptation systems (Masten, 2001). There are protective factors that promote resiliency including high self-esteem, resourcefulness, desire and ability to help others, faith, and opportunities for meaningful action and activities, in addition to being more aware of vicarious trauma and countertransference (Meichenbaum, 2007). Maintaining healthy boundaries with patients as well as with the working environment also supports resilience.

The view that individuals can be changed in a positive way and grow from trauma, a crisis or a major stressor is an ancient theme cited in literature. However, researchers from a variety of disciplines have just recently begun to systematically understand this phenomenon of trauma-related positive change, which has been named post-traumatic growth (PTG). Calhoun and Tedeschi (2006) offer that PTG allows for one to have greater appreciation for life and may significantly impact the existential, and for some, religious or spiritual realms, allowing for deep consideration of purpose and the meaning of life, greater connection to other people, and increased compassion for those who suffer.

Healthy work environments: Culture and community

The work environment can bolster or conversely undermine self-care efforts. Infrequent clinical supervision, inadequate continued education, lack of training, as well as an implicit "culture of silence"—the belief that vicarious trauma signifies professional weakness—may exacerbate symptoms of vicarious trauma and burnout (Robins et al., 2009). A work environment that supports staff to maintain professional identity, engagement, and resilience explicitly prioritizes clinician wellbeing, balance and sustainability, and supports optimal patient care.

A sense of community amongst colleagues may buffer the impact of feelings of isolation and inequity at work (Truchot and Deregard, 2001). One of the greatest pleasures of my work is the sense of community that has been fostered as a result of collaborating with the interdisciplinary team, which reaffirms a shared sense of values. The "caring for the caregiver" culture within the palliative care ethos brings forth a fortuitous environment in which to explore personal self-care practices, how I may promote self-care in others through my role as an art therapist, and to bear witness to these caregiving stories.

Therapeutic arts interventions to support staff: A review

Klein's (1973) early interest in adapting art therapy interventions to support staff in exploring countertransference founded the use of art in addressing work stress. Since then, staff created collaborative group art-making tasks, including "Caring Quilts," which have been shown to be effective in engaging with and reducing stress, identifying positive workplace resources, discovering commonality, and decreasing feelings of isolation through increased team support (Vachon, 1995; Van Der Vennet, 2003; Italia, Favara-Scacco, Cataldo, and Russo, 2007). Numerous creative arts and mindfulness-based arts interventions have been developed for work-related stress to support medical, nursing, and psychosocial staff experiencing secondary traumatic stress in general healthcare, oncology, and palliative care (Huet, 2015). Belfiore (1994) explored the effects of art therapy on doctors' and nurses' experience of burnout, citing positive experiences where staff could reflect on the emotional impact of their work. Salzano, Lindemann, and Tronsky (2012) confirmed the effectiveness of collaborative art making for hospice staff in reducing burnout and increasing social support.

While art therapists who provide art-based support within a work environment are not providing therapy due to the importance of maintaining professional and ethical boundaries, the value of having art therapists lead such groups has been recognized. Art making may trigger emotional responses that may be best understood by an art therapist, who is trained to maintain a group's psychological safety and containment, and has knowledge of and practice with art materials (Huet, 2015).

The use of therapeutic art experiences in addressing vicarious trauma

We now understand, as it has been widely documented, that typical brain function is disrupted by trauma (Lusebrink and Hinz, 2016; van der Kolk, 2005; van der Kolk, Burnbridge, and Suzuki, 1997). Cognitive processes, language, memory, and our ability to regulate our emotional climate are all compromised in the shadow of a trauma. In considering the phenomenon of vicarious trauma in healthcare environments it is essential to identify the correlation in behavior, emotional response, and deficit in verbal processing for those that bear witness, in much the same way that we would assess a firsthand or primary trauma response and provide supports where possible. Trauma imprints are "stored as fragmented sensory and emotional traces, rather than being organized by the higher brain's autobiographical self" (van der Kolk, Burnbridge, and Suzuki, 1997;

van der Kolk, 2001, 2005) and are difficult to integrate into a cohesive narrative.

While neurobiologically informed art therapy research is in its early stages, art therapists appear uniquely positioned to integrate and implement psychotherapeutic interventions grounded in principles of neuroscience to enhance outcomes (Hass-Cohen and Carr, 2008; King, 2016). Creative expression bypasses verbal and linear pathways to communicating traumatic memories (Hass-Cohen and Carr, 2008; Gantt and Tinnin, 2008), while the sensory quality of the art materials themselves elicits self-soothing, stabilizes body responses and supports self-regulation, supporting processing and integration. With recent advances in the intersection of art therapy, neuroscience, and traumatology, clinicians are gaining new insights into how the art therapy process (the therapeutic relationship cultivated as well as the process and practice of art making) is restorative and generative, not only from an emotional perspective but also neurocognitively and neurobiologically. A recent example from Lusebrink and Hinz (2016) explores the expressive therapies continuum through a neurobiological lens as a way of supporting "cognitive restructuring," integration of memory and experience, as well as the integration of a "trauma narrative" (p.43) that may be helpful in addressing vicarious trauma, and cultivating resilience and post-traumatic growth. Perry (2006) advocates for neurodevelopmental approaches to therapy with trauma survivors, emphasizing the necessity of expressive activities that are relational, repetitive, relevant, rewarding, and rhythmic.

In practice

The following therapeutic arts group was facilitated in response to patient deaths witnessed in the hospital environment. Weaving to Explore Awareness of Vicarious Experience (WEAVE) was a group implemented with pediatric staff following a traumatic patient death on the pediatric intensive care unit.

WEAVE: Weaving to explore awareness of vicarious experience

WEAVE is a three-step arts-based group experience to address vicarious trauma(s), grief and loss in the work environment. WEAVE was initially created following a traumatic and unexpected death that several of our staff members witnessed on the pediatric intensive care unit. The cumulative effect of the many losses impacted a variety of clinicians in their respective roles, who reported feelings of distress, guilt, helplessness, and profound sadness surrounding these patient cases. The Child Life and Creative Arts Therapy department surveyed departmental staff to identify needs and assess clinician experiences. Staff indicated that an opportunity to process recent events would be helpful. All clinical staff members within the department were invited to attend WEAVE. Attendance was optional. The group was held in a private, closed space.

The goal of WEAVE was to support staff in identifying coping and self-care strategies, increase awareness, and foster connection to community through group art and weaving intervention. A large piece of canvas cloth was primed with white gesso beforehand for step 1. A medium-sized canvas with slits made with an X-Acto knife was also prepared before the group for step 3. See other materials offered in "Protocol: Weave" below.

One music therapist and five child life specialists participated in WEAVE over an hour and a half during work time at the end of the day. The two facilitators, dually certified art therapists and child life specialists, facilitated the group but also participated in art making and discussion. The group began with facilitators acknowledging specific losses that the group had experienced, established a confidentiality agreement, and introduced art interventions.

On one large piece of canvas cloth, participants were invited to explore personal symbols of loss/grief that were specific to the patients who had recently died. Some members verbalized feelings of nervousness or hesitation in engaging with memories of the patient by participating in the group experience, but acknowledged the need to do so. All group members participated in art making. As previously mentioned, facilitators also participated in art making.

After 20 minutes, participants were invited to share the meaning of their symbols and comment on other symbols on the canvas cloth. Four staff members felt comfortable verbally sharing symbols and personal meaning, which welcomed storytelling. Symbols and themes that came up during painting included a dog, the color red, blood, goriness, and feelings of helplessness and disgust. The sharing of symbols led the group to organically process events and learn more about the order of events that led to the patient's death. Staff also commented on the art process, noticing how participants were reaching out nonverbally to one another using paint on canvas. Group discussion revolved around lack of, and need for, boundaries and space; our unique work environment as it related to boundaries; and memories of patients and how staff cope with loss while at work.

The next ten minutes were dedicated to the second step of WEAVE. Participants were instructed to create strips out of the canvas cloth. Group members verbally shared their resistance to destroying the canvas cloth. Unfortunately, a photograph was not taken of the canvas cloth, and in retrospect taking a photograph could have helped the group in being able progress to the next stage of the art experience, as well as document the transformative creative process. The facilitators reassured group members that creating strips would eventually lead to a purposeful process that we hoped would be restorative and symbolic for the group. One group member began scoring the cloth with an X-Acto knife, and others joined in with scissors and ripping with their hands. Some group members intentionally preserved certain symbols from step 1 by cutting around these symbols.

After ripping the canvas cloth, group members commented on the rhythm, physical release and cathartic quality of ripping. In looking at the pile of strips, the group spoke about encountering fragmented symbols and the feeling of invading others' space. The group processed the collective difficulty of maintaining physical and emotional boundaries in the art experience and explored similarities in the work environment and more specifically, one patient's death. The group also noticed that participants were more aware of their bodies during this step of WEAVE, and how the art directive oriented participants to their bodies. Group members later shared how this step was most helpful in externalizing feelings of anger, fragmentation, helplessness, and brokenness. It appears that the physical act of mindful ripping may have contributed to grounding in the present experience of group art making.

The remainder of the time was spent on the final step of WEAVE. Participants were invited to reweave strips onto a pre-slit stretched canvas, which moved the group into a more kinesthetic and tactile space. Group members began weaving, knotting, and connecting strips of canvas cloth through the slits and with other strips. The group displayed increased physical movement, physical touch, problem solving and increased verbal communication with other group members as they attached the strips to the canvas (Figure 13.1). Group members connected over the communal act of weaving and integrating fragments, locating symbols from step 1 as well as discovering areas of beauty. Members spoke of the importance of ritual in loss, and explored the symbolism of creating, destroying, and reweaving to "move through" loss. The group shifted from sharing memories of the patient and became more focused on the present moment. The group collectively decided which way the canvas should hang and where it should live. In a post survey, staff reported positive feelings towards the weaving intervention, recognizing the inherently integrative process, and expressed feeling supported in the work environment (Figure 13.2).

Figure 13.1 Weaving   *Figure 13.2 Final weave*

WEAVE: Reflections and testimonial

It is important to evaluate participants to understand feelings and effects of the group. In addition to using SurveyMonkey to collect specific data, staff were also able to write their own impressions of the experience. The following is an anonymous testimonial from a staff member:

> I found the arts bereavement group to be very impactful. There was a therapeutic rhythm of sharing memories while simultaneously creating art that brought staff members' emotions to the surface. I appreciated that people shared specific memories, such as what staff members did with the patient, or what about her made them laugh, or even songs that still make us think of her. The next day I saw that all of the art was put up on the walls, which definitely brought the power of the group and our collective healing to life.

The group experience was a much-needed pause for myself, and even though I was co-facilitating, I benefited from art making and listening to stories about the patient. Aside from the validation and support the group provided, what really struck me was seeing the vulnerability of my co-workers, and their willingness and need to share, and to hear, these stories. I remember thinking how sacred this space was. Despite the pain and revisiting of trauma, empathy, compassion, and kindness sprouted and took root in our group.

Stories need to be shared and received. Some stories need to be contained, stored away, but still accessible. Our communal weave served this purpose. WEAVE was a beautiful reminder to engage with my own vulnerability, to care for myself, and when capable and appropriate, provide a supportive space for others.

Protocol: Weave

Objective

To support staff in identifying coping/self-care strategies, and increase awareness and foster connection to community through group art and weaving intervention.

Material goal

To complete a woven canvas in service of the objective.

Duration

One two-hour session is offered within a week of discharge. If a client is unable to attend, a second opportunity may be offered to allow for scheduling difficulties.

Curriculum

The following is the curriculum used for WEAVE. It can be adapted to the needs of the group and is meant to be a guide.

These are the materials you will need:

- a large piece of canvas cloth primed with white gesso for step 1

- a medium-sized canvas with slits made with an X-Acto knife prepared before step 3

- acrylic paint, a variety of paint brushes in different sizes, sharpies, fine-tip markers, tissue paper, magazine clippings, Mod Podge, glue sticks, scissors, and tape.

STEP I CREATION OF INDIVIDUAL AND GROUP TRAUMA NARRATIVE

Facilitators state the purpose of the group, explain the rules of confidentiality, acknowledge specific losses, and introduce art intervention. Group members are invited to share the meaning of their symbols and comment on other symbols on the canvas cloth.

STEP 2 DECONSTRUCTION

The group facilitators introduce the concept of deconstruction in relation to healing and catharsis. They then invite participants to deconstruct the canvas cloth by cutting, shredding, and tearing the canvas using their hands, scissors, X-Acto knives. Members verbally share and process the action of destruction and feelings that come up in this process.

STEP 3 TRANSFORMATION/RECONSTITUTION

Participants are invited to reattach their strips to a new pre-slit canvas to create a new symbolic visual narrative. Members verbally share and process the action of weaving and feelings that come up in this process. The canvas is hung in a public place to serve as a touchstone for staff.

References

Alexander, D.A. and Klein, S. (2001) 'Ambulance personnel and critical incidents: Impact of accident and emergency work on mental health and emotional well-being.' *The British Journal of Psychiatry 178*, 1, 76–81.

Back, A.L., Rushton, C.H., Kaszniak, A.W., and Halifax, J.S. (2015) '"Why are we doing this?" Clinician helplessness in the face of suffering.' *Journal of Palliative Medicine 18*, 1, 26–30.

Barnsteiner, J.H. and Gillis-Donovan, J. (1990) 'Being related and separate: A standard for therapeutic relationships.' *The American Journal of Maternal/Child Nursing 15*, 4, 223–228.

Belfiore, M. (1994) 'The group that takes care of itself: Art therapy to prevent burnout.' *Arts in Psychotherapy 21*, 2, 119–126.

Bober, T. and Regehr, C. (2005) *In the Line of Fire: Trauma in the Emergency Services.* New York: Oxford University Press.

Calhoun, L.G. and Tedeschi, R.G. (2006) *The Handbook of Posttraumatic Growth: Research and Practice.* Mahwah. NJ: Lawrence Erlbaum Publishers.

Christopher, J. and Maris, J. (2010) 'Integrating mindfulness as self-care into counseling and psychotherapy training.' *Journal for Counseling and Psychotherapy Research 10*, 2, 114–125.

Collins, S. and Long, A. (2003) 'Too tired to care? The psychological effects of working with trauma.' *Journal of Psychiatric and Mental Health Nursing 10*, 17–27.

Figley, C.R. (1995) 'Compassion fatigue as secondary traumatic stress disorder: An overview.' In C.R. Figley (ed.) *Compassion Fatigue: Coping with Secondary Traumatic Stress Disorder in Those Who Treat the Traumatized.* New York: Brunner-Routledge.

Gantt, L. and Tinnin, L.W. (2008) 'Support for a neurobiological view of trauma with implications for art therapy.' *The Arts in Psychotherapy 36*, 148–153.

Hass-Cohen, N. and Carr, R. (eds) (2008) *Art Therapy and Clinical Neuroscience.* London: Jessica Kingsley Publishers.

Hatfield, E., Cacioppo, J., and Rapson, R. (1994) *Emotional Contagion.* Paris: Cambridge University Press.

Huet, V. (2015) 'Literature review of art therapy-based interventions for work-related stress.' *International Journal of Art Therapy 20*, 2, 66–76.

Italia, S., Favara-Scacco, C., Cataldo, A. and Russo, G. (2007) 'Evaluation and art therapy treatment of the burnout syndrome in oncology units.' *Psycho-Oncology 17*, 676–680.

King, J.L. (ed.) (2016) *Art Therapy, Trauma, and Neuroscience: Theoretical and Practical Perspectives.* New York: Routledge.

Klein, R. (1973) 'Art therapy with staff groups: Implications for countertransference and treatment.' *Art Psychotherapy 1*, 3–4, 247–253.

Lusebrink, V.B. and Hinz, L.D. (2016) 'The expressive therapies continuum as a framework in the treatment of trauma.' In J.L. King (ed.) *Art Therapy, Trauma, and Neuroscience: Theoretical and Practical Perspectives.* New York: Routledge.

Masten, A.S. (2001) 'Ordinary magic: Resilience processes in development.' *American Psychologist 56*, 3, 227–238.

Meichenbaum, D. (2007) 'Self-care for trauma psychotherapists and caregivers: Individual, social and organizational interventions.' Handout at Melissa Institute, 11th Annual Conference, May 4, 2007. Available at http://melissainstitute.com/handouts.html, accessed on July 3, 2016.

Pearlman, L. and Saakvitne, K. (1995) 'Treating therapists with vicarious traumatization and secondary traumatic stress disorders.' In C.R. Figley (ed.) *Compassion Fatigue: Coping with Secondary Traumatic Stress Disorder in Those Who Treat the Traumatized.* New York: Brunner-Routledge.

Perry, B. (2006) 'Applying principles of neurodevelopment to clinical work with maltreated and traumatized children: The neurosequential model of therapeutics.' In N.B. Wedd (ed.) *Working with Traumatized Youth in Child Welfare.* New York: Guilford Press.

Robins, P., Meltzer, L., and Zelikovsky, N. (2009) 'The experience of secondary traumatic stress upon care providers working within a children's hospital.' *Journal of Pediatric Nursing 24*, 270–279.

Sabin-Farrell, R. and Turpin G. (2003) 'Vicarious traumatization: Implications for the mental health of health workers?' *Clinical Psychology Review 23*, 3, 449–480.

Salzano, A.T., Lindemann, E., and Tronsky, L.N. (2012) 'The effectiveness of a collaborative art-making task on reducing stress in hospice caregivers.' *The Arts in Psychotherapy 40*, 45–52.

Truchot, D. and Deregard, M. (2001) 'Perceived inequity, communal orientation and burnout: The role of helping models.' *Work and Stress 15*, 347–356.

Vachon, M. (1995) 'Staff stress in hospice/palliative care: A review.' *Palliative Medicine 9*, 2, 91–122.

van der Kolk, B.A. (2001) 'The assessment and treatment of complex PTSD.' In R. Yehuda (ed.) *Traumatic Stress*. New York: American Psychiatric Press.

van der Kolk, B.A. (2005) 'Developmental trauma disorder: Toward a rational diagnosis for children with complex trauma histories.' *Psychiatric Annals 35*, 5, 401–408.

van der Kolk, B.A., Burbridge, J.A., and Suzuki, J. (1997) 'The psychobiology of traumatic memory: Clinical implications of neuroimaging studies.' *The Annals of the New York Academy of Sciences 821*, 99–113.

van Dernoot Lipsky, L. and Burk, C. (2009) *Trauma Stewardship: An Everyday Guide to Caring for Self While Caring for Others*. San Francisco, CA: Berrett-Koehler Publishers.

Van der Vennet, R. (2003) 'A study of mental health workers in art therapy group to reduce secondary trauma and burnout.' Dissertation Abstracts International: Section B: The Sciences and Engineering 63, 9-B, 4389. US: University Microfilms International.

Weiss, D., Marmar, C., Metzler, T., and Ronfelt, H. (1995) 'Predicting symptomatic distress in emergency services personnel.' *Journal of Consulting and Clinical Psychology 63*, 3, 361–368.

Figure 6.1 Image from childhood

Figure 6.2 Fetus in womb of warmth

Figure 6.3 Skull and candles

Figure 7.1 Front side stone mandala

Figure 7.2 Adding the black yarn, front

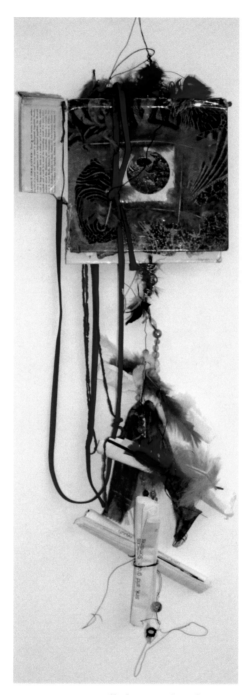

Figure 8.1 All about earthquakes

Figure 8.2 A green-hearted tree

Figure 9.1 Final weaving

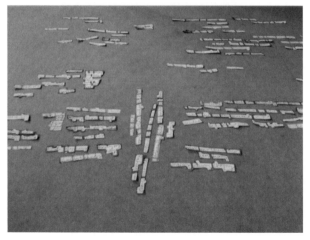

Figure 9.2 Small piece of the mind map from my journal

Figure 10.1 Prepping the box with Grandma

Figure 10.2 The finished memory box

Figure 11.1 Acceptance on the river

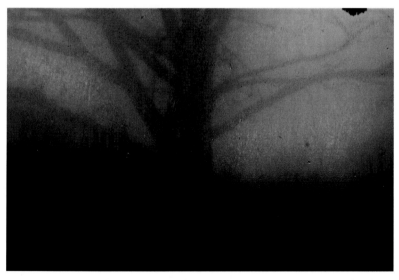

Figure 11.2 Window covered with mist

Figure 11.3 Front trees out of focus

Figure 11.4 The reeds stand in tranquility

Figure 12.1 Woman who dreams

Figure 13.1 Weaving

Figure 13.2 Final weave

Figure 14.1 Aden's family heart

Figure 14.2 Mother and child handprints

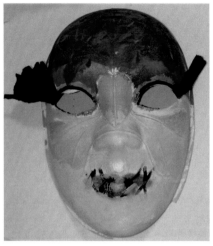

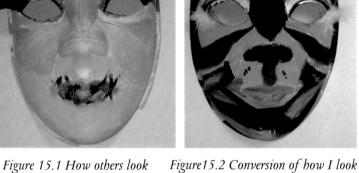

Figure 15.1 How others look at me—Barb

Figure 15.2 Conversion of how I look at myself into an animal—Barb

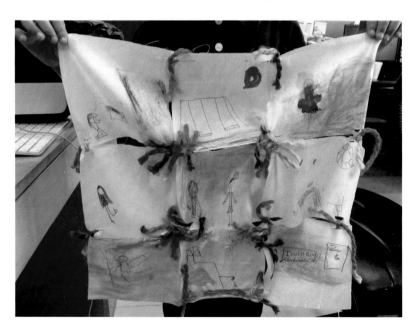

Figure 16.1 Memorial quilting with Jaiden

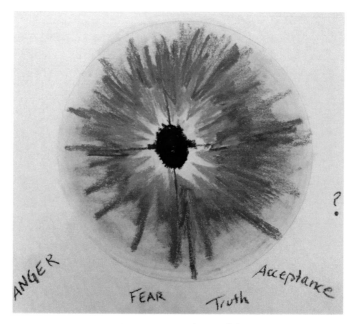

Figure 17.2 Pat's mandala

Figure 17.3 Pat's box top view

Figure 18.1 Kinetic Family Drawing

Figure 18.2 Doll

Figure 18.5 Memory box, bottom of box

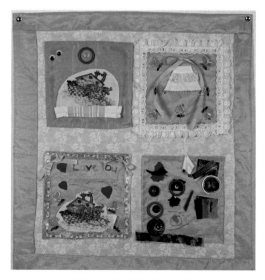

Figure 18.6 Family quilt

Figure 19.1 The inner and outer profiles of PC's shoe

14

Can You Help Me Say Goodbye?

Sibling Loss and Bereavement Support in the Healthcare Environment

Lauren D. Smith and Sarah Yazdian Rubin

It's the thing that nobody dares talk about: the death of a child. For if we say the words, then they become real, and the unimaginable chasm of such profound loss stretches open its gaping mouth, threatening to swallow us whole. How then, can we approach this unspeakable, unthinkable thing? As clinicians in pediatric critical care settings, we join families in those unspeakable moments, providing a therapeutic bridge or a transition from one space to the next, from now to then, from hospital to home, from holding a hand to letting it go. So often society focuses on the impossible trauma of loss as it impacts the bereaved parent. The loss is so great that there is not even a word in the English language to describe it as there exists for other losses, e.g. widow/widower/orphan. But what too of the loss of a sibling? We cannot underestimate the attachment bond of siblings and the equal complexity of grief or sometimes guilt when a child is lost to serious illness or trauma. There is richness in this work, straddling the liminal space of a hospital, between here and there. We have opportunities to build foundations for healing in the bleakest of moments. As art therapists we learn to bring form, symbolism, and connection to the disorganizing feature of grief and loss.

Medical art therapy in pediatric acute care and critical care settings

While an ordinary hospital admission can be disruptive to children and families, for those facing chronic, life-shortening, or terminal illness the complexity of navigating an unfamiliar medical–surgical environment, comprehending the language of medicine, and enduring potentially invasive and painful testing and treatments can produce a profound state of psychological, emotional, physical, and spiritual turmoil. Medical art therapy with children is utilized in hospital settings thoughout the country and internationally to support coping and adjustment to hospitalization and illness (Hart and Rollins, 2011; Sourkes, 1991).

Defined as the "specific use of art therapy with individuals who are physically ill, experiencing trauma to the body, or undergoing aggressive medical treatment such as surgery or chemotherapy" (Malchiodi, 1993 as cited by Rode, 1995), medical art therapy plays a vital role in pediatric medicine, supporting the psychosocial needs of children and families as physiological and biological states are compromised. The art therapist practicing within a medical–surgical setting must remain adaptive and integrative (Rode, 1995), operating within a holistic model that recognizes the child in relationship to place, person, illness, and time. This position is integral to the treatment team, for in addition to addressing internal conflicts, the art therapist must also be prepared to navigate the aspects of disease and disability that can interrupt the normal course of a child's development (Councill, 1993). Art therapy within the pediatric critical care setting has the potential to restore a sense of repair, empowerment, and psychoemotional growth.

Secondary attachment figures: The sibling bond in the cycle of grief

While early attachments are primal, our unique sibling bonds may be the strongest and truest bonds that sustain us throughout life. Within the family system, the sibling subsystem also operates to support childhood identity formation, relational bonds, and secure attachment. Preserving this ongoing bond or attachment (Packman et al., 2006), particularly with secondary attachment figures such as siblings, can be sustaining and even transformative for the bereaved, resulting in post-traumatic growth or adapted coping and attachment styles. In working with bereaved siblings of deceased patients, expressive and reflective interventions may support the formation and/or preservation of a continuing or ongoing bond of attachment.

Myth of the mourning child

Unfortunately, children are frequently shielded from grieving rituals or mourning processes. Kirwin and Hamrin (2005) discuss myths around children's grief, such as children are incapable of grieving or able to rebound quickly with minimal emotional consequence. Children who do grieve are believed to suffer "maladjustment" as adults. Grief, however, is a human experience that transcends the bounds of age and psychological development; all people, including children, are capable of experiencing loss, grief, and a bereavement process. Through a developmental lens, we know that indeed children of all ages and developmental abilities perceive the complexity of loss and enter into their own grief work and process. Even infants perceive loss and separation, and grief can be observed through behavioral and somatic disturbances in toileting, sleep, and feeding patterns. Toddlers have difficulty grasping the concept of permanence, therefore may believe that the deceased will return after the funeral, or after the hospitalization. School-age children may develop an exaggerated fear of illness or the common cold, fearing that any illness results in death. Adolescents, occupied with social relationships, self-concept and bodily identity may develop deep anxieties around life-threatening illnesses (Raymer and McIntyre, 1987).

Aden's family heart

Aden was a previously healthy, active, and charismatic eight-year-old boy who was diagnosed with severe heart failure after falling ill in gym class at school. Over the course of ten months, this therapist (Lauren) had the opportunity to work with Aden and his brother, Ben and their family during periods of extended admission in the pediatric cardiac intensive care unit as he underwent treatment and awaited a heart transplant.

Aden received regular individual creative arts therapy sessions as well as psychological and emotional preparation and procedural support for both transplant and cardiac assist devices. As Aden's condition worsened and his long-awaited heart transplant ultimately failed, he passed away. During the time leading up to his death and immediately following, this therapist alongside the psychosocial team provided family-centered sibling support during long separation and the anticipatory grief period.

Aden was a prolific artist while in the hospital, and art was ultimately the tool that provided his younger brother and family with a healing container as they navigated the unfathomable terrain of grief and loss. As will be articulated in the following protocols, Aden's family engaged in a legacy-building handprint intervention at bedside at the time of Aden's death, with the support of this therapist as well as a post-bereavement art therapy session. Ben and Aden's youngest cousins then engaged in a memory box making and wish writing intervention, in order to provide containment, education about death and dying, and open new healing channels to integrate Aden's vibrant memory into this new phase of their family life. The following are excerpts from Aden's brother and cousins:

We wish that you are playing baseball.

We wish that you could come back to life.

We wish you could eat all the pizza in the world.

We wish you will watch over us.

We wish the transplant worked well.

At the end of their session, the children presented their box and wishes to Aden's parents and his aunt read the wishes aloud to the group, which included the therapist and primary social worker (Figure 14.1).

Figure 14.1 Aden's family heart

Creative arts therapy interventions at end of life and bereavement

Family-centered bereavement support in a pediatric medical surgical setting can be viewed in two parts: 1) during end of life or at time of death and 2) following a child's death in a post-mortem grief counseling session. In the later, family or sibling-based art therapy session, developmentally appropriate psychoeducation surrounding death is provided and modeled for caregiver and siblings. It is imperative to provide as much autonomy in decision making as possible during this time (Kenner, Press, and Ryan, 2015), as individuals frequently feel an overwhelming sense of loss of control and disorganization.

At the time of an end-of life intervention, whether the death is anticipated or unanticipated, the creative arts therapist has symbolic tools at their disposal to facilitate an intimate, containing ritual for the family that may serve as a meaningful transition from anticipatory grief and mourning into the actual active bereavement phase of grief work.

Creative arts therapy interventions, fundamentally nonverbal in nature, can serve to enhance other channels of communication that may be blocked in times of crisis due to existing relational conflicts or the effect of traumatic loss on neurobiological verbal functioning processes (van der Kolk, 2005). Children who engage with familiar art materials may experience a sense of mastery and competence in the face of disorganization and uncertainty. The sensory stimulating nature of certain organic materials (fiber or textiles, earth clay, etc.) in an art therapy intervention may be experienced as soothing and regulating, or may stimulate non-threatening memories of the deceased loved one while providing enough psychic distance so as not to trigger an emotionally destabilizing or acutely anxious response.

In the context of the vastness of grief and loss, many individuals feel themselves obscured or lost or displaced. Certain art therapy interventions that introduce concretized objects for containment (boxes, vessels, envelopes, etc.) may promote a possibility for emotional containment, closure, and groundedness. Art making created within the safety and boundedness of the therapeutic alliance also provides an opportunity to externalize deeply held beliefs, fears, and misconceptions about death and dying or reveal patterns of cognition and behavior that may provide great insight for clinicians helping children and families to cope with death and loss.

Short-term bereavement interventions

There are myriad possibilities for facilitating short-term bereavement interventions with patients and families in an acute medical setting; these are only a sampling. In our experience, it has been best to present simple and concrete interventions with an open framework to allow for exploration of material, process, and relationship. The important concepts to grasp are those of safety, containment, and transition. These interventions are intended to bridge the experience of illness and hospitalization with the experience of grief and mourning outside of the hospital environment. The medical art therapist specializes in providing support in times of physical, emotional, psychological, and spiritual crisis. It is the role and responsibility of the medical art therapist to provide these emotional supports through a family's most vulnerable time of trauma and loss, so that they are able to safely connect with more permanent coping supports in their community following their child's death.

A one-time intervention, offered following a patient's death
Following a patient's death, siblings and family of the child are invited back to the hospital for a post-bereavement session, allowing for an opportunity to verbally and nonverbally process themes of loss, grief, complicated grief, anger, etc. During this session, siblings who have perhaps not had the opportunity to say goodbye in person may visit the hospital again and gain greater orientation to the experience of loss (particularly for children in more concrete developmental phases). This often allows children the space to ask questions about death and dying (e.g. What happens to the body? What does cremation mean? Will my sibling come back?), especially when primary caregivers may not know how to answer or may be unable to provide the necessary emotional supports as they tend to their own grief and shock. The trained therapist in this session will be able to model to caregivers developmentally appropriate language around death and offer a variety of symbolic art therapy interventions to support memory making, legacy, and containment.

Children may engage verbally or nonverbally. We frame the session as a safe space to remember their sibling or ask questions or simply make art together without talking, if that is where they are most comfortable. Asking child-centered open-ended questions such as, "What questions do you have?" can help in setting a tone for the work. It's important to address misconceptions around death, especially for young children who may not yet grasp the concept of permanence. Developmentally appropriate, honest language provided by the therapist can convey that their sibling has died and that means that their sibling's body has stopped working and they can't play, walk, breathe, or do any activities they used to enjoy anymore.

It's important to emphasize that they didn't do anything to cause their sibling's death and that their sibling didn't do anything wrong to cause their own death. Many school-age children internalize a sense of guilt or shame around the cause of their sibling's death, deeply held sentiments that may only reveal themselves in the art-making process. Utilizing compassionate and developmentally appropriate language is a proactive and body-positive approach, asserting and acknowledging both the deceased child's physical body and the sibling in relationship thereto.

In such a destabilizing time as in immediate grief, it is important first to communicate emotional and physical safety to the surviving child, normalize expressions of grief, and orient siblings to the purpose of the art therapy session. For example:

> We are here in the hospital today to make art together and remember [sibling's name]. You might have some questions about [your sibling] and why they died. We can talk about it together. It is very normal to feel lots of different feelings after someone has died. Sometimes you might feel very sad and want to cry and be alone; other times you might feel very angry or want to break something. You might feel worried about your [parent/caregiver] too. All of those feelings are very normal. You did not do anything to cause this. [Your sibling] was very sick and died but it is not your fault.

This language is a sample and must be modified and tailored to fit appropriate developmental stages and the needs of individuals and families. During art therapy sessions, children may display a wide range of emotions. Some children will cry and verbalize their experience of loss. Others may engage quietly in art making, and others may not engage differently or acknowledge loss or sadness at all in the session. Others still will reveal their level of coping through their engagement with the art material itself. All responses are developmentally appropriate and should be supported equally by the therapist. This is an appropriate opportunity for the art therapist to observe and assess a child's engagement with the creative arts therapy process, their interaction with materials, and their ability to verbally or nonverbally express a feeling state. Doing so will assist the therapist in providing appropriate bereavement referrals to the family's community resources.

Additionally, we typically provide mixed media, developmentally appropriate art materials, and materials that provide for affect expression but limited regression as this is a single session and siblings may become dysregulated easily in the art making. We tend to avoid paints, clay, and wet materials and move towards oil pastels, markers, colored pencils, tissue paper in a wide variety of color, glue sticks and objects such as boxes that can be ornamented and serve as containers. For therapists who have the opportunity to facilitate longer-term bereavement support, modification of art materials is of course appropriate. Two interventions we have found to be useful:

- *Memory box.* The box itself is an obvious form of containment. In the early stages of grief, it is important to provide familiar and not overly complicated materials to which a family or sibling may easily attach and that can serve as a symbolic object. We introduce a pre-made box that can be altered or ornamented to siblings and family as an opportunity to dedicate the object to their deceased sibling, to work on the surface of the box, or move to the interior spaces. Siblings frequently create messages or drawings for their sibling and place them inside of the box during the session. This is something that the family can take home and utilize in other moments of memory making.

- *Saying goodbye—letters and wishes.* Writing wishes for the deceased sibling can serve as a powerful container for a variety of emotional responses ranging in tone from playful to somber and reflective. If wishes are written, it is important to offer a means of containment, either in a specially designated envelope, or to be placed inside the memory box or something similar. Again this supports the concept of safety when children are expressing their most vulnerable feeling states. For older children and adolescents, or for younger children through the assistance of the art therapist, letter writing might afford a more concrete opportunity for acknowledgment of a sibling's death. Offering the opportunity to write a letter provides another form of safe containment for the expression of a range of emotions, wishes, hopes, desires, frustrations, regrets, etc. The letter can be accompanied later by a visual response, and may be utilized as a first tool in supporting the expression of grief and mourning.

The legacy handprint

The legacy handprint intervention is a powerful process, both in which to actively participate and to witness (Figure 14.2). Inherent in the art making itself is the metaphor of transformation. The algin impression material changes first from powder to liquid to gel and eventually to solid. The gel solid eventually is transformed to plaster or stone. The grief process is likewise fluid and sometimes feels weighted or stagnant. We are moved from one emotional state to the next, sometimes with little preparation. The experience of death and dying is a changing of states, from life, to end of life, to death. It is within these liminal and transitional moments that the creative arts therapist can provide stewardship, comfort, and safety.

Figure 14.2 Mother and child handprints

This intervention encourages transparency and intimacy in times of great fear and anxiety. The material itself as well as the structure within which the art therapist orients families to the process is a holding environment. We have witnessed many families experience this intervention and every family processes this experience in a manner unique to their family dynamic, cultural, and/or spiritual belief system. There is no correct path through grief. As art therapists working with bereaved individuals, we can only serve as guides and provide tools to ease the passage.

Protocol: Legacy building handprint intervention

Objective

To support families in acute or anticipatory loss and grief through tactile, sensory-stimulating interventions to preserve memory, legacy, and impact of the deceased person.

Material goal

To provide safe, family-centered containment to facilitate as much autonomy and choice as possible within the process.

Duration

This is a one-time intervention. The materials have their own drying process that must be incorporated into the intervention. Completed prints are mailed to families following hospitalization, in post-bereavement sessions or, when possible, processed with the family prior to the child's death.

Curriculum

Presenting a legacy handprint intervention to families is emotionally charged and brings complex conscious and unconscious responses connected to the family's culture, spiritual or belief system, family dynamic, and comfort level with death and the dying process. The clinician should note the timing of introduction and maintain interdisciplinary communications to ensure the highest levels of empathy and attunement. Utilize orienting language, explain the process step by step, and offer as much choice within the process for families to participate or observe, depending on their level of comfort.

These are the materials you will need:

- mixing bowl and spatula

- spoon or scooping tool

- cool water

- a sturdy, flat, mobile surface such as a tray or panel

- plaster of Paris or other art plaster

- an appropriately sized circular silicon mold (basic baking molds work well)

- a high-algin-content impression material such as Jeltrate® Alginate Impression Material designed for making dental impressions.

STEP 1 MIX THE IMPRESSION MATERIAL

First, bring the impression material, water, mixing bowl, spatula, and flat surface into the room where the prints will be taken. After mixing the material with the water (instructions may vary by product) it will almost immediately begin to change into a more solidified, malleable form, so be prepared to mix the material in the bowl and transfer it onto the flat surface right away.

STEP 2 CREATE THE IMPRESSION

The hand, fingers, or foot must be pressed firmly into the material and held for a minute or two so that the material can fully gel into a more solid state. It is helpful when possible to bring a colleague with you at the time of the intervention to assist with the more logistical aspects and so that you can focus your attention on providing the family with support and containment throughout the process. Many parents wish to press their child's hand into the impression material independently, while some prefer to observe the therapist, and some prefer to work in tandem with the therapist. There is no correct mode or method, and sometimes the caregiver will need support in the middle of the intervention, so the therapist must be grounded, present, and flexible in the moment to shift roles or positions unexpectedly.

STEP 3 PLACE THE GEL IMPRESSION IN THE SILICON MOLD

After a satisfactory impression of the child's hand or foot has been created, the therapist will place the gel impression in the silicon mold, print side facing up, and mix the plaster and warm water in a separate container.

STEP 4 POUR THE PLASTER

Pour the plaster evenly over the impression and tap the silicon mold against a flat surface gently to release any air bubbles. The drying time will likely take between 24 and 48 hours, after which the gel impression can be easily removed from the plaster mold. A relief of the child's hand will remain and can be further enhanced with the use of sculpture tools, a fine-grain sand paper, etc.

Author's note: In some cases, such as when an autopsy must be performed, utilizing an algin-based impression material may be contraindicated. In these situations, Model Magic may be substituted. The art therapist should always check with the medical team prior to providing or introducing this intervention.

References

Councill, T. (1993) 'Art therapy with pediatric cancer patients: Helping normal children cope with abnormal circumstances.' *Art Therapy: Journal of the American Art Therapy Association 10*, 2, 78–87.

Hart, R. and Rollins, J. (2011) *Therapeutic Activities for Children and Teens Coping with Health Issues.* Hoboken, NJ: Wiley.

Kenner, C., Press, J., and Ryan, D. (2015) 'Recommendations for palliative and bereavement care in the NICU: A family-centered integrative approach.' *Journal of Perinatology 35*, S19–S23.

Kirwin, K.M. and Hamrin, V. (2005) 'Decreasing the risk of complicated bereavement and future psychiatric disorders in children.' *Journal of Child and Adolescent Psychiatric Nursing 18*, 2, 62–78.

Packman, W., Horsley, H., Davies, B., and Kramer, R. (2006) 'Sibling bereavement and continuing bonds.' *Death Studies 30*, 817–841.

Raymer, M. and McIntyre, B.B. (1987) 'An art support group for bereaved children and adolescents.' *Art Therapy 4*, 1, 27–35.

Rini, A. and Loriz, L. (2007) 'Anticipatory mourning in parents with a child who dies while hospitalized.' *Journal of Pediatric Nursing 22*, 4, 272–282.

Rode, D.C. (1995) 'Building bridges within the culture of pediatric medicine: The interface of art therapy and child life programming.' *Art Therapy: Journal of the American Art Therapy Association 12*, 2, 104–110.

Sourkes, B. (1991) 'Truth to life: Art therapy with pediatric oncology patients and their siblings.' *Journal of Psychosocial Oncology 9*, 2, 81–96.

van der Kolk, B.A. (2005) 'Developmental trauma disorder: Toward a rational diagnosis for children with complex trauma histories.' *Psychiatric Annals 35*, 5, 401–408.

15

Mask Making and Dialectical Behavior Therapy With Homeless Young Mothers

Divya Sunil Gulati

Overview

Most individuals have experienced times of getting upset, when nothing seems to go right. One of the worst pains can come from self-inflicted suffering and self-criticism. As Albers (2013) notes, I am good enough and I accept and love myself for the way I am are words we don't often say to ourselves.

> Noticing one's suffering, being kind and caring towards that suffering, and realizing that imperfection is a part of human experience are key for developing compassion for the self. Acknowledging loss and the pain it has caused requires mindfulness. (Neff, 2011, n.p.)

Mindfulness is an awareness and acceptance of thoughts, feelings, behaviors, and behavioral urges (Arnold, 2008). Mindfulness stems from dialectal behavioral therapy (DBT) and is the core basis of DBT. This acceptance is tough for many of us, and particularly people who have faced severe trauma or have had a difficult childhood with traumatic pasts. People with traumatic pasts typically have a distorted sense of self and thus, developing self-compassion is often difficult for them (Ot'alora, 2012).

For this chapter, I focused on using expressive mask making art therapy intervention as a means of developing mindful self-compassion in traumatized homeless adolescent mothers. My goal is to provide a platform upon which psychotherapy practitioners interested in the study of neuroscience, art psychotherapy, and narrative therapy might reorganize knowledge into collective research vehicles that serve a broader need for individuals with a history of trauma, including disrupted attachments.

Homelessness in adolescence

Homelessness is a serious problem in the United States, and various efforts to rectify this serious problem have failed (Panter-Brick, 2002). In addition to the developmental challenges adolescents face, homelessness and motherhood add a significant level of stress. According to The National Child Traumatic Stress Network (NCTSN) (2007), homeless youth experience significant mental health problems, including depression, anxiety disorders, PTSD, suicidal ideation, and substance abuse disorders. One of the most frightening trauma symptoms is when the individual holds himself responsible for what happened (Kammerer and Mazelis, 2006), and this self-blaming can lead to a lack of self-compassion.

Adolescence has been considered, almost by definition, as a period of heightened stress (Spear, 2000) due to the array of transitions being experienced naturally, including physical maturation, drive for independence, increased salience of social and peer interaction, and brain development (Blakemore, 2008; Casey, Getz, and Galvan, 2008; Casey, Jones, and Hare, 2008). There are four important aspects the clinician should consider in working with this population.

1. From a psychoanalytic perspective, adolescence is a sensitive time because it involves a reconjuring of early childhood separation–individuation issues, which heightens the risk of maladaptive attachments and identity confusion.

2. Adolescents are in a biological upheaval involving neurological changes that impact their decision making.

3. Most adolescents in homeless shelters have experienced some type of childhood trauma and significant loss.

4. Most adolescents in homeless shelters face unique challenges, including substance use, sexual orientation and identity issues, and pregnancy.

Mindfulness and Dialectical Behavior Therapy

Mindfulness is the core basis of DBT, which incorporates Eastern meditative practices (Arnold, 2008). DBT developed from the synthesis of opposites, particularly acceptance and change, which is the core of DBT philosophy. Mindfulness, as defined by Rappaport and Kalmanowtiz (2014), is "a practice of bringing awareness to the present moment with an attitude of acceptance and non-judgment" (p. 1). By being present, one is more aware of his or her thoughts, feelings, behaviors, and behavioral changes. Also, one feels more empowered to be in charge of self in a different way (Arnold, 2008). One of the most important aspects of DBT is realizing that feelings and thoughts are not facts (Arnold, 2008).

Mask making as a means of developing a trauma narrative
DEVELOPING A TRAUMA NARRATIVE

Schiffer (as cited in Klorer, 2005) suggests that the traumatized child maintains feelings of trauma and perspectives in one half of the brain (right hemisphere) while the other half matures. According to Munns (2000), the right hemisphere controls sensorimotor perception and integrations. Creative art therapy gives access to the right hemisphere, thus revealing these suppressed memories (Klorer 2005).

It takes a great deal of effort for the brain to deal with trauma. Whether because of PTSD or the many adaptive behaviors that victims use instinctively in threatening situations, the traumatized brain is constantly in a state of high alert, particularly its lower regions, where survival instincts originate. As Klorer (2005, pp.5–6) states, these children and adolescents "need play outlets, they need to be able to use symbolism, they may need to draw or paint or create things with their hands because there are no words available."

MASK MAKING

Over the years, mask making has been used as an important art therapy intervention to deal with crisis and explore present and possible future selves (Markus and Nurius, 1986). Mask-making activities used with clients dealing with a personality crisis, as a result of trauma and or significant loss, might include creating a mask that represents the "past self, present self, and future self" (Brumleve, 2010, p.1). This activity is closely related to the theory of possible selves by Markus and Nurius (1986). Possible selves represent individuals' ideas of what they might become, what they would like to become, and what they are afraid of becoming, and thus provide a conceptual link between cognition and motivation. Art has the ability to act as a buffer in this process, allowing the individual to view this other side from more of a distance.

In practice

The period of adolescence, spanning roughly from 12 to 18 years of age, is marked by puberty, with increasing drive pressures and rapid physical, cognitive, and social challenges. Uncontrollable and unpredictable mood swings, rapidly changing interests, behavioral changes, and other transient symptoms sometimes blur the boundaries between normality and pathology. Psychic turbulence and imbalance is necessary to the adolescent process; how well a teen navigates the turbulence depends on how well the teen mastered early childhood.

Perhaps most importantly, adolescence is a crucial developmental period in which the teenager strives to more permanently individuate from his or her family of origin. A balance is struck between base desires and a social conscience with the revival of infantile traumas and fixations. Early ideals are re-examined; we start to understand our parents and their values in a greater, somewhat disempowering context. Cognitive advances allow us to put our feelings of shame, anxiety, and guilt into context as well, allowing for a sense of instinctual freedom of feeling, thought, and action.

For the homeless teen, a premature severance is most likely the result of a traumatic experience or rejection by the family unit. This suggests ruptures in the early attachment relationships that would have otherwise helped to facilitate a healthy process of individuation and developing an independent sense of identity. For the homeless, teenage mother, she now not only needs to meet her own basic needs, but those of her child. She is charged with the difficult responsibility of resolving any arrestments in her own childhood individuation process (and grieving the loss of those experiences), while at the same time entering into a necessarily merged relationship with her infant child. Art therapy, a safe and non-threatening approach, is well suited for the task of repairing attachment disturbances in the young mother, in order to foster a healthy and independent sense of self.

This chapter examines a case study in which DBT interventions and expressive mask making were used in a group setting to help homeless young mothers explore these aspects of themselves, providing for mindful, self-compassion (the group activity was conducted for the purposes of completing my master's thesis project). Themes that arose in the group process—and in the responses of this case participant—were motherhood, trauma narratives, loss and grieving, lack of self-compassion/self-esteem and empowerment gained or felt due to converting the mask into an animal. Finally, self-compassion appeared to have developed as a result (at least in part) of participating in this intervention.

Motherhood

The theme of motherhood played an important role throughout the entire study. The participants were very involved with their infants and discussed them at the beginning and end of the sessions. As stated by Miller (1986), young people are in the separation and individuation phase and their children act as the transitional object, which serve the need for symbiosis and separation/individuation.

During the study Barb, an 18-year-old Hispanic female who always had her hair tied in a ponytail, came to the session with her seven-month-old daughter. She seemed attuned to her daughter's needs, which was evident when she would constantly check on her daughter, adjusting her blanket and giving her milk at the scheduled time. Her masks also represented her need to be Winnicott's (1960) good-enough mother. According to Winnicott, a good-enough mother is a mother who is connected to her infant and is attuned to his or her needs. In this case, Barb could be aiming to be the mother she did not have; Miller (1986) might suggest that Barb's behavior could be a reflection of her wish to have a good-enough mother.

Trauma narrative

Many symptoms of trauma were visible in the artwork of the group participants. Barb's mask in particular seemed to serve as a trauma narrative for her (Brumleve, 2010). On her mask, the glitter under the eye looks more like tears, and the fans on two sides of the eyes look like two extra eyes, perhaps because she is hypervigilant of the environment around her (see Figure 15.1). Barb's hypervigilance was also evident in her "how I look at myself" mask as it has a third eye and two feathers on the corners of the eyes, highlighting and exaggerating the eyes. Additionally, the forehead of Barb's mask had harsh strokes indicating that trauma may have affected her head.

Figure 15.1 How others look at me—Barb

LACK OF SELF-COMPASSION

The theme of lack of self-compassion was visible in the mask and in the verbal interaction. Lack of self-compassion can emerge for many reasons, namely homelessness, the age of the individuals (as they are fighting through identity issues), and blaming themselves for the trauma they have experienced.

Like many people, these young women lacked self-compassion. Many of the statements used by the young women during the study depicted that they lacked self-compassion and were harsh towards themselves. One of the important things that I noticed is that many of the participants realized that they never sat back and looked at "self" from a distant perspective. According to Neff (2011), people avoid looking at the self for fear of having to accept shortcomings.

Even though Barb noted she didn't like how others look at her, she still chose to change "how I look at myself" into a powerful animal. Her choice of wanting to convert the "how I look at myself" mask showed that she was not happy with the way she looks at herself, thus indicating that she looks at herself in a less compassionate way (see Figure 15.2).

Figure 15.2 Conversion of "how I look at myself" mask into an animal—Barb

MINDFULNESS

As established earlier, mindfulness is the art of being present in the moment. In this case mindfulness was achieved by most of the young women during the process of art making. They were present and accepting towards feelings and emotions that came up during the creative process. Many of them were straightforward and upfront about their feelings and did not hesitate to accept and share them with others and myself in the group. The words in the note written by Barb help us understand how Barb felt more mindful of herself after she made her mask. Her written words, "Who is Barb" demonstrate that this exercise made her mindful of who she really is. The following comment as noted in Barb's note indicates further self-reflection: "I had somewhat of a wakeup call, that I need to be more in tune with myself."

EMPOWERMENT

The art-making process initiated mindfulness in most of the participants. The conversion of the mask into powerful animals seemed to serve the purpose of empowerment. The young women were able to link the animal strengths to their strengths, hence giving them an opportunity to acknowledge their own positive attributes. The animal that emerged most frequently was the tiger.

Barb said that tigers are respected, and this statement could be her desire to be respected herself. The covering of glitter under the eye on her mask could reflect that she felt empowered after viewing herself as a powerful animal (Figure 15.2). The strong bright colors over the timid white mask seem to be empowering because of their boldness and intensity. From the list of strengths, she noted being strong and a good-enough mother seemed to be prominent for her.

DEVELOPMENT OF SELF-COMPASSION

As the participants became more mindful and were able to recognize their strengths, I noticed self-compassion in their written words during the "write a note" intervention. They seemed more connected and attuned with self after the study. Barb referred to the study as a "wake-up call" towards self. This intervention also helped to develop self-compassion in her. Barb stated, "I realized that how others see me, [which] bothers me. So, to change that or make it better I will be the best me I can be. If people still see me as something else I will not mind because I will not be putting up a 'mask' I will be all me and whoever cannot accept me that does not need to be a part of my life." These statements indicate that she was able to achieve self-respect and compassion through the process of sitting back and asking herself who she is (mindfulness).

Barb achieved the DBT concept of mindfulness, which involves change and acceptance. In addition, Barb felt more aware of her feeling of dislike towards how she feels others look at her. This attunement with her feelings and compassion towards self was achieved through mask making for Barb.

Protocol: Mask making and developing mindful self-compassion

Objective

To provide traumatized, homeless young women with the ability to increase self-compassion (mindfulness) and decision-making skills in processing feelings of grief and loss.

Material goal

To complete two masks and one transformation of either of the two masks, in service of the objective.

Duration

As is appropriate to the setting and time constraints. Ideally, each session should be at minimum one hour and 15 minutes in length, once per week, until the goal is achieved.

Curriculum

SESSION 1 SELF-ESTEEM

Directive: How you see yourself.

Description: The young women are asked to use available materials and make a mask depicting how they feel when they see themselves. The aim is to be present in the moment through art making and gaining mindfulness about self. The concept of self-discovery and self-understanding was explored through this directive (Daniels, 2004, p.1).

Materials: Scissors, glue sticks, pre-made papier-mâché masks, feathers, beads, Mod Podge (matte), sets of markers, sets of Cray-Pas, pencils, different types of tissue paper, limited choice of paints. Adjust the quantity according to the number of participants.

Interview questions:

1. What was your experience in making the mask?

2. Can you describe any feelings that came up?

3. How did viewing the mask as "how you look at yourself" feel?

4. Do you feel more thoughtful (mindful) about self after this experiential learning?

5. How did viewing the mask as "how others look at you" feel?

6. After converting your mask into a strong animal mask how do you feel about yourself?

7. Do you feel more respectful and compassionate towards self after this experiential learning?

8. How was the experience of listing your strengths after the experiential learning?

9. Were you able to identify any goals linked to those strengths?

10. Which mask did you choose to convert and why?

11. How was your overall experience of making these masks?

SESSION 2 SELF-AWARENESS
Directive: How others look at you.

Description: The young women are asked to use available materials and make a mask depicting how they feel others see them. In this directive the masks are used as a container of trauma, to give participants an ability to form a trauma narrative. Trauma caused by the judgments of others, verbal, physical, emotional abuse and its effects on our self-esteem and compassion are the focus of the directive. Mask making closely connects to Jungian concept of archetypes and shadows. Mask making can be used to bring to consciousness how one sees the world and how one feels the world sees that person (Malchiodi, 2010).

Materials: Scissors, glue sticks, pre-made papier-mâché masks, feathers, beads, Mod Podge (matte), sets of markers, sets of Cray-Pas, pencils, tissue paper, limited choice of paints. Adjust the quantity according to the number of participants.

Interview questions:

1. What was your experience in making the mask?

2. Can you describe any feelings that came up?

3. How did viewing the mask as "how you look at yourself" feel?

4. Do you feel more thoughtful (mindful) about self after this experiential learning?

5. How did viewing the mask as "how others look at you" feel?

6. After converting your mask into a strong animal mask how do you feel about yourself?

7. Do you feel more respectful and compassionate towards self after this experiential learning?

8. How was the experience of listing your strengths after the experiential learning?

9. Were you able to identify any goals linked to those strengths?

10. Which mask did you choose to convert and why?

11. How was your overall experience of making these masks?

SESSION 3 SELF-WORTH AND STRENGTHS

Directive: Conversion of masks into animals. The young women are asked to convert one of the two masks into their favorite animal mask and then write the strengths of the animal inside the mask. The aim is to experience that change can be empowering. This directive followed the DBT model of acceptance and change.

Materials: One of the previously made masks, scissors, glue sticks, feathers, beads, markers, Mod Podge (matte), sets of markers, sets of Cray-Pas, pencils, animal fur, felt, animal print tissue paper, limited choice of paints. Adjust the quantity according to the number of participants.

Interview questions:

1. What was your experience in making the mask?

2. Can you describe any feelings that came up?

3. How did viewing the mask as "how you look at yourself" feel?

4. Do you feel more thoughtful (mindful) about self after this experiential learning?

5. How did viewing the mask as "how others look at you" feel?

6. After converting your mask into a strong animal mask how do you feel about yourself?

7. Do you feel more respectful and compassionate towards self after this experiential learning?

8. How was the experience of listing your strengths after the experiential learning?

9. Were you able to identify any goals linked to those strengths?

10. Which mask did you choose to convert and why?

11. How was your overall experience of making these masks?

SESSION 4 NOTE WRITING

Directive: Ask the young women to write a note expressing their overall experience mask making and what they learned about themselves after making these masks. The aim is to summarize the experience and gain mindfulness about the experience itself, and to develop the realization that if they were able to experience mindfulness and self-compassion this one time there is an ability to do it again.

Materials: Scissors, glue sticks, sets of markers, sets of Cray-Pas, pencils, colored chart papers. Adjust the quantity according to the number of participants.

Interview questions:

1. What was your experience in making the mask?

2. Can you describe any feelings that came up?

3. How did viewing the mask as "how you look at yourself" feel?

4. Do you feel more thoughtful (mindful) about self after this experiential learning?

5. How did viewing the mask as "how others look at you" feel?

6. After converting your mask into a strong animal mask how do you feel about yourself?

7. Do you feel more respectful and compassionate towards self after this experiential learning?

8. How was the experience of listing your strengths after the experiential learning?

9. Were you able to identify any goals linked to those strengths?

10. Which mask did you choose to convert and why?

11. How was your overall experience of making these masks?

References

Albers, S. (2013) '3 ways to be kinder to yourself: Expert advice.' *Psychology Today.* Retrieved from http://www.psychologytoday.com/blog/comfort-cravings/201311/3-ways-be-kinder-yourself-expert-advice, accessed on March 23, 2017.

Arnold, T.G. (2008) 'Core mindfulness: Dialectical behavior therapy (DBT).' *GoodTherapy.org,* January 23. Available at www.goodtherapy.org/blog/dialectical-behavior-therapy-dbt-core-mindfulness, accessed on December 16, 2016.

Blakemore, S.J. (2008) 'The social brain in adolescence.' *Nature Reviews Neuroscience 9,* 267–277.

Brumleve, E. (2010) 'Expressive mask making for teens: Beginning insights.' Alexandria, VA: American Art Therapy Association. Available at www.arttherapy.org/upload/News&Info/ExpressiveMaskMakingForTeens.pdf, accessed on November 22, 2016.

Casey, B.J., Getz, S., and Galvan, A. (2008) 'The adolescent brain.' *Developmental Review 28,* 1, 62–77.

Casey, B.J., Jones, R.M., and Hare, T. (2008) 'The adolescent brain.' *Annals of the New York Academy of Sciences 1124*, 111–126.

Daniels, M. (2004). *Self-discovery the Jungian way: The watchword technique.* New York: Routledge.

Kammerer, N. and Mazelis, R. (2006) *Trauma and Retraumatization.* After the Crisis Initiative: Healing from Trauma after Disasters. Expert Panel Meeting. Available at www.academia.edu/4001045/After_the_Crisis_Initiative_Healing_from_Trauma_after_Disasters, accessed on December 16, 2016.

Klorer, P.G. (2005) 'Expressive therapy with severely maltreated children: Neuroscience contributions.' *Art Therapy: Journal of the American Art Therapy Association 22*, 4, 213–220.

Markus, H. and Nurius, P. (1986) 'Possible selves.' *American Psychologist 41*, 9, 954–969.

Malchiodi, C. (2010) 'Cool art therapy intervention #8: Mask making.' *Psychology Today*, March 2. Available at www.psychologytoday.com/blog/arts-and-health/201003/cool-art-therapy-intervention-8-mask-making, accessed on December 16, 2016.

Miller, N. (1986) 'Unplanned adolescent pregnancy and the transitional object.' *Child and Adolescent Social Work Journal 3*, 2, 77–86.

Munns, E. (2000) 'Theraplay with zero- to three-year-olds.' In C.E. Schaefer, S. Kelly-Zion, J. McCormick, and A. Ohnogi (eds) *Play Therapy for Very Young Children.* New York: Jason Aronson.

NCTSN (2007) *Trauma among Homeless Youth.* Available at www.nctsnet.org/nctsn_assets/pdfs/culture_and_trauma_brief_v2n1_HomelessYouth.pdf, accessed on December 16, 2016.

Neff, K. (2011) *Self Compassion: The Proven Power of Being Kind to Yourself.* New York: William Morrow.

Ot'alora, M. (2012) 'Possibilities for growth: Working with trauma.' *Treating PTSD with MDMA-Assisted Psychotherapy.* Available at www.mdmaptsd.org/testimonials/65-possibilities-for-growth.html, accessed on December 16, 2016.

Panter-Brick, C. (2002) 'Street children, human rights, and public health: A critique and future directions.' *Annual Review of Anthropology 31*,147–171.

Rappaport, L. and Kalmanowtiz, D. (2014) 'Mindfulness and dance/movement therapy for treating trauma.' In L. Rappaport (ed.) *Mindfulness and the Arts Therapies: Theory and Practice.* Philadelphia, PA: Jessica Kingsley Publishers.

Spear, L. (2000) 'Neurobehavioral changes in adolescence.' *Psychological Science 9*, 4, 111–114.

Winnicott, D.W. (1960) 'The theory of the parent–infant relationship.' *International Journal of Psycho-Analysis 41*, 585–595.

16

Art and Grief

Working with At-Risk Youth Who Have Lost a Parent

Ariel Argueso

Overview

During my first internship of graduate school, I became familiar
with the community residing in the Chelsea-Elliott Houses in
Chelsea, New York, where I provided art therapy treatment to
children individually and in classrooms at a multiservice community
organization serving those in the immediate area with a focus on
those in need, or now commonly referred to as "at risk." At-risk, or
youth in danger of negative future events, was a unique population
for me to begin working with, after working with more privileged
youth in Westchester for about ten years. After I completed my
internship there, I recognized how strong an attachment I had
established with the community. The teacher turnover rate was high
and the children had inconsistent and unstable lives at home—
moving in and out of foster homes, shelters, and regularly adjusting
to different caretakers. In my treatment termination with one client,
I remember feeling the heartbreak that came with his words, "You're
leaving too?" Through processing the guilt that lived on for quite
a bit, I processed what would be the most important aspect of my
work—that no matter how long I stayed and continued working

with any of them, treatment was never about changing their lives, their environments, or their families.

Treatment was focused primarily on helping clients to develop coping skills and strategies to survive in their given environment. I continued my work with at-risk youth and families at a foster care agency in Brooklyn, New York, where I facilitated treatment between children and their biological parents throughout the reunification process. Experiencing the significant impact of therapeutic intervention within the foster care system solidified my interest in the at-risk population.

One doesn't know empathy until a parent is sobbing next to you, telling you that you would be better at raising her kids, or until a five-year-old is telling you he doesn't need to live because his mom hates him and never says "I love you." And one truly doesn't know empathy until a child tells you they have lost a parent and that you can't do anything to change that. I never gave full meaning to the African proverb "It takes a village to raise a child" until I became a part of the village. Sometimes I hear about lost teeth, broken arms, losing a basketball tournament, or losing a student ID card. Other times, about losing friends, losing grandparents, and most common, losing a caretaker or parent.

Losing a parent: Disturbances in attachment

Childhood bereavement is chronically painful. Growing up in a society that avoids the mention of death and grief, and does not encourage kids to talk about their loss—what child wouldn't suffer in silence to save others from the burden of their grief? This comes with emotional, psychological, and behavioral difficulties that will extend for as long as the pain goes unaddressed. Survivors of childhood trauma are left to grieve not only for what was lost, but also for what was never theirs to lose. The childhood and foundation of basic trust and the belief in a good parent disintegrates as the child is left to solely fly from the nest.

Severe separations and losses leave emotional scars on the brain. Studies show that early childhood losses make us sensitive to losses we encounter later on (Viorst, 2002). Therefore, our response to a death, divorce, loss, or any other form of separation in mid-life may result in a depressed response, similar to that of the helpless, hopeless, and angry child that experienced loss too early to comprehend. Now what is the cost of loss if the cost of love is grief? While we can develop strategies that defend against the pain of separation, time to process must be prioritized among the instincts to invest in developing defenses. Viorst (2002) describes three such defenses:

1. *Emotional detachment* or the idea that we cannot lose someone we care for if we don't care.

2. A *compulsive need to take care of other people.* Rather than attempting self-care, we know that by taking care of someone else, we are guaranteed to feel better.

3. *Premature autonomy*, learning at a young age not to let survival depend on the help or love of anyone but the self.

It is a normal reaction to disconnect and dissociate from the experience of a loss. However, if a child builds such defenses at a young age, they will continue implementing such defenses in future cases of grief. The loss will not be processed effectively and therefore, the death may not be integrated into the griever's ongoing life. For this reason, it is absolutely critical that a child is given the space to mourn.

The mother within

Separation as a child wasn't easy, for me, you, or the next person, and the effect of separation varies dependent on affectional ties or *attachment*, a term that has now gained usage among psychologists and theoretical models. The first tie is most likely to be formed to the mother (Ainsworth, 1969). As children, we could let our mother go or eventually leave our mother, by internalizing and establishing a permanent mother within us, also known as object constancy.

The baby now perceives his mother as separate and has an internalized representation of the mother. In a similar way we internalize the people we have loved who have deceased. The ones we have lost are loved objects within us that continue to impact our existence.

In the younger years, we may not grasp our experience of being left, seeing it as an abandonment because we are unlovable, bad, or undeserving. Our intuitive response may be feelings of helplessness and guilt, terror and fury, or unendurable sadness. Unfortunately, we may not have the resources, internal or external, to cope with these feelings and process the experience. Children may mourn a death, but may not be able or know how to mourn in a way that lets them work through the enormity of the loss, failing to fully resolve childhood losses in childhood, which, if not resolved, may continue to dwell within us all our life (Viorst, 2002).

At-risk population: Implications of grief

Exposure to loss and grieving is common among the at-risk population. McWhirter *et al.* (1998) postulated that as stressors accumulate in a child's life, he becomes more at risk of negative outcomes; these risk factors or stressors are a "series of steps along a continuum" (p.7). The first step is having specific demographics. For example, living in an impoverished neighborhood, having a low socio-economic status, or being a member of a minority ethnic group. Children are not at risk because of such personal circumstances, but because children with this background often have reduced access to adequate services, such as school, insurance, and housing, which may additionally result in personal or material racism (Camilleri, 2007).

The next stressor identified by McWhirter *et al.* (1998) involves family and school environments. If a caring, nurturing, predictable, and safe environment is provided, the child can develop a sense of security and confidence, whereas families and schools that are chaotic, dangerous, and unpredictable can instill fear and hopelessness. A lack of stable home and school environments "reduces access to positive adult role models and potential support networks," according to Camilleri (2007, p.18).

The third stressor is "experiencing negative psychosocial or environmental events such as divorce, death, suicide, teenage pregnancy, abuse, incarceration, loss of a job and insurance, and eviction" (Camilleri, 2007, p.18). Not only can these factors cause psychological trauma, but they can also create physical circumstances such as homelessness, foster care, hunger, poverty, or illness.

The fourth factor is psychological make-up. Personal characteristics, such as coping mechanisms and stress reactions determine how children deal with a given situation and how they will be affected. Undoubtedly, the more negative their attitude, the more at risk a child will be. Further, if the child's outlook is hopeless, it can lead to symptoms of depression, anxiety, and aggression. Such negative psychological states can lead to dangerous activities and behaviors a child chooses to develop, which can be self-destructive or harmful to others.

According to Camilleri (2007), each of these circumstances individually can lead to a child being at risk; however, the risk increases as stressors accumulate "without adequate moderating effects" (p.19). Societal stressors such as racism, poverty, and violence, in addition to environmental stressors such as housing, education, healthcare, and employment, often coexist among domestic stressors. Domestic stressors such as parenting, domestic conflict, parental mental health, and child abuse are frequently the most prevalent and negatively impacting stressors among youth who are at risk. Brought up to be ready to throw a defensive punch at any time, it is uncommon for at-risk youth to reflect on and acknowledge significant loss. Art making and processing loss through creative expression in a safe space with an art therapist is one way to address and ameliorate the impact of the loss.

Creative expression to ameliorate loss

If you stop to think about the drawing that you did as a child, you probably recall more of the feelings that came from drawing than the actual content of the drawing that you did. It is crucial to let children know that it is okay to express themselves in their own language—whether it's verbally, physically, or visually. A good deal of my time as a therapist is spent explaining that there are languages other than spoken ones. We talk about body language and how movement, facial expressions, and sound relay messages. We talk about mindfulness and how yoga, meditation, and breathing can inspire conversations with the self. Most of all, we talk about art and using materials, space, and visual narrative to communicate nonverbally. Arnheim (1992, p.170) observed that art serves as:

> a helper in times of trouble, as a means of understanding the conditions of human existence and of facing the frightening aspects of those conditions, [and] as the creation of a meaningful order offering a refuge from the unmanageable confusion of the outer reality.

The use of art to interpret emotions has become an incredible outlet and form of therapy for working with children experiencing trauma. Focusing on communication, control, and emotional resolution, creative expression and art making often leads to catharsis, allowing space for repressed emotions, thoughts, and ideas to surface.

Traumatized children experience a wide range of emotions, as well as psychological pain including anxiety, helplessness, fear, loneliness, depression, vulnerability, and despair (Malchiodi, 1998). Seeing as feelings are the root of any loss, art therapy provides space for an individual to grieve, express their emotions, and create a new view of their life after the loss. Art therapy is not only an outlet to express the trauma or loss, but a process that allows for repair, restoration, and healing.

In practice

Mindfulness is a foreign concept to at-risk youth growing up in fast-paced, rapidly growing, and progressively gentrifying urban areas. An understanding of therapy is an even more foreign, unexplored concept and resource. Families are often silent when it comes to life stressors and loss. Raising awareness and breaking the stigma around therapy is critical in working with this population. We have to talk about the importance of seeking professional support and working towards being healthy and emotionally happy because families and youth are suffering in silence. Processing feelings shouldn't feel like a chore, but a healthy habit.

Quilting in memory of a loved one was used in the following case study to identify and explore feelings associated with mourning, as well as develop constructive coping mechanisms to create a new view of life after loss. Quilting was used specifically to utilize comforting material as well as create a transitional object to aid in the mourning process.

Mindfulness, breathing, and grounding exercises were used to create a safe space for processing. The client was able to adjust to the routine of using guided meditation to transition into the space. Further, he developed the ability to identify emotions and explore coping mechanisms to self-soothe. The client successfully worked through resistance to healing and used quilt making to aid in the healing process. Although exhibiting some forms of repression, rejection, guilt, and sadness, he was engaged in the art-making process and took full responsibility for sewing and/or tying the quilt squares together, with limited assistance from the therapist. Often seeking validation or approval from the therapist when finishing a piece of the quilt before moving forward was indicative of a sense of perfectionism in honoring the loved one that was lost.

In summarizing, the client appreciated the creative process and transitional object as a product of his work. The directives promoted creativity development and an exploration of materials to parallel the exploration of feelings and thoughts. The incorporation of mindfulness created a safe, transitional space that was held by the therapist. Finally, the client developed a healthy therapeutic relationship with the therapist.

Case study: Jaiden

Jaiden is a six-year-old boy who lost his aunt, who was his primary caretaker. Jaiden was referred for therapeutic services by his grandmother and teachers at his after-school program, where he was tired, crying constantly, and not eating.

When the client started therapy, he had heavy bags under his eyes and a flat affect. In just the first session, Jaiden shared that he had just lost his aunt who he referred to as "the only person that understood me." In speaking about her loss, Jaiden explained that he was told she passed away in her sleep at the hospital. He said that he was afraid to sleep in case he might not wake up, like her.

Asking many questions, Jaiden was engaged throughout treatment. During sessions, he talked about memories he had of his aunt, or details about his drawings. When asked about her, he often worried no one would understand him as she did. Jaiden said that no one talked about her, making him feel like everyone was trying to forget about her. He then shared that his memorial quilt would be his way of remembering her forever.

After about two sessions, Jaiden began awaiting therapy sessions. His flat affect and bags under his eyes began to change. Staff reported his engagement in class was more regular and he seemed happy more often than not. He was given the chance to process his feelings and mourn the loss.

In the final session, Jaiden was ready to tie his quilt together. He picked out a colorful thick yarn and tied each square one by one until the isolated pieces became a quilt. He held it up and said with a smile, "I can't wait to hang her up." Jaiden showed his finished quilt to his grandmother when she picked him up (Figure 16.1). He explained each of the individual squares and asked to hang it at home. The therapist reinforced the importance of caring for the quilt and continuing to process feelings that surface around the loss.

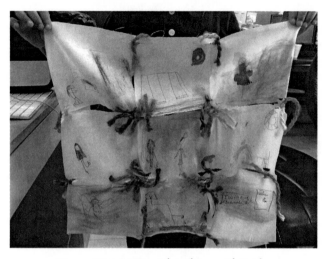

Figure 16.1 Memorial quilting with Jaiden

Protocol: Art and grief with at-risk youth

The following directive is intended to be used in individual treatment.

Objectives

- To identify and explore feelings associated with mourning, as well as develop constructive coping mechanisms to create a new view of life after loss.

- To use materials that provide comfort and focus on creating a transitional object to aid in mourning process.

Material goals

- Client will gain insight with regards to common defense mechanisms such as denial and repression that may surface in response to grief and mourning, as evidenced by at least one art project and one verbalization.

- Client will be able to identify emotions and explore coping mechanisms to self-soothe, as evidenced by at least one art project and one verbalization.

- Client will process the stages of grief in order to frame coping strategies and prevent resistance to healing, as evidenced by at least one art project and one verbalization.

- Client will use the creative process of quilt making to aid in the healing process, as evidenced by the completion of the quilt.

Duration

Six sessions to be conducted as is appropriate to the population and setting. Forty-five minutes is recommended per session.

Curriculum

SESSION 1 THE FIRST STEP

Begin the individual session with an introduction and brief guided meditation exercise. Following the exercise, provide oil pastels, colored pencils, and markers to allow the client doodling time while bringing the discussion around to loss and grief. What losses have they experienced? How did those losses affect them—their emotions, their relationships with others, their attachment styles? What stage of the grieving process are they currently working through? What has aided or supported the healing process?

With these questions in mind, ask the client to create a representation of their current state of emotion in relation to the parent being mourned.

End the session with a discussion of the work and any other pertinent material. If needed, provide a closing exercise as well, such as a grounding visualization or breathing exercise.

SESSION 2 SAYING GOODBYE

Begin the individual session with a guided meditation to promote mindfulness, and transition the client into the space. Following the exercise, speak to the client about what saying goodbye means.

- When do we say goodbye?

- How do we say goodbye?

- How do we feel when we say goodbye?

Explain to the client that over the next few sessions, you will be creating a memorial quilt to say goodbye to, and remember, the loved one who has been lost. Once a discussion has been opened, provide the client with lined paper they will use to complete statements to be used later on when making the quilt. Offer pens, colored pencils, or fine-lined markers for writing. One by one, begin each statement listed below for the client to complete on paper:

I remember a time we _____

It was fun when _____

I wish we _____

I feel _____

I hope _____

Thank you for _____

You taught me _____

Something I want you to know is _____

I will always remember _____

When all the sentences are complete, ask the client to read them aloud and propose a few processing questions.

- How did it feel to complete these statements?

- Why do you think it is important to think about someone we lost?

- Is there any statement that stands out to you the most?

Allow the client to talk about their processing for as long as necessary before closing with a grounding exercise. Have the client sit, planting both feet on the ground, with his or her eyes closed. Ask the client to take three deep breaths before returning to the space. Finally, remind the client you will begin creating the memorial quilt in the next session.

SESSION 3 MEMORIAL QUILTING

Begin the individual session with a guided meditation to promote mindfulness, and transition the client into the space. Following the exercise, review the completed statements from the previous session. Ask the client to read them aloud and propose a few processing questions.

- How do you feel reading the statements you wrote last week?

- Would you change any of them if you were to rewrite them today?

- Which one stands out most?

Following the discussion, provide the client with materials that will be used for the quilt such as fabric, fabric markers, and fabric paint, showing him/her how to use them. Chalk pastels can also be used for background or shading of fabric. Once the materials have been provided, the therapist should allow the client to begin representing his processing statements visually on the fabric—one statement per square. The therapist can facilitate this process by reading a statement for the client to think about.

- When you hear this statement, what images or colors come to mind?

- What do you think about most when you hear this statement?

- If you could put this statement into a drawing, lines, or color, what would it look like?

End the session with a discussion of the work and any other pertinent material. If needed, provide a closing exercise as well, such as a grounding visualization or breathing exercise. Be sure to show the client that you are placing their artwork to dry in a safe space, and remind him/her that you will continue working on the quilt the following week.

SESSION 4 CONTINUING THE QUILT

Begin the individual session with a guided meditation or breathing exercise to promote mindfulness, and transition the client into the space. Following the exercise, provide the client with materials that will be used to continue the quilt. The therapist can facilitate the continuation of the process by reading a statement for the client to think about.

- When you hear this statement, what images or colors come to mind?

- What do you think about most when you hear this statement?

- If you could put this statement into a drawing, lines, or color, what would it look like?

End the session with a discussion of the work and any other pertinent material. If needed, provide a closing exercise as well, such as a grounding visualization or breathing exercise. Be sure to show the client that you are placing their artwork to dry in a safe space, and remind him/her that you will continue working on the quilt the following week. The client should finish the majority of the quilt squares during this session—but can add finishing touches in the following session.

SESSION 5 FINISHING TOUCHES

Begin the individual session with a guided meditation or breathing exercise to promote mindfulness, and transition the client into the space. Take out all the quilt squares and inform the client that the goal of this session is to add any finishing touches and complete each square. Once the client has completed each piece, pose a few reflective questions as you and the client look back on the completed work.

- How do you feel about the completed pieces?

- What colors or forms do you see most?

- Do you notice anything interesting about your work?

- Do you feel this is a representation of your current state in the grieving process?

- If there is anything you could add or take away, what would those things be?

End the session with this discussion. If needed, provide a closing exercise, such as a grounding visualization or breathing exercise. Be sure to show the client that you are placing their artwork in a safe space, and remind him/her that you will be sewing it together to be taken home the following week.

SESSION 6 PUTTING THE PIECES TOGETHER

Begin the final session with a guided meditation or breathing exercise to promote mindfulness. Lay out all the quilt squares and allow the client to organize them in the order that he/she would like them sewn. Assist the client in sewing the squares together to form one quilt. Be sure that all threads have been tied so the quilt will remain intact once it is taken home. For younger children, it is best to use a larger needle that is not as sharp, and possibly thicker thread as thinner sewing thread can cause frustration. An alternative is having the therapist sew all pieces together previous to the final session, and allowing the young client to sew the last piece, completing the quilt. It is in the therapist's best interest to gauge whether the client is more interested in the process or product, and assist with both parts so the client does not feel alone or helpless during this process.

Once all the pieces are sewn together, allow the client to look at and absorb the final product. Pose reflective questions such as the following:

- How do you feel about your finished quilt?

- What does it remind you of?

- Do you feel this is an accurate representation of whoever was lost?

- What is your favorite part? Least favorite part?

- Where would you like to put the finished quilt? What are some emotions that have come up while thinking about this person and what helps you work through those emotions?

This discussion should be as detailed as possible. The idea is for the client to understand the emotions from the start of the grieving process, throughout the process of creating the quilt, and looking back at a memorial object. It is a good idea to photograph the artwork in case something happens to it, so it can be reprinted for the client. Provide a closing exercise, such as a grounding visualization or breathing exercise. If possible, place the finished quilt, folded or not, between cardboard or in a folder to keep safe when giving it to the client to take home.

Author's notes:

- It is important to notify the parent/guardian(s) that the product should be displayed, should the child so desire, and recognized as an aid in the grieving process.

- The edges of fabric squares can be finished with no-fray fabric glue, and number of squares and size of fabric can be determined by the therapist.

References

Ainsworth, M. (1969) 'Object relations, dependency, and attachment: A theoretical review of the infant–mother relationship.' *Child Development 40*, 969–1025.

Arnheim, R. (1992) *To the Rescue of Art*. Berkeley, CA: University of California Press.

Camilleri, V.A. (ed.) (2007) *Healing the Inner City Child: Creative Arts Therapies with At-Risk Youth*. London: Jessica Kingsley Publishers.

Malchiodi, C. (1998) *Understanding Children's Drawings*. New York: Guilford Press.

McWhirter, J.J., McWhirter, B.T., McWhirter, A.M., and McWhirter, E.H. (1998) *At Risk Youth: A Comprehensive Response*. Pacific Grove, CA: Brooks/Cole Publishing.

Viorst, J. (2002) *Necessary Losses: The Loves, Illusions, Dependencies, and Impossible Expectations That All of Us Have to Give Up in Order to Grow*. New York: Free Press.

17

The Women's Womb

Archetypal Imagery and Grieving Lost Self-Parts

Marie Caruso-Teresi

A changing self-concept

It is reported that 600,000 women in the United States undergo hysterectomies annually (US Department of Health and Human Services, Centers for Disease Control and Prevention [CDC], 2017). Negative psychosocial outcomes include reduced sexual interest, arousal, and orgasms as well as elevated depressive symptoms and impaired body image (Flory, Bissonnette, and Binik, 2005). Following hysterectomy, little support is offered for women to process the loss of their uterus by way of counseling or mental health follow-up (Darling and McKoy-Smith, 1993). This has led to negative outcomes, such as impaired body image and depressive symptoms (Flory *et al.*, 2005) as well as a loss of self-concept (Darling and McKoy-Smith, 1993).

One major aspect of the loss of a sex organ is a woman's inability to menstruate or bear children physically. These two female events not only significantly impact gender identity but also affect women's lives socially (Elson, 2004). Inner changes that connect a woman to her body, self-concept, and to other women are to be considered. As this population ages alongside female peers who have not experienced hysterectomy, developmental milestones specific to women, such as childbirth and menopause, may cause feelings of grief, conflict, and isolation. Without proper psychological support, women do not have a proper way to fully integrate their new identity post-hysterectomy.

As Elson (2002) noted, medical sociologists (e.g. Bury, 1982; Charmaz 1983; Corbin and Strauss, 1987; Schneider and Conrad, 1983) have found that medical events have power to generate biographical disruptions or turning points; the individual's concept of who she or he is may never be the same as before. We can define "self-concept" as the individual's belief about herself, how she thinks about herself and perceives her value regarding who and what she is in relation to the world. It can include how the individual sees herself and how she believes others see her.

Reconstruction: Fostering meaning

Meaning is the integration of an individual's experience physically, emotionally, and cognitively. A meaningful experience is one that holds insight of importance to the individual for the purpose of integration and psychological growth. Post-hysterectomy, few opportunities are offered to support women to process their experience. Without proper psychological support, women do not have a proper way to fully integrate their new identity post-hysterectomy. Art therapy helps to find meaning related to the experience of living without a uterus and to encourage an integrated self-concept post-hysterectomy.

A study by Appleton (2001) further illustrated the significance of creative core and developing personal symbolic imagery. Art therapy aids in the process of accessing stored imagery of personal experience and is an effective method for integrating trauma and improving self-concept. Appleton identified four trauma stages and associated art therapy goals: 1) impact and creating continuity; 2) retreat and building therapeutic alliance; 3) acknowledgment and overcoming social stigma and isolation through mastery; and 4) reconstruction and fostering meaning.

Fostering meaning is a key component in reconstruction of an improved self-concept. Meaning and associations attached to images produced during art therapy sessions are subjective to the art maker and become the vehicle for gaining insights into one's unconscious world. The universal use of symbols in imagery has long been considered in the realm of art as well as psychology. Well-known art therapist Margaret Naumburg (1955) emphasized the role of symbol and meaning, stating, "We have…become aware of the importance of symbolic images…derived from the unconscious through the development of psychoanalysis" (p.435). Additionally, speaking of the importance of art, Naumburg stated, "Art as symbolic speech plays a major role in both the conscious and unconscious cultural expression of man throughout the ages" (p.435).

Bodily schema and personal symbolism

Living without a uterus presents a unique situation in the sense that there is no outward alteration in a woman's appearance. A post-hysterectomy assumption may be that a woman's sense of bodily schema remains the same, that the woman's pre-surgery neural representation of her body will be constant. On the surface a woman is unchanged; however, without proper psychological support, women do not have a proper way to fully integrate their new bodily schema post-hysterectomy.

Studies that research women's art to illuminate the existence of a bodily schema for productive inner space versus outer space are helpful in considering art therapy for women post-hysterectomy. Bassin (1982) stated that women's psychobiological development must be further understood, based on women's inner images and symbols that are unique to them, not based on simply not being male. Language and metaphors can reveal symbolization from inner space. Creativity allows women to reach into inner space to bring forth and externalize experience. Bassin also looked at women's metaphoric womb with regard to containment and holding of self, finding interpretations of designating the experience of inner space that supports women's interiority, not their inferiority.

Art therapy and archetypes

Research supports art therapy as a mood stabilizing modality that helps increase self-awareness through the process of discovering unconscious and conscious negative imagery and externalizing it creatively. Through externalization, positive and negative experiences become integrated in the psyche. The image-making process helps subjects engage in self-care as well as bolster ego strength and self-identity (Luzzatto and Gabriel, 2000). Thus, art therapy would be a good fit to help postsurgical subjects develop coping mechanisms to deal with negative mood and pile-up stressors.

Archetypal imagery in art therapy sessions provides a pathway to the exploration of self-concept related to gender identity and body image. This creative process will allow women to process feeling of loss, find meaning, and gain insights to a more integrated sense of self-concept and bodily schema.

Jung (1968) discussed the power of archetypes, noting that archetypes have their own initiative and their own specific energy. These powers enable them both to produce a meaningful interpretation and to interfere in a given situation with their own impulses and their own thought formations. Archetypes can help provide meaning to experience.

Lauter and Schreier Rupprecht (1985) noted several key elements of feminist archetypal theory, including:

> a commitment to raising the unconscious, the de-ontologized concept of the archetype, a post-Jungian approach to the female psyche, a spirit of "animity" [a way to live with the fathers as equals] toward ourselves which allows us to engage our forebears in productive dialogue, and an affirmation of the psychophysical unity of the human person. (p.231)

Additionally, Estella Lauter's work suggests that it will be fruitful to examine the images created by women in the nonverbal arts in order to understand their relationship to the gender-linked archetypes that have long been familiar. Such efforts will yield re-descriptions or additional descriptions of archetypal patterns that accord with reported female experience (Lauter and Schreier Rupprecht, 1985, p.232).

Art therapy can be considered one approach that may offer benefits to both physical and psychosocial aspects of women's experience of having a hysterectomy. The art therapist can act as educator to facilitate a woman exploring her personal meaning and connections to the loss of her sex organ. Following the loss of a gender-identified organ, art therapy can offer a way to integrate a new self-concept. Archetypal patterns of being a mother, being mothered, shadow self and repression of aggressive tendencies, and body image concerns were all described as clients shared verbally and nonverbally in artwork. Art therapy with archetypal imagery helps in discovery and release of repressed internalized beliefs, negative and ambivalent feelings of loss, and allowed women to create and report their own female experience.

In practice

Women's psychosocial issues are overlooked post-hysterectomy; women often isolate and repress feelings connected to grieving lost parts, their infertility, and suffer in silence, or in many cases rely on secondary defense behaviors, such as repression and reaction formation. Women internalize gender roles and standards that inhibit authentic expression of feelings, especially when dealing with loss and grief, and art therapy helps women to access inner, implicit feelings. By integrating archetypal imagery and through the creative process, women create images related to authentic expression and contain feminist archetypal power not based on external sources.

The womb as a symbol holds archetypal content related to containment, protection, and shelter. Women in this study were prompted, through guided meditation, to consider their womb-space, meaning the space which once held their uterus.

Archetypal imagery was utilized and discussed in all four art directives. Mandalas were discussed as symbolic of a developmental sense of self. The MARI® (Mandala Assessment Research Instrument) speaks of developmental stages on the Great Round (see "Session 1" of the protocol below), through which clients revealed insights pertaining to their sense of identity and relationships. The theme of clay pots and shells as being symbolic of the female uterus and vulva was also discussed in the second session. Pre-printed imagery symbolizing body, relationships between men and women, maiden, mother, crone, nature, lioness, wolves, family, cyclicity, labyrinths, shadow, persona, and the self were made available for collage purposes during the box directive. The use of boxes creates an interior space and allows clients to experience a sense of inner and outer, providing an opportunity to unite opposites (Farrell-Kirk, 2001).

Following this chapter's art therapy protocol, clients gained the following insights about ambivalence about infertility: rejection and suppression of negative feelings such as grief; feelings of lack of support; perfectionism and control issues; and compromised sense of body image.

It was evident that there is a sense of struggle between internal feelings and external sources or relationships. Infertility issues were varied; however, the clients shared a need to repress grief and negative or ambiguous feelings regarding their hysterectomies. Art therapy sessions aroused their feelings of confusion and grief over loss of fertility, loss of their gender identity, and struggles with gender role pressures from external sources. For example, statements made by women were: "I am taken aback by my emotional response to seeing a pregnant woman after my surgery. How dare I feel the loss?" "A part of my identity was taken; but I look for new ways to be productive, so that I don't feel the sadness connected to the loss." "Most people don't get it."

Each session's materials and directives held the opportunity for clients to explore and reveal new insights into their experience. Directives were intended to allow clients to gain access to their inner space and explore the materials and art-making process. Each of the four sessions began with a three-minute guided meditation with music and an art directive, followed by an art-making phase of 40 minutes. Ten minutes were made available to view the artwork produced, with an opportunity to share personal responses to the art or the art making process. A closing three-minute meditation ritual ended the session.

Case study: Pat

Pat is a 46-year-old married mother of a ten-year-old girl. She had her surgery within the last year. She planned to have additional children prior to her surgery. Her hysterectomy was medically necessary due to fibroids and very heavy clotting periods. Her husband was helpful and supportive during her surgery and post-operatively.

Despite the support she received, Pat stated that she did not feel she had enough time to emotionally heal or grieve the loss of a part of her identity. During art therapy sessions, Pat shared her earliest memories of knowing that she, as a female, was connected to the ability to become a mother, and she also shared that she currently felt conflict regarding that part of her identity. Pat struggled with mourning the loss of her ability to give birth to another child. This feeling of loss was quickly followed by a sense of gratitude for having a child and already being a mother, creating a sense of conflict within her. This conflict created an inability to seek support in her processing of her feelings of loss.

Post-hysterectomy, she struggled with negative body image due to weight gain, a decrease in energy, increase of depression, and lowered self-esteem. Additionally, a decrease in sexual satisfaction was noted, related to poor body image.

Pat easily shared her experience during the art-making process. Pat had a good level of self-awareness and the ability to verbally express her reactions to the materials in the moment. Pat stated, "I don't want to," often when attempting to keep materials under control. Aspects of perfectionism, repression, and rejection of negative feelings were addressed during sessions.

Pat discussed the issue of beginnings, such as a project in her home or seeking a new career path, stating that she starts with a great deal of energy and fizzles out. An inability to access and integrate external support seems to hold Pat back from fully realizing her potential. As observed in the clay pot directive, Pat began to make handles on the sides of the pot but then removed them, stating that she might have been complicating things. Handles on the pot could symbolize a way to access external support; however, Pat felt that the handles were difficult for her to create in a satisfying way, which "complicated" the process.

When Pat sought support, she would not feel a sense of satisfaction and she would internalize feelings of frustration. Further into the clay pot directive, Pat became overwhelmed by frustration and destroyed the piece by collapsing it into itself. Pat discussed having experienced a great sense of relief, or a catharsis, in the destruction of her first pot. Pat reworked the clay into another pot; she felt satisfied by the strength of it in her hand and by its shape. Her destruction of the first vessel was a way to release repressed frustrations related to unsatisfied needs and repressed negative feelings.

Figure 17.1 Pat's clay pot

Body image and gender identity discussions emerged as Pat verbalized responses to the 44 images during the box directive. Pat shared feelings of dissatisfaction with weight gain post-hysterectomy. Images that held rounder, fuller female shapes were rejected by Pat. Pat discussed the issue of being female and being a mother, directing attention to her earliest memories of learning that she could become a mother. She said, "The first thing you learn about as a little girl is that you can be a mommy; you learn about your mommy, and you can be a mommy."

Pat reported having struggled with feelings of being "damaged goods" as a result of prior miscarriages and of needing a hysterectomy; however, she felt that she had worked through this in the past and she felt more at peace with herself at the present time. Pat reported:

> Most helpful were the feelings I walked away with. Learning that I am not maimed or deformed or not a woman in the true sense of the word. Instead that a new "me" has emerged and that could be a very good thing. The therapy helped me to see that: 1) new decisions and new outlooks can be positive; 2) my opinions on women's issues and how I feel about myself as a woman are still worthy; 3) I am a creative woman.

For Pat's artwork, see Figures 17.1–17.3.

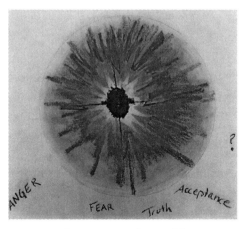

Figure 17.2 Pat's mandala

Figure 17.3 Pat's box top view

Protocol: Archetypal imagery and grieving lost self-parts

Objective

To encourage an integrated self-concept post-hysterectomy, thereby reducing negative symptomology and feelings of loss and grief, such as ambivalence about infertility, feeling lack of support, perfectionism and control issues, and a poorer sense of body image.

Material goal

To complete three artworks in support of the objective, using archetypal imagery.

Duration

As is appropriate to the individual, group, and setting. Ideally, sessions will last for between an hour and an hour and a half, at least once per week until the goal is achieved. Each session involves the following activities:

- five minutes of deep breathing, centering meditation

- five minutes of instruction/description of materials for the art-making process

- thirty-five minutes of art-making time

- ten minutes of art process

- five minutes of deep breathing, centering meditation.

Curriculum

SESSION 1 MANDALA—MARI® DISLIKE CARD FOCUS

The MARI® (Mandala Assessment Research Instrument) is a projective assessment instrument that uses symbols and colors to tap into the individual's unconscious thought processes. Art therapist Joan Kellogg developed the MARI® Card Test as a result of her years of studying mandalas with her patients. The MARI® system contains 13 stages on a "Great Round" which aligns 39 symbols to specific developmental stages in the mandala (Takei and MARI®, 2006).

Materials: Cray-Pas and 9-inch diameter, pre-drawn circle on white paper 12 by 12 inches.

Description: During Session 1, a mandala and MARI® assessment is conducted. The MARI® is a projective assessment instrument that uses symbols and colors to tap into the individual's unconscious thought processes. Art therapist Joan Kellogg developed the MARI® Card Test as a result of her years of studying mandalas with her patients. The MARI® system contains 13 stages on a "Great Round" which aligns 39 symbols to specific developmental stages in the mandala. A mandala was drawn and compared to the MARI® cards on the Great Round as part of this assessment.

Author's note: If a practitioner is not trained in this assessment, alternative mandala-making activities with the incorporation of archetypal images may be used.

SESSION 2 CLAY POT

Materials: Red air-dry clay, clay tools, water, shells.

Description: During the second session, clients are instructed to create a clay pinch pot. The art therapist demonstrates the technique briefly, offering clay, water, clay tools, and gloves if needed.

SESSIONS 3 AND 4 BOX WITH ARCHETYPAL IMAGERY BOX
Materials: Pre-made, unpainted, small wooden boxes, archetypal pre-printed images for collage, glue, scissors.

Description: During Session 3, and for as many sessions as are required subsequently, clients are offered a pre-made, unpainted wooden box to decorate together with collage materials, markers, paints, shells, stones, mirrors, and printed archetypal images.

References

Appleton, V. (2001) 'Avenues of hope: Art therapy and the resolution of trauma.' *Journal of the American Art Therapy Association 18*, 1, 6–13.

Bassin, D. (1982) 'Woman's images of inner space: Data towards expanded interpretive categories.' *International Review of Psycho-Analysis 9*, 191–203.

Bury, M. (1982) 'Chronic illness as biographical disruption.' *Sociology of Health and Illness 5*, 168–195.

Charmaz, K. (1983) 'Loss of self: A fundamental form of suffering in the chronically ill.' *Sociology of Health and Illness 5*, 168–195.

Corbin, J. and Strauss, A.L. (1987) 'Accompaniments of chronic illness: Changes in body, self, biography, and biographical time.' In J. Roth and P. Conrad (eds) *The Experience and Management of Chronic Illness: Research in the Sociology of Health Care.* Vol. 6. Greenwich, CT: JAI Press.

Darling, C.A. and McKoy-Smith, Y.M. (1993) 'Understanding hysterectomies: Sexual satisfaction and quality of life.' *The Journal of Sex Research 30*, 4, 324–335.

Elson, J. (2002) 'Menarche, menstruation, and gender identity: Retrospective accounts from women who have undergone premenopausal hysterectomy.' *Sex Roles Mental Health Journal 46*, 1, 37–48.

Elson, J. (2004) *Am I Still a Woman? Hysterectomy and Gender Identity.* Philadelphia, PA: Temple University Press.

Farrell-Kirk, R. (2001) 'Secrets, symbols, synthesis, and safety: The role of boxes in art therapy.' *American Journal of Art Therapy 39*, 88–92.

Flory, N., Bissonnette, F., and Binik, Y.M. (2005) 'Psychosocial effects of hysterectomy: Literature review.' *Journal of Psychosomatic Research 59*, 3, 117–129.

Jung, C.G. (1968) *Man and his Symbols* (M.-L. Von Franz and J. Freeman, eds). London: Dell.

Lauter, E. and Schreier Rupprecht, C. (eds) (1985) *Feminist Archetypal Theory: Interdisciplinary Re-Visions of Jungian Thought* (2nd ed.). Knoxville, TN: The University of Tennessee Press.

Luzzatto, P. and Gabriel, B. (2000) 'The creative journey: A model for short-term group art therapy with posttreatment cancer patients.' *Journal of the American Art Therapy Association 17*, 4, 265–269.

Naumburg, M.N. (1955) 'Art as symbolic speech.' *The Journal of Aesthetics and Art Criticism 13*, 4, 435–440.

Schneider, J.W. and Conrad, P. (1983) *Having Epilepsy: The Experience and Control of Illness.* Philadephia, PA: Temple University Press.

Takei, S. and MARI® (2006) *Color at Stage: Level One* [Training manual]. Raleigh, NC: MARI®.

U.S. Department of Health and Human Services Centers for Disease Control and Prevention (2017) *Data and Statistics.* Available at www.cdc.gov/reproductivehealth/data_stats, accessed on February 27, 2017.

18

Multimedia Approaches in Childhood Bereavement

Sarah Vollmann

Overview

Childhood and adolescent bereavement

The grief of children is often misunderstood or overlooked in our society. As the presentation of a child's grief differs from that of an adult, misconceptions sometimes occur and adults may erroneously conclude that a child is not deeply impacted by a loss. While adults frequently mourn with intensity for an extended amount of time after losing a loved one, children are emotionally unable to immerse themselves thoroughly in grief because of their developmental level. Mourning children need to take frequent breaks from the intense affects induced by a loss; they will often fluctuate between moments of sadness and moments of diversion. Their play sometimes serves to provide needed distance, and it also may be used as a vehicle to understand or master a loss. Play which appears to be carefree to an unsuspecting adult might be dense with symbolic re-enactments and references to the loss.

Developmental considerations in childhood bereavement

A child or adolescent's ability to understand a loss will shift as they age, and is largely influenced by his or her developmental level. As we seek to understand the bereavement experience of children we need to be aware of their developmental aptitude to comprehend and process the loss.

- *Infants from 0 to 2 years old* experience death as a separation. While they will not comprehend the meaning or finality of death they will react to a separation and feel a sense of loss. They will also respond to changes in their routine, and to parental and familial grief. Recommendations for this age group include maintaining a reliable routine, and close and comforting physical contact.

- *Children from 2 to 5 years old* are concrete thinkers. They do not conceive that death is irreversible. They may engage in magical thinking, using fantasies to make sense of the death. Due to egocentric thinking they may believe that they are responsible for the death. They will react to familial grief and to routine changes. Recommendations for this age group include developmentally understandable explanations of the death, reassurance if needed that they are not to blame for the death, a consistent routine, and comforting physical contact.

- *Children from 6 to 12 years old* are beginning to understand that death is final, and that it is an event which could happen to them or to others. They may ask many questions as they attempt to absorb the significance of death and loss. Recommendations for this age group include providing opportunities for discussion and questions, maintaining a predictable routine, and providing comforting.

- *Adolescents* gradually conceptualize death with the cognition of an adult. They may realize intellectually that death could happen to them but might also feel invincible, not fully believing that they could die. They may feel some spiritual or emotional confusion about death, and could engage in risky behaviors. Recommendations for this age group include providing opportunities for open discussion, and comforting (Davies, 1999; Gibbons, 1992).

Family grief

A family systems perspective informs us that all family members are deeply impacted by one another as a co-existing group. When a familial death occurs, grieving children face not only the loss of a loved one but also the subsequent alterations and grief in the family, perhaps including a shift in their care or in the emotional availability of their caregivers. Family art therapy sessions can be an important component of treatment, providing insights about a grieving family's functioning and relationships and allowing for therapeutic intervention:

> While the family is engaged in creating an art product, the clinician watches the *process*... The family members' approach to the art gives the art therapist an opportunity to observe the gestalt of the family's structure, assigned roles, alliances, behavioral patterns, communication systems, and style. (Landgarten, 1981, pp.21–22)

The family's art product will provide additional information and opportunities for intervention, highlighting the family's ego-strengths, defenses, unspoken messages, and secrets (Landgarten, 1981).

In practice

Case study

An eight-year-old girl, Charlotte, was referred to me for treatment after the death of her baby sister. In the intake I learned that Charlotte's sister died a few hours after birth due to swelling in the brain. The death was unanticipated as the pregnancy was deemed to be healthy.

Charlotte was the first-born child and she had a four-year-old brother. After her brother's birth, her parents had three miscarriages, of which Charlotte was aware. Charlotte's parents were consequently anxious throughout the last pregnancy, and her mother had been on bed rest. They were devastated by the baby's unexpected death, and were considering separating. Charlotte's mom was severely depressed, rarely leaving her bed or her bedroom. She was too distressed to be emotionally available for her family. Charlotte's dad seemed overwhelmed by his caretaking role and the familial grief. It was determined that Charlotte and her family members would all benefit from treatment. One of my colleagues would work with the parents, another would see Charlotte's brother, and Charlotte would work with me.

Charlotte's parents described their child's anxiety. She was reluctant to go to summer camp, often refusing; she was fearful that something bad might happen while she was gone. She also expressed dread about returning to school in the fall. She felt that she was now different from peers, and worried that she would not be able to contain her upset feelings at school. Her anxiety about separating from her parents was rooted in a fear of leaving her mom alone. Like her mom, her grief often seemed to be overflowing and she broke down frequently in tears.

A MULTIMEDIA APPROACH

When I met with Charlotte she presented with shyness, but I could sense her desire to connect. Her mother's acute grief and the family dynamics around the loss were huge factors in this case and in the transference. Charlotte was clearly hungry for an available mother figure who could be present for her. I felt empathy and a strong connection to Charlotte. As I considered my countertransference I knew that I saw myself in her in some ways. I felt a protective urge to mother her and to compensate for her mom's current inability to be emotionally available. I was aware that my reaction stemmed in part from my own struggles of growing up in a grief-stricken home.

In our first session, I asked Charlotte to make a Kinetic Family Drawing (K-F-D), suggesting that she could "draw a family doing something." Charlotte engaged easily with the art supplies. Interestingly, she drew the baby who died, and also made an additional person who she then crossed out. It was a poignant and accurate family portrait; the baby's presence and the void that she left were both represented. All family members were portrayed as cut-off figures with no legs, indicative of their lack of movement and their helplessness. She linked all family members together with hand-holding, a representation of her wish to hold the family together (see Figure 18.1).

Figure 18.1 Kinetic Family Drawing

In the next session, I offered doll-making supplies. Charlotte engaged with absorption. She named the doll after her deceased sister, and made her a hat to replicate her sister's hat from the hospital. She wrote the names of her sister and mother on the hat, perhaps as an indication of a dual loss of her sister and of her mom, who had been so withdrawn since the death. After making a blanket she carefully swaddled the doll in a nurturing manner, enacting her wishes about being a big sister as well as symbolizing her own needed nurturance. She then created five ribbon links, one to represent each member of the family, and attached the links to the doll's hat, hinting at her need to hold on to her sister and to keep the family whole and linked together. This mirrored her K-F-D drawing, which showed all family members linked with holding hands.

The doll symbolized and held several meanings. In her doll making Charlotte was able to construct a tangible representation of her sister, fostering a deeper processing of the loss. One of Charlotte's sorrows was that she did not meet or hold her sister. The doll was a helpful symbol, bringing her sister into the room in a palpable representation and allowing Charlotte to play out and imagine aspects of their relationship. Charlotte's doll was also a symbol of self. With her doll she was able to touch and nurture the baby sister she had hoped for while also mothering herself as a needy infant. Between us, I felt the space opening up as she revealed deeper concerns about her family and built a sense of trust and safety (see Figure 18.2).

Figure 18.2 Doll

I suggested creating a "Big Sister Book" in another session, and Charlotte agreed enthusiastically. She began her story with a page about her brother, writing about their relationship and creating an elaborate frame for her drawing of self and brother. Her choice to focus first upon her brother showed her need for defenses and for pacing herself as she explored the loss. I supported this and followed her lead. I reflected that she seemed to be holding everything together with the ample frame, and she agreed.

The next page was devoted to her sister. Charlotte's anxiety was apparent; she made more mistakes in her writing and her penmanship became uneven. She wrote that her sister "lived for seven hours and then she died." She drew an image of the baby, adding arms holding the baby to represent her wish to hold her sister. Her anxiety increased as she added herself to the picture. She requested a pencil for the first time and erased repeatedly. She depicted herself as a much smaller figure than the baby; she was marginalized, on the edge of the page, while her sister was colorful and central. Her own figure remained a colorless and faint pencil drawing, pointing to her struggle with her affect state and to her fragility. I reflected upon the size and placement of the two figures, commenting that "your sister is so big in everyone's mind right now." She agreed. She again created a frame, and added sequins all over the inside, using the sparkles in a seeming attempt to brighten her despair. The chaotic nature of her image indicated a high level of emotion, and the frame illustrated her need to contain the turmoil (see Figure 18.3).

Figure 18.3 Big sister book, drawing of self and sister

The book was continued in several sessions. Wishes, fantasies, and feelings of loss were all represented in her pages, and frames around her images were a constant. She ended the book with a drawn image of herself with her pregnant mom. This image held some positive memories of connecting with her sister and of a more emotionally available mom. I also think that it represented a shift in treatment; she was beginning to allow herself to own her feelings without being quite so frightened of being annihilated by them, and there was a slight loosening of the rigid frames (see Figure 18.4).

Figure 18.4 Big sister book, self with pregnant mother

After the book's completion I offered the option of creating a memory box. Charlotte began eagerly, painting many layers of color on the top of her box. I wondered aloud if the layers were perhaps like feelings, and said that I could imagine that Charlotte might have a lot of layers in her too. Charlotte nodded and named her feelings as "happy, sad, hurt, and mad." She decided to color code those feelings, claiming that yellow was for anger, red was for love, purple was for hurt, and blue was for sad. She then created a unique process of mixing colors, one that she repeated for many sessions, which seemed ritualistic; she stirred and stirred mixtures of paint, trying to devise the correct shade to represent different affect states. She would assess and adjust the paint color as she mixed, informing me for example that she now needed a bit more sadness, or a bit more love. In this way she tried to pinpoint, control, and express the complexity of her feelings and experience.

Charlotte painted the inside of the box, added sequins, and stated, "We can't forget the borders," clearly remembering our prior conversations about frames and needs for containment. I asked her what would happen if the borders were not in place; she replied, "That would be very bad. Everything would fall apart." In the inside of the box she glued images of babies, a smiling family, and a birthday cake. I reflected upon her sister's birthday, which had been anticipated as a joyous occasion. The inside of the box clearly represented her wish for a happy family and a healthy baby; images of food also pointed to needs for nurturance. She ran out of time to finish at the session's conclusion and asked me to "finish the borders," indicating her growing trust and my role as a container.

Charlotte arrived late to the following session; her dad reported that Mom was "having an episode" and that they had been unable to leave the house. Charlotte's presentation was withdrawn and sorrowful. After briefly describing her mother's distress she engaged vigorously with the box, letting out some aggression in a playful yet frustrated manner with the materials, saying forcefully "Stay up, macaroni!" and "Come here, glue!" I wondered aloud if sometimes she has angry feelings, perhaps about seeing her mom cry so much, and she responded with a nod, saying, "She cries all the time! She never used to cry like that."

Charlotte moved to the sandbox, where she set up figures whom she identified as her family. She surrounded them with signs. I commented upon the many rules surrounding the family and Charlotte said that they were needed "to hold everything together." She agreed that they were like her boundaries. She created a hole near the family, and informed me, "It is a lake." This seemed to illustrate her needs for defenses and distance. The hole was an apt representation of the family's loss, of a void, and of her buried sibling; however, it could simultaneously represent a lake, perhaps a symbol of desired peacefulness or of murky deep waters.

In future sessions Charlotte continued to mix colors and to paint her box. She added more layers of color, symbolizing her layers of emotions and her process of covering up and burying feelings which felt too hard to manage. She avoided painting the bottom of the box for some time, leaving it bare. It seemed to represent a vulnerable spot, perhaps the core of her grief, which was still untouchable. After several weeks, she flipped the box over to begin, and mixed some blue paint, her color for sadness. As she mixed she verbalized her concerns about returning to school and her fears about leaving her mom alone. She admitted to some angry feelings about her mom's state.

She drew a circle on the bottom of the box, writing "blue" inside; the circle was a spontaneous mandala, perhaps drawn to foster centering as she broached this difficult well of feelings. She began creating borders around the box edges, completing only one side, and then painted with the blue paint. She regressed, dipping her fingers into the paint and pouring a small amount of paint onto her box. I commented that it looked as if her border would be unable to hold all of that sadness, and wondered what would happen. She mixed some glue and blue paint and continued dripping increasing amounts on the box, which soon overflowed; it began to run onto the table, and she continued to pour. I offered paper and the option of creating "sadness prints" off of the box, to express and contain these overwhelming feelings while allowing the overflow and expression to continue. She created a series of many prints, continually adding glue and blue paint as I quietly reflected upon the depth and huge quantity of sadness.

When she finished printing, she painted over the blue with a putrid green color, mixing in a bunch of sequins and googly eyes and creating a final "mess" on the box's bottom. I observed that maybe those were the distressing feelings underneath all of the layers. She declared that her box was finished. This seemed fitting, as that final "mess," symbolic of those hard-to-tolerate feelings, was now fully expressed and contained, and it had its place on the bottom of the box, just as she held her painful feelings underneath the surface (see Figure 18.5).

Figure 18.5 Memory box, bottom of box

APPROACHING TERMINATION

Charlotte returned to school in the fall. It was a bumpy beginning, but progress was apparent. Charlotte's mother began medication as a part of her treatment, and she was becoming more able to join the family and to heighten coping skills. After several more sessions the concept of termination was broached. As Charlotte's grief was so firmly linked to familial grief and dynamics some family sessions were planned, to include Charlotte, her parents, and her brother. I would work jointly in these family sessions with my co-worker who had been treating Charlotte's parents. Due to our ongoing collateral sessions I had already established a strong rapport with Charlotte's parents. I suggested the option for the whole family to create a memorial quilt for the baby.

All family members engaged willingly in the directive, which was worked on for two sessions. The familiar theme of boundaries and containment was quickly presented as both Charlotte and her mom created borders on their quilt squares, pointing to mirroring and similar grieving styles and needs. Charlotte's brother was also containing, drawing shape outlines which he subsequently colored in. Intense energy and sadness came from Dad, who had rarely expressed his own emotions as he was deeply focused on caretaking for Mom and crisis management. He asked for permission to cut the fabric; this seemed to hint at his need for permission to own and express repressed feelings. Both children showed interest in their father's artwork. He initially refused to show it to them, in an apparent effort to protect them from his grief. He then stopped working on his square, appearing increasingly emotional and choked up.

Mom worked carefully, creating a frilly, "girlish" design, which was initially without much of a center. She reflected that she knew that she was doing better as she was there and participating, stating that she would not have been able to do this a few weeks ago. She said that she chose "pink things for my little girl" and also "ribbon, because I would have liked to put ribbon in her hair." This illustrated some of her wishes and fantasies about her deceased daughter, and aptly represented her sense of loss.

Charlotte's brother needed containment and structure. He sat on the floor and began cutting, demonstrating a need to distance himself from the intensity of the family and some underlying anger. His image followed the family pattern of contained shapes and structures. He chose a picture of a baby dinosaur in an egg, symbolic of the baby who had just "hatched."

Dad depicted the baby as a little bunny who was contained by a circle, which represented the family. Both children seemed surprised by Dad's tears; this session seemed to be one of the first times that he took a little space for his feelings, rather than being a caretaker for Mom and the kids. Mom's heightened coping and the family sessions seemed to provide an opening for some of his feelings.

Charlotte's image mirrored both of her parents, demonstrating her mirroring of their grieving styles and her need to connect with them. She used the same Noah's ark image as her father, and placed decorations around her quilt block in a pattern resembling her mom's square. Her image was contained by a border, like much of her prior artwork done in our sessions. The theme of containment was seen in all four squares; this family clearly coped by holding tightly to feelings (see Figure 18.6).

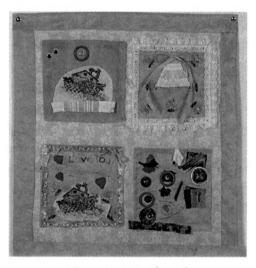

Figure 18.6 Family quilt

SAYING GOODBYE

In our last individual session, Charlotte and I looked through the many art pieces done in our time together; we used this activity to review her treatment, revisit our history and connection, and explore her process and progress. She demonstrated pleasure and pride in her art pieces. Interestingly, as we read through her "Big Sister Book," she looked back at the drawing of self and sister (see Figure 18.3) and casually reversed their identities without realizing that she was doing so; she now saw herself as the central figure, and her sister as the one on the sidelines. This was such a positive indicator of the healthy shifts in her family, in her grieving process, and in her self-concept.

She had regained center stage in her own life story, which was a poignant enactment of a primary goal of bereavement therapy.

She and I then created a book about saying goodbye, to honor our connection and facilitate a positive separation process. She used her feeling colors, and expressed love, sadness, and anger; I normalized and validated these feelings. I also felt great sadness about saying goodbye to her; our attachment and connection were strong. We exchanged photos, and created a goodbye bag as a container to hold and carry her artwork home. She used a fabric marker to write notes to me on her bag, writing, "I love you, I'll miss you," and "mad." I responded with loving notes in reply. In this way, I symbolically sent her home with tools to contain, and with messages of care.

Protocol: Options for bereaved children, adolescents, and families

Objectives

- To assess a patient's family functioning and dynamics, so that the patient and the loss can be understood from within the familial context.

- To encourage expression, exploration, and processing of feelings regarding the loss, using art therapy to foster meaning making and mastery.

- To reduce feelings and symptoms of anxiety and depression while building positive coping skills and heightening self-esteem.

Material goals

- Patients will be able to identify feelings about the loss, and gain insights about their reactions, defenses and needs, as evidenced by at least one art piece and one verbalization.

- Patients will take the lead in their own grieving process within the session, using art and play both to process the loss and to self-soothe, as evidenced by at least one art piece and one verbalization.

Duration

Ideally, sessions will last for one hour and occur at a frequency of once per week, until the goals are achieved and some healthy progress is noted.

Curriculum

The following art therapy directives are designed as optional suggestions. Every patient and case is unique, and it is always advisable to provide choices, to be mindful of respecting defenses, and to be ready and open to follow the patient's lead.

SESSION 1 ASSESSMENT

Materials and recommendations: Ask the child to create a drawing of a family doing something. Ideally, the child should be encouraged not to draw stick people. Observe the child's presentation, affect, process, use of art supplies, and final product, as well as his or her interactions and developing rapport with you.

Provide: Pencils, erasers, colored markers or colored pencils, white drawing paper.

The Kinetic Family Drawing or K-F-D (Burns and Kaufman, 1970) provides valuable insights for the therapist to inform future treatment. The completed drawing as well as the patient's process and reaction to materials will furnish understanding about the patient's self-perception within the family unit, and their sense and experience overall of the functioning and health of the family.

SESSION 2 DOLLS

Materials and recommendations: It is usually beneficial to provide an open-ended doll-making directive, allowing the child to create any type of doll that he or she chooses and allowing for the child's process, defenses, and authentic expression. While many children may choose to create a doll of the deceased, unlimited choices are obviously possible, and many dolls hold several identities and symbolic meanings. It is important to create opportunities for doll play as well as for the creative process.

Provide: A blank doll figure, fabric markers, fabric, sewing supplies, tacky glue, yarn, googly eyes, buttons, ribbons, feathers, sequins.

In my experience, grieving children frequently choose to make a doll of the deceased, and it becomes a powerful way for them to touch, hold, and process their loss. A doll may symbolize the deceased while also being a symbol of self; as with all art therapy creations, the doll can simultaneously contain an array of meanings.

SESSION 3 MEMORY BOOK

Materials and recommendations: The patient may choose to bring in photos of the deceased to include in the book; color Xeroxes of the photos may be helpful so that the originals remain intact, and the patient has the freedom to cut and collage the photos as he or she wishes.

Provide: Sheets of paper to be bound, book-binding supplies (such as yarn, string, or staples), pencils, erasers, markers, cut-out magazine images, decorative papers, glue sticks, glue, feathers, fabric scraps, ribbons.

The creation of a memory book allows a child to use drawing and storytelling to document his or her loss and memories of the deceased, and to take control of his or her own narrative. The format of a book promotes some type of organization and sequencing, which may provide needed structure, containment, and clarity. The directive of the book is directly linked to the deceased from the onset, and it serves a clear purpose as a memorial object.

SESSION 4 MEMORY BOX

Materials and recommendations: The patient should ideally have a variety of box shapes and sizes to choose from. Blank boxes made of wood or hard cardboard may be used. The box should be blank, sturdy, and large enough to fit a collage of various images.

Provide: An assortment of boxes, acrylic paints in a variety of colors, metallic pens, glue, feathers, fabric, googly eyes, sequins, cut-out images from magazines, decorative papers, photos/Xeroxed photos of the deceased, if the patient so chooses.

A memory box is a literal container, and it can symbolically hold feelings and experiences. The inside of a box may provide a safe place to express hidden or deeper feelings, while the outer shell can represent defenses and the outward persona which one shows to the world. Bereaved patients may choose to keep mementos of their loved one in their memory box.

SESSION 5 SANDPLAY

Materials and recommendations: Introduce the modality of sandplay to the patient. Allow him or her to select miniature figures and objects to create a world within the sandbox. You may choose to intervene as needed, perhaps providing witnessing, support, reflection, and assistance with containment.

Provide: The traditional set-up for sandplay includes two sandboxes, placed on a table, which each measure approximately 23 by 28 by 4 inches. One sandbox is for wet play and one is for dry. The bottom and sides of the boxes should be painted blue, to represent water and sky. An assortment of miniature figures is also needed, including a range of people, animals of all types, trees, bushes, fences, houses, bridges, cars, trucks, planes, and fantasy figures. While the traditional set-up is ideal I have also seen therapists use only one sandbox, where wet and dry sandplay are combined. A camera is needed to photograph the sandbox in its final state.

Sandplay therapy is a narrative process which allows for complex symbolic representations that can be assimilated into the whole self. Children select miniature objects and figures and create worlds and stories in the sandbox. The expression of the unconscious is revealed in the choice and placement of figures, the cohesion of the created world, the molding of the sand, and the interactions with the therapist.

SESSION 6 FAMILY QUILT

Materials and recommendations: Each family member should be given a blank quilt square to decorate. The family may choose to bring in fabric from the clothing of the deceased, or other meaningful charms or belongings to sew into the quilt.

Provide: Blank quilt squares, quilt backing, an assortment of fabrics, sewing supplies, tacky glue, pom-poms, ribbons, lace, fabric markers, embroidery thread.

The creation of a family memorial quilt is an art therapy intervention that fosters a shared and expressive act of remembrance. A memory quilt is a poignant container which may hold loving tributes to the lost family member, feelings of loss, memories of the deceased, hopes, wishes, and regrets, and it becomes a tangible artifact for the family to keep as a bonding object.

References

Burns, R.C. and Kaufman, S.H. (1970) *Kinetic Family Drawings (K-F-D)*. New York: Brunner/Mazel.

Davies, B. (1999) *Shadows in the Sun: The Experiences of Sibling Bereavement in Childhood*. Philadelphia, PA: Brunner/Mazel.

Gibbons, M. (1992) 'A child dies, a child survives: The impact of sibling loss. *Journal of Pediatric Health Care 6*, 65–72.

Landgarten, H. (1981) *Clinical Art Therapy: A Comprehensive Guide*. New York: Brunner/Mazel.

19

Exploring Attachment and Grief through Shoe-Alteration Techniques

Kelsey Dugan

Overview

The symbolic implications of shoes are seen in literature time and time again: as the saying goes "walk a mile in someone's shoes." Shoes are significant because they represent something personal that takes us from one place to another on our own journey. They travel with us through our experiences, particularly our experiences of grief and loss. Shoes protect the soles of our feet from the harshness of the Earth's surface so that we can continue on our journey. By experiencing the world from the perspective of those who decided to take that first crucial step when their lives were on the line—by walking in their shoes—and developing a deeper understanding, this study was designed to present a more authentic image of domestic violence survivors and provide them with a safe place to break their silence, and explore their grief over severed attachments.

For most of us, taking that first step can be scary, whether it's leaving home for the first time, ending a long-term relationship, or moving to another city. But for a victim of domestic violence to take those similar first steps and leave also puts them at a 75 percent greater risk of being killed by their abuser if they try and leave (Center for Relationship Abuse Awareness, 2015). The Public Policy Office of the National Coalition Against Domestic Violence (2015) found that in the United States a woman is assaulted or beaten every nine seconds and that domestic violence is the leading cause of injury to women, more than car accidents, muggings, and rapes combined. This chapter focuses on how abused women in a safe-house experienced the self-reflective process of art therapy, through shoe-altering techniques aimed at fostering self-efficacy for survivors of domestic violence, so they can continue to thrive independently.

Survivors of domestic violence

The case example from this chapter is derived from a thesis study conducted with women who have fled the grip of their abusers, in hopes of finding shelter in confidential safe housing.

Women generally need ongoing support for a period of time after becoming free of violence in order to work through the denial, minimization, anger, low self-esteem, grief, and other effects it produced. Some victims may develop PTSD, and have difficulty trusting others and future relationships. Sometimes, the anger and stress that victims feel may lead to eating disorders, depression, and suicidal ideation. Often, these behaviors were developed as coping strategies for survival while the women were in the relationship, but once they are independent the same strategies can impede their growth.

Art therapy with abused women

FORCED SILENCE

Domestic violence survivors often are unable to verbalize the horrific abuse they've endured due to an unbearable fear of consequences for disclosing and sensory memories of trauma and depression, withdrawal, and shock associated with violent episodes. Their stories feel impossible to forget, but survivors also need to confront them and acknowledge the shame, ambivalence, and fears associated with their trauma, in order to begin the process of grieving and recovery. Art can serve those who have not yet reclaimed their voice. Art can also help these women become more aware of the effects of their trauma.

ART AS A VOICE

While many programs use art to help survivors of domestic abuse access their voices, this approach first emerged in the 1990s through the Clothesline Project. Inspired by the AIDS Quilt, visual artist Rachel Carey-Harper created the idea of hanging shirts on a clothesline as a way to raise awareness of the violence perpetrated against women in the United States. Her initiative was designed from the culture-based notion that laundry had always been considered a woman's job (women often used to exchange information over backyard fences while hanging their clothes out to dry). Today, thousands of women each year share their stories with the public by decorating t-shirts to hang on clotheslines at domestic violence programs throughout the United States. In addition to visually telling their personal journeys of struggle and survival, many women often commemorate victims who have passed away as a result of domestic violence.

ART THERAPY IN DOMESTIC VIOLENCE SHELTERS

Art programs like the Clothesline Project opened the door to using art therapy with women and children living in domestic violence shelters and safe houses across the United States. Art therapy helps stabilize emotions, reduce anxiety and fear and validate feelings; it helps families adjust to living in shelters, and acts as a preventative measure to stop the cycle of abuse and enable planning for safety. Art therapy helps women address separation and loss, single parenting, socioeconomic problems, and gender roles. Shelters have also integrated group family art therapy interventions and found that art facilitates communication between mothers and children during their residency (Malchiodi, 2011). Domestic violence programs take both time constraints and the immediate needs of shelter residents into consideration, and thus treatment goals typically include safety and social support, crisis intervention, psychoeducation on the cycle of abuse, and mother–child interventions (Malchiodi, 2011).

In practice
Case example: Participant C

On the day she contacted the Emergency Shelter Screening Hotline, Participant C reported that she was not safe to stay in her current location. She had endured ruthless emotional, psychological, and verbal forms of abuse and had a history of major trauma. Participant C contacted the Hotline, via her prior agency's referral, to see if her family could be immediately transferred to this shelter. During that call, Participant C reported that her landlord had physically and emotionally abused her 15-year-old daughter. She further disclosed that the perpetrator had molested her daughter. Later on in the study, it became evident that Participant C's 15-year-old daughter had given birth two weeks earlier to a daughter. Participant C never commented on the identity of her granddaughter's biological father.

The severity of her family's situation had been acknowledged as life threatening. Their landlord was, and probably still is, relentless in his efforts to track her family down. The forcible discharge from her previous crisis shelter left Participant C's family with no other living arrangement options. For the first half of this study, Participant C lived on the second floor of the shelter, referred to as the "safe" floor. Participant C, her daughters, and granddaughter transitioned down to the first floor of the shelter, referred to as the "thrive" floor, towards the end of the study. Participant C speaks primarily Spanish and translations were used throughout the study. However, to maintain authenticity, the grammar was not modified within her translations. Each of the following quotes are Participant C's genuine words.

Figure 19.1 The inner and outer profiles of Participant C's shoe

ATTACHMENT AND LOSS

Participant C and her daughters had moved to the United States from Mexico approximately a year and a half previously. Her support systems live back in Mexico and she does not have any reliable family in this country. Participant C began the study by immediately identifying significant people on her shoe (see Figure 19.1). In her journal, Participant C reported at Directive #1:

> The white circular petals are my problems. These are the obstacles of my life that I have overcome. On the right side, I put the little shells to represent the ones who were always there for me... up until today. These are the important people in my life back in Mexico.

For Participant C, this first session brought up culturally influenced feelings of isolating separateness from family, which exposed her to the *multiple losses* she's experienced over the last two years.

She eagerly gravitated towards natural materials that she found reminiscent of family and Mexico altogether. In the art for Directive #2, Participant C used shells, white feathers, and dried tulip petals, all of which were metaphorically indicative elements of Participant C's *grieving process*. Participant C reported:

> The feathers represent my daughters, and the seashells represent my brother that was taken from us, and my mother and other brothers. The orange petals are the good people who are gone from our lives. The white feathers represent the most important people that are gone from my life.

Each material had its own backstory and, thus, was chosen with purposeful intention. In covering the entire inner side of her shoe with dried tulip petals, Participant C had asked me what kind of flower it was that these petals came from. She expressed joy in hearing that it was a tulip, in verbally reporting, "Aaah, *el tulipán!*" Participant C explained how in her country tulips are particularly special because they only blossom and survive in the cold weather.

For her, the feathers were similar to those of the Quetzal, which is the bird of Mexico. After Directive #2, Participant C introduced the researcher to her newborn granddaughter, who was named after this bird. She provided further insight by expressing that Mexico is a very poor country and it saddens her to hear about how people don't see Quetzal birds flying around anymore, like they used to. This brief encounter led the conversation towards a profoundly traumatic disclosure: the ex-communication of one of her brothers (due to his sexuality), and the kidnapping and murder of another brother in Mexico. Participant C began to cry as she formed a gun with her hands and put it up to her head.

Moments after this encounter, Participant C quickly shook off her tears, then referred to this brother as her guardian angel, and reported how her granddaughter was "named in honor of him, which is a beautiful thing." This traumatic experience was understandably difficult for Participant C to talk about. However, her behavior directly after disclosing such horrific information shows Participant C's deficits in affect regulation leading to *grief-related defenses*.

GRIEF-RELATED DEFENSES

In order to avoid confronting the emotional pain associated with her grief, Participant C attempts to rationalize her experiences through *comparison and minimization*. This is demonstrated in her immediate behaviors and verbal responses after disclosing anything she felt was "negative" about her life experiences. Participant C became visibly upset when the murder of her brother was brought into light and in order to alleviate her internalized pain she communicated how lucky she was to have him as a guardian angel and a grandchild she could name in honor of him. Participant C also feels upset that she doesn't speak with her other brother, but again rationalizes this form of a loss to avoid her feelings. During Directive #2, she verbally reported, "money equals happiness for him," then pointed towards her granddaughter as she continued, "but for me family and children are true happiness." In this statement, Participant C is essentially saying:

> I may feel sad because my only living brother won't speak to me, but at least I have other family, which is really great! And my brother and I have different perspectives on what's actually important in life anyways.

This helps her continue to ignore internalized emotions so that she won't appear "selfish" in feeling them. At the same time, she does verbally specify that family is her primary source of happiness while rationalizing the lack of connection (loss) of her ex-communicated brother.

ONGOING ATTACHMENTS

Participant C's grieving process appears to impact her ongoing relationships. Her difficulties with differentiating self and other are most visible in her family dynamics. Participant C identified her daughters as her prominent source of self-worth and motivation. She reported using the feathers and shells to metaphorically represent her daughters and "how they depend on her." She doesn't even visualize herself on the shoe, but others, indicating a false sense of self and her co-dependency, as if she wouldn't exist without the other. The flowers may be a symbol of a healed and whole self, which Participant C feels she is not, but she seems to believe that her daughters are a more suitable fit for that representation.

CULTURAL INFLUENCES

Deficits in Participant C's self-concept, separation individuation processes, and boundary issues could be indicators of her *cultural influences.* Cultural underpinnings are seemingly intertwined within all of her essential themes. Falicov (1996) further justifies this notion in reporting, "Migration transports Mexican families to a new social terrain. Bombarded with differences, they attempt to recreate elements of the culture they left" (p. 172). Participant C's tendency to only depict the important people in her life back "home" on her shoe communicates how she sees herself as part of a whole. But because her part has been irreparably split off from its other parts, she may have developed an over-identification with a false self, or persona, an outward projection of identity that is detached from the individual's internal resources and experience. She compensates for the internal depreciation of her false self, by adopting Roland's "familial self" (see Falicov, 1996, p.175). Her use of splitting is also part of a systemically approved and reinforced aspect of identity.

During Directive #1, she reported using flower petals to represent her mom among many others whom she considers to be "now gone from her life." These feelings of loss and separation from her mother would initially communicate Participant C's attachment deficits. However, for Mexican Americans, maternal love is the most sacred form (Falicov, 1996, p.176). Isolation is a common problem for Mexican Americans because relocation disrupts the structures of support and assistance that social constructs like family had provided in the past (Falicov, 1996 p.172). For Participant C, religion and the church provide the support that she's lacking while simultaneously allowing her to continue focusing on the external for internal organization. Using her children as a narcissistic arm is also influenced by Participant C's culture. Mexican culture is strongly dedicated to family unity and family honor. She uses her daughters to honor what she considers "good" and sees them as her primary source of happiness, unlike her brother, who is more independent, part of the counterculture, and (according to Participant C) only interested in material gain. Thus, to contend with this loss, he has been split off and labeled "bad" through defensive rationalization.

Community and family are valued above the individual in many Latino cultures. From a socio-cultural perspective, her attitude is dutiful "marianismo" (MacWilliam, personal communication, 2016). This was seen when Participant C brought her daughters and granddaughter unannounced to the study and then eventually asked permission for her daughter to join that one session. Participant C's inability to address her daughter did show issues with her separation–individuation processes, but also can be explained by her Mexican culture. According to Falicov (1996), "the process of separation/individuation, so highly regarded in American culture, is deemphasized in favor of close family ties" (p.175). Family collectivism, inclusiveness, and parent–child lifelong connectedness are central to Mexican Americans, and boundaries are easily expandable to in order maintain these components.

ART, INTEGRATION, AND INDEPENDENCE

Participant C indicated a final theme of *independent strivings* at the end of the study. This experience provided her with personal insight in learning how she's "not alone" and "it's not good holding so much in," as she wrote in her journal. During Directive #2, Participant C reported, "Beautiful feelings came up for me today and every time I go downstairs to work on the shoe I feel better. The difference between before and now is that today I can see things with more tranquility" indicating an increase in personal clarity which would as a result enhance problem-solving skills. Participant C identified her favorite session as the last one because for her, the final product evoked a "beautiful feeling of satisfaction." Upon completing the study, Participant C reported:

> Yes, I'm satisfied with my piece. I feel much better and much more realized. There's nothing I'm unhappy with or would want to change. Before [beginning this study], I felt blocked and emotionally very bad but this therapy helped a lot.

She reported feeling that the art therapeutic process helped "take off the heaviness." Participant C suggested that the shelter should do more projects like this because she believes it can help anybody in any situation. When asked her final thoughts about this experience as a whole, Participant C reported:

> Yes, I learned something—to look at more solutions and to see that the world is beautiful and be thankful every day and give thanks that there is help and that they put beautiful people in these shelters to help us.

Protocol: Stepping forward

Objective

The purpose of this protocol is to explore the process of self-reflection through shoe altering and observe how incorporation of product acknowledgment plays into therapeutic treatment for survivors of domestic violence. Further, this study looks to discern whether or not telling one's personal journey in a nonverbal modality could be successful in fostering independent striving and healthy integration with victims of domestic violence.

Material goal

Participants—a closed group of between four and six clients—will complete an altered shoe over the course of four sessions, as well as engage in self-reflective journaling and discussions regarding the artwork. Participants will gain awareness on how far they've come in their own healing process after experiencing domestic violence, explore any triggers that might surface, and choose to process with the group as a whole if they wish.

Duration

Four 150-minute sessions (timeframe negotiable), including orientation and a final debriefing session.

Curriculum

Materials (to be given weekly):

- Each participant will be given a new blank shoe at the first session. They will continue to work on that shoe for the duration of the study.

- Natural materials, hot glue, brushes, glue sticks, tissue paper. Participants will be encouraged to bring in found objects as they wish.

Each participant will also receive blank paper to record their process after each session.

SESSION 1 ORIENTATION—OVERVIEW AND EXPLORATION

Discuss participant questions and consent. Discussion should include:

- informed consent

- risks (triggering personal issues)

- benefits

- limits to confidentiality

- consent for work to be photographed, to share written entries or processes with the principal investigator, and to have artwork displayed publicly—if they choose to do so

- establishing group rules (confidentiality, respect, listening, phone free)

- briefly presenting shoes done by past participants in a similar group setting and discussing the concept of creating the shoes

- introducing materials that will be available weekly for art making, and distributing blank shoes and paper for written processing.

Participants are encouraged to explore the provided natural art materials, and are welcome to start working on their shoe if they wish. After having time to play with the materials, they are instructed to begin working on their shoe. Participants are also encouraged to go on walks outside before the next session and bring in any found objects they would like to incorporate into their shoe.

Journaling questions:

1. What have you added to your shoe today? What thoughts came up for you? Explain your process today if you are able to. What would you want to tell someone about your shoe (your journey) in regards to what you've created today?

2. What were your initial thoughts when you found out this shoe was an expression of your personal journey? Did any thoughts/ concerns come up for you?

3. How was it for you to think back to the beginning of your experience as a victim of domestic violence?

4. What was it like for you to be in the group? Is there anything you'd like to change for next week's session?

5. Where do you want to go from here? Do you have any thoughts about this experience?

6. Is there anything you wanted to say about your journey but weren't able/ready to?

7. Is there anything you wanted to say about the group but weren't able/ready to?

SESSION 2 FROM THE BEGINNING

Reiterate the group rules (confidentiality, respect, listening, phone free), and do a "check-in" with each group member to view their progress and find out how they are feeling. After having time to play with the materials, again have the participants begin working on their shoe. Share the following prompts with the group to consider as they work on their shoe.

- Where did I start?

- How did I get here?

- What do I feel confused about?

- Am I drawn to any material specifically?

- Why do I think that is?

- What do I need to say about my personal journey?

- What would I want my children to know about my journey?

- What would I want to tell someone struggling with leaving his or her abuser?

Towards the end of the session, prompt the clients to process the following questions.

- What have you added to your shoe today?

- What thoughts came up for you? Explain your process today if able.

- What would you want to tell someone about your shoe (your journey) in regards to what you've created today?

- Now look at your shoe and write as little or as much as you'd like about what you see/think/feel. Jot down whatever it is that comes to your mind in your journal.

Journaling questions:

1. What do you like? What don't you like? Are you more drawn to one part of the shoe than the other?

2. How do you feel when you look at the piece?

3. What story do you think this shoe is telling so far?

4. What's missing?

5. Do you feel more or less connected to any of your group members after today's session?

6. How do you feel right now? Write down three words/phrases describing today's process.

SESSION 3 CONTINUATION

Reiterate the group rules (confidentiality, respect, listening, phone free), and do a "check-in" with each group member to view their progress and find out how they are feeling. Have the participants continue with their pieces. If they feel "stuck" then direct them to reflect back on what they wrote in their journals last week. If necessary, verbalize the following, or something similar:

Let the art materials speak to you. What jumps out at you? You don't have to force your artwork. This process in itself is a journey too. Take a deep breath. You will have plenty of time. Take this step by step.

Journaling questions:

1. What have you added to your shoe today? What thoughts came up for you? Explain your process today if you are able to. What would you want to tell someone about your shoe (your journey) in regards to what you've created today?

2. What do/don't you like? Are you more drawn to one part of the shoe than the other?

3. How do you feel when you look at it? What story do you think this shoe is telling so far?

4. What's missing?

5. Do you feel more or less connected to any of your group members after today's session?

6. What's different now?

7. What wouldn't you want to share about your piece? Why not?

8. Did any thoughts/feelings come up for you today that you didn't expect?

9. How do you feel right now? Write down three words/phrases describing today's process.

SESSION 4 FINISHING TOUCHES, GROUP
REFLECTION, AND DEBRIEF

Reiterate group rules (confidentiality, respect, listening, phone free), and do a "check-in" with each group member to view their progress and find out how they are feeling. Have the participants walk around the room and look at everyone's shoe from a different angle/perspective. Encourage them to write down any last thoughts they have about this experience.

Was it helpful? Did you learn anything about yourself you weren't aware of before? Is there anything you wish was different? Add your final touches to your shoe. Take your time and really process this entire experience in your journal.

Journaling questions:

1. What is your shoe saying to you? Is anything left unsaid?

2. Are you satisfied with your piece? If you are what does that feel like for you? Do you feel accomplished?

3. If you aren't satisfied, what are your thoughts about it? Is there anything you would change? What's it like to not get satisfaction? Can you still move forward? If not, what's holding you back?

4. Were you more hesitant, resistant, or blocked to one of the sessions? Please describe. Why do you think that happened?

References

Center for Relationship Abuse Awareness (2015) 'Barriers to leaving an abusive relationship.' Available at http://stoprelationshipabuse.org/educated/barriers-to-leaving-an-abusive-relationship, accessed on December 1, 2015.

Falicov, C.J. (1996) 'Mexican families.' In M. McGoldrick, J.K. Pearce, and J. Giordano (eds) *Ethnicity and Family Therapy*. New York: Guilford Press.

Malchiodi, C.A. (2011) *Handbook of Art Therapy*. Second edition. New York: The Guilford Press.

National Center for Injury Prevention and Control (2003) *Costs of Intimate Partner Violence Against Women in the United States*. Atlanta, GA: Department of Health and Human Services, Centers for Disease Control and Prevention. Available at www.cdc.gov/violenceprevention/pdf/ipvbook-a.pdf, accessed on December 1, 2015.

National Coalition Against Domestic Violence (NCADV) (2015) 'What is domestic violence?' Available at www.ncadv.org/files/National%20Statistics%20Domestic%20Violence%20NCADV.pdf, accessed on February 1, 2016.

National Coalition for the Homeless (2009) *Domestic Violence and Homelessness*. Washington, DC: National Coalition for the Homeless. Available at www.nationalhomeless.org/factsheets/domestic.html, accessed on December 1, 2015.

Contributors

Ariel Argueso, MPS, LCAT-LP

Creative Arts Therapist for Community-Based Programming

The Coalition for Hispanic Family Services, Brooklyn, New York

Ariel obtained her Bachelor of Arts in Psychology and Bachelor of Arts in Studio Art from Binghamton University. She obtained her Master of Professional Studies in Art Therapy and Creativity Development from Pratt Institute in May 2015. Utilizing her educational and fieldwork experience, she developed art therapy programs at four community centers in Brooklyn, NY where she embraces her passion for serving at-risk youth and families.

Anne Briggs, MS, MPS, LPC

Professional Therapist at The Art Station, Fort Worth, Texas

Anne currently is an art therapist at the Eating Recovery Center as well as The Art Station, a non-profit art therapy agency that offers services to a wide range of populations. Her experience includes facilitating individual and group art therapy sessions at homeless shelters, psychiatric and substance abuse hospitals, and public schools. She also holds social skills groups for children with autism and process groups for teens struggling with anxiety and depression. Anne graduated from Pratt Institute in 2015 with a master's degree in Professional Studies in Art Therapy and Creativity Development. She had previously obtained a master's degree in Science in Counseling Psychology from Abilene Christian University and a Bachelor of Arts in Politics, Philosophy, and Economics from the King's College.

Kimberly Bush, MFA, ATR-BC, LCAT

Creative Arts Therapist and Adjunct Assistant Professor
Pratt Graduate Creative Arts Therapy Program, Brooklyn, New York

Kimberly is a licensed Creative Arts Therapist, practicing artist, and psychoanalytically trained therapist in private practice in New York City and Brooklyn. She has been working therapeutically with adults, children, and families for over 20 years. Her education and training has taken place at Parsons School of Design, Pratt Institute, and the Westchester Institute of Psychoanalysis and Psychotherapy. She holds certifications as a Sandplay Practitioner and Open Studio Process Facilitator. Kimberly teaches in the Graduate Creative Arts Therapy Program at Pratt Institute. She is also the Creative Arts Therapy Supervisor at the League Education and Treatment Center, Brooklyn, NY and a developmental consultant in various school and hospital settings. Her areas of expertise include working with young children who have developmental challenges/autism, as well as children, adolescents, and adults dealing with anxiety, loss, and trauma/recovery issues. She has additional experience in bereavement and grief work, medical art therapy, and the supervision/training of creative arts therapists.

Marie Caruso-Teresi, MPS, ATR-BC

Art Therapy Registered and Board Certified, Creative Arts Therapist
Private Practice, Northern New Jersey

Marie holds a master's degree in Art Therapy and Creativity Development from Pratt Institute and is a registered, board certified art therapist. Post-graduate certification training includes: NJ Domestic Violence Training Program, Dorothy B. Hersh Child Protection Center "Child Sexual Abuse/Complex Trauma," Trauma Informed Practices and Expressive Arts Therapies Institute "Trauma Informed Art Therapy," and HAP EMDRIA, EMDR level 2 practitioner. Marie has worked with children, adults, and families at various sites such as outpatient settings, school-based and community-based programs, and in-home art therapy services. She held the position of Creative Arts Coordinator at the YWCA Union County, NJ PALS (domestic violence counseling program), and currently serves clients in her private practice in northern New Jersey. In 2014, Marie was honored to present her thesis study "The Women's' Womb: Art Therapy with Women Following Hysterectomy" at the American Art Therapy Association Conference in San Antonio, Texas. Positive feedback following the presentation validated her passion to further advocate for the efficacy of art therapy with this population.

Julie Day, MPS

Creative Arts Therapist

Kate's Club, Atlanta, Georgia

Julie recently relocated to Atlanta, Georgia, where she now works as an art therapist and community liaison for Kate's Club, a program that helps children and teens establish healthy support systems and develop the necessary skills to cope effectively with their grief after the loss of a parent or sibling. She has also spent time at Hospice of the Golden Isles where she was privileged to help process end-of-life issues with patients and develop a creative arts bereavement program for grieving families. Julie's experience also includes adults and adolescents dealing with addiction, mental illness, behavior issues, physical limitations, and trauma. She received her master's degree in Professional Studies in Art Therapy and Creativity Development from Pratt Institute.

Kelsey Dugan, MPS

Creative Arts Therapist

GenPsych PC, Central New Jersey

After graduating from the Savannah College of Art and Design with a bachelor's degree in Fine Arts in Illustration, Kelsey attended Pratt Institute's Creative Arts Therapies program in Brooklyn, New York, earning her master's degree in Professional Studies and Creativity Development. She has provided art therapy services to clients in Adult and Child Outpatient Departments, Adolescent Intensive Outpatient Departments for young girls recently discharged from hospitalization for self-mutilation and attempted suicide, Dual Recovery Intensive Outpatient Service Programs for adults recovering from substance abuse amongst other co-occurring disorders, and to adult and child survivors of domestic violence and sexual abuse, at Richard Hall Community Mental Health Center, SAFE in Hunterdon, and SAFE's Emergency Shelter. Her creative focus is on the juxtaposition of traditionally rendered portraits with mixed media by incorporating elements of fiber art, natural materials, and found objects.

Kateleen Foy, MPS

Creative Arts Therapist

After graduating from Hoftsra University with two bachelor's degrees in Psychology and Fine Art Photography, Kateleen attended Pratt Institute's creative arts therapies program in Brooklyn, New York, earning her master's degree in Professional Studies and Creativity development. She has provided art therapy services to children on the autism spectrum and developmentally disabled adults at the Heartshare School and The League Treatment Center. Her creative focus is on photography and art therapy.

Karen Gibbons, MFA, MPS, ATR-BC, LCAT, PYT

Creative Arts Therapist

Founder of Yoga and Art NYC

Karen holds a master's degree in Art Therapy from the School of Visual Arts, as well as a master's degree in Fine Arts from Hunter College. Karen is a board certified and New York State licensed art therapist and has been practicing for more than 12 years. She has worked with varied populations including children in schools, people who are mentally ill/chemically addicted, and court involved youth. Currently working in private practice and with the Art Therapy Outreach Center, Karen's specialty is combining yoga with art therapy. She has practiced yoga for many years, became a registered yoga teacher in 2003, and completed the Integrative Yoga Therapy's Professional Yoga Therapist certification in 2013. Additionally, Karen is a published author; her most recent book is *Integrating Art Therapy and Yoga Therapy: Yoga, Art, and the Use of Intention.*

Divya Sunil Gulati, MPS, ATR-BC, LCAT

Creative Arts Therapist

Flatbush Addiction Treatment Center at Catholic Charities of Brooklyn and Queens, New York

Divya is the Creative Arts Therapist for Flatbush Addiction Treatment Center at Catholic Charities of Brooklyn and Queens. Divya earned her master's degree in Professional Studies in Art Therapy and Creativity Development from Pratt Institute in May 2015. She obtained her bachelor's degree in Fine Arts from Lasalle College of the Arts, Singapore. Her focus lies in serving under-served populations, mainly looking at complex trauma, bereavement, and addressing substance use disorders.

Maya Rose Hormadaly, MA

Drama Therapist

Maya is a graduate of New York University's drama therapy program where her thesis research focused on exploring the use of therapeutic performance to process intergenerational loss and grief. Her clinical experience has focused on working with adults in acute inpatient and forensic psychiatry, as well as veterans in an outpatient program. Maya has practiced clinically at the Nordoff-Robbins Center for Music Therapy where she combined music and drama therapy techniques to assist individuals living with severe and persistent mental illness. She recently completed a teaching assistantship focusing on clinical applications in drama therapy at NYU. In addition to her clinical work, Maya has been involved in an arts-based research project utilizing therapeutic theater to explore the relationship between people living with disabilities and their able-bodied caregivers. Additionally, Maya is an accomplished playwright and artist–researcher, whose play *Concerta for Eight*, about the lived experience of learning disabilities, is currently being performed throughout Israel and was chosen by the Ministry of Education of Israeli Government as a mandatory training tool for students and educators. Maya's research has been presented and performed in local, national, and global arenas.

Danielle Klingensmith, MS, LCAT, MT-BC

Board-Certified Music Therapist and Creative Arts Therapist (Limited Permit)
MJHS Hospice and Palliative Care, New York, New York
Private Practice, New York, New York

Danielle is a music therapist at MJHS Hospice and Palliative Care in New York, NY, where she works in home, hospital, and healthcare facility settings with pediatric and adult patients, families, and grieving and bereaved children. Though a range of physiological, cognitive, psychosocial, emotional, and spiritual goals are addressed, grief work and bereavement processing are woven throughout. In addition to her work at MJHS, Danielle maintains a small private music therapy practice, primarily serving children with ASD and other neurodevelopmental disorders in Manhattan and Queens. Previously, Danielle taught Special Education/ELA in a Brooklyn high school while completing graduate coursework in education at The City College of New York; she remains a member of the Educator Advisory Board for Classroom, Inc., a non-profit organization dedicated to supporting education in high-poverty communities. Danielle holds a master's degree in Science in Creative Arts Therapy from Nazareth College of Rochester and a bachelor's degree in Arts in Music and Humanities from Houghton College.

Laurel Larson, MPS, ATR

Art Therapy Registered, Creative Arts Therapist
Hospice and Veterans Affairs, Cleveland, Ohio

Laurel is a practicing art therapist with Menorah Park Hospice in Cleveland, Ohio. Laurel enjoys being an integral part of a clinical team that works holistically to provide end-of-life care for patients and bereavement services for their families. Laurel is also the sole art therapist at the Veteran's Domiciliary at Wade Park with Volunteers of America of Greater Ohio, serving veterans struggling with homelessness, addiction, PTSD, and military sexual trauma. At Wade Park Laurel focuses on art therapy studio groups with the Women's Treatment Program, the Cognitive Behavioral Therapy cohorts and the homeless veterans residing in the Domiciliary. Laurel coordinates veteran art shows throughout the city of Cleveland and does so to promote the veteran story and the importance of art therapy as an imperative part of their treatment.

Laurel has been a presenter at The Buckeye Art Therapy Association's Annual Symposium, The Cuyahoga Community College's Art Therapy Symposium, and enjoys facilitating staff workshops pertinent to her work as an art therapist. Laurel is a graduate from Capital University with a bachelor's degree in Fine Art and Art Therapy and holds a master's degree in Professional Studies in Art Therapy and Creativity Development from Pratt Institute. She is a new mom and enjoys living the good life with her sweet little family in Cleveland, Ohio.

Susan Leopold, MPS, MSW, RSW

Creative Arts Therapist, Registered Psychotherapist, MSW Clinical Social Work

Susan is a registered psychotherapist, an award-winning illustrator, and a visual artist and educator who became interested in the therapeutic benefit of expressive and creative therapies for diverse populations. She is particularly interested in working with complex trauma. Leopold completed her MA at UCSF, her MPS at Pratt Institute, and her MSW in Clinical Social Work at Smith College. She has over six years of clinical training including: Catholic Family Services Toronto, York University Personal Counseling Services, Toronto General Hospital (UHN) and the Hincks Dellcrest Centre for Children's Mental Health. She has extensive direct experience and training working with diverse clients (age, culture, race, gender, sexual identity) facing many personal life challenges and providing services to individual adults, children, youth, and their families. She provided creative/expressive and play therapy to children and adolescents in residential treatment, and gained broad knowledge of community resources for children and youth. In addition, her Hincks-Dellcrest experience included collaborative work with the Trauma team, treatment services, Assessment, Individual Art and Play therapy, Family therapy and Group work with parents, children, and adolescents. She maintains a private art therapy studio in Toronto, where she works relationally with clients, using a variety of creative approaches such as creative arts therapy, play therapy, sand, and other expressive arts therapies. Her interests focus on children and family mental health and improving developmental outcomes for children and youth in the child welfare system. She is a board member of the Children in Limbo Task Force in Toronto and part of the Known Donor Research Team at Smith College School for Social Work.

Melissa Meade, MS, R-DMT, NCC

Dance/Movement Therapist

Melissa earned a master's degree in Science in Mental Health Counseling from Capella University and completed the alternate route curriculum at the Pratt Institute for registration as a Dance/Movement Therapist. Melissa has conducted individual and group psychotherapy sessions, including dance/movement therapy, with a variety of clients. She has worked with grieving children through Hospice of Chattanooga and supported cancer patients at Memorial Hospital. She has also worked with individuals diagnosed with HIV, and patients with eating disorders and addictions. She has advocated for Dance/Movement Therapy, introducing the profession to the Chattanooga area. Melissa has presented at professional conferences and workshops to build understanding of creative arts therapies and their benefits.

Romona Mukherjee, Ed.M, LMHC

Licensed Mental Health Counselor

Therapy to Evolve, LLC, New York, New York

Romona earned her master's degree in Education, Emphasis in Counseling Psychology at Teachers College, Columbia University. She is also a certified yoga instructor and teaches yoga and meditation at Reflections Center for Conscious Living. As a therapist, Romona specializes in mindfulness-based psychotherapy, utilizing a blend of Eastern wisdom practices with Western psychology and theory to create a space for releasing old wounds, healing beyond them, and expanding one's sense of self. She worked extensively with trauma. providing therapy to women and children survivors of domestic violence at Sanctuary for Families in New York City. After leaving Sanctuary, she spent time working internationally with Kolkata Sanved, an NGO in West Bengal, India which provides dance movement therapy to street children who were trafficked into sex or domestic labor. At present she works with adults who suffer from mood disorders, grief, trauma, and relationship conflicts in private practice. Her approach infuses the practice of meditation, breath, and somatic awareness techniques alongside insight-oriented talk therapy. In her years of working in the field, she has found the practice of mindfulness to be tremendously effective in bridging the fragmented and dissociated state individuals experience after suffering loss or trauma.

Dina Schapiro, MPS, ATR-BC, LCAT

Acting Assistant Chair and Director of the Art Therapy Program

Pratt Graduate Creative Arts Therapy Program, Brooklyn, New York

Dina earned her master's degree in Creative Arts Therapy from Pratt Institute. She began working at Housing Works as the Director of the Art Therapy Department where her interest in creating an inclusive therapeutic environment for her clients was a priority, integrating horticulture therapy with the creative arts therapies. After leaving Housing Works and the Renfrew Center to pursue her private practice specializing in eating disorders and addictions, Dina was asked to teach at both the Pratt graduate art therapy program and the New School Creative Arts Therapy Certificate Program. Soon after starting to teach at Pratt, Dina became the practicum coordinator and after ten years of teaching and doing practicum work, Dina took on the position of Assistant Chair and Director of the Art Therapy Department at the Pratt Graduate Art Therapy Program. In 2014, Dina and her partner started an artists residency program in Vermont called the Marble House Project, where the arts and the environment are in the forefront of their project.

Lauren D. Smith, MPS, LCAT, ATR-BC, CCLS

Licensed and Board Certified Creative Arts Therapist and Certified Child Life Specialist
Child Life and Creative Arts Therapy Department
Kravis Children's Hospital at Mount Sinai Medical Center, New York, New York

Lauren is a Senior Child Life and Creative Arts Therapist, KidZone TV producer and Video Therapy Coordinator at Kravis Children's Hospital at Mount Sinai Medical Center in New York. She facilitates individual and group creative arts therapy sessions for children, adolescents, and families in the pediatric inpatient, intensive care, cardiac intensive care units, outpatient clinics and in end-of-life support. Lauren provides patient and family-centered art therapy and child life interventions to support psychological coping, reduce anxiety, and diminish the potential for traumatization resulting from the stress of hospitalization and serious childhood illness. Lauren also produces creative content for KidZone TV, an interactive, closed-circuit, in-house broadcast studio and channel, producing three live programs per day, seven days a week. Lauren supervises graduate-level art therapy interns and clinical staff within the Child Life department at Mount Sinai. Lauren has presented nationally and internationally on creative arts therapy trauma interventions and medical art therapy in pediatric acute care settings. Lauren holds a master's degree in Professional Studies in Creative Arts Therapy and Creativity Development from Pratt Institute.

Juliana Thrall, MPS, ATR

Art Therapist
Clara's House at St Cloud Hospital, St Cloud, Minnesota
Ars Bellum Foundation, Minnesota

Juliana received her master's degree in Professional Studies in Creative Art Therapy and Creativity Development from Pratt Institute in Brooklyn, New York. She has worked in a variety of facilities, including Adult Inpatient Mental Health, free programs for children with autism, and group homes for adults with disabilities. Juliana serves as the Treasurer of the Minnesota Art Therapy Association, where she helps develop fundraising opportunities, community education, and art therapy awareness in Minnesota. Juliana works as an art therapist at Clara's House, part of St. Cloud Hospital. In this role, Juliana facilitates group and individual art therapy sessions with adolescents who have mental health and/or chemical dependency diagnoses, using trauma-informed art therapy. Juliana conducts trauma-focused group art therapy for the Ars Bellum Foundation, which provides free art therapy services to veterans with PTSD in Minnesota. She engages with many materials in her practice including clay, painting, drawing, printmaking, plaster work, and fiber arts.

Dana George Trottier, MA, RDT, LCAT

Drama Therapist

Dana is a registered drama therapist with the North American Drama Therapy Association and a licensed creative arts therapist working predominantly with adults in acute inpatient psychiatry and in private practice in New York City. In private practice he offers therapeutic services to adults, children, and groups as well as clinical supervision and career consultation for therapists. He provides training and supervision for burgeoning therapists through the Drama Therapy graduate program at New York University. In addition to his clinical work, Dana is an arts-based researcher utilizing performance and other art modalities to explore the human experience and expand the body of knowledge in clinical practice. His arts-based research has focused on a variety of topics including the playability of race, the lived experience of traumatic loss, and the use of client embodiment in clinical training and practice. His research and workshops have been presented at local and national conferences, colleges and universities, and healthcare organizations throughout New York City.

Sarah Vollmann, MPS, ATR-BC, LCAT, LICSW

Licensed Independent Clinical Social Worker, Creative Arts Therapist
Buckingham Browne and Nichols School, Cambridge, Massachusetts

Sarah has specialized in working with children, adolescents, and families, and her practice has spanned school settings, a pediatric medical hospital, a residential treatment facility, mental health clinics, and a private practice. Grief and loss have been an area of clinical focus throughout Vollmann's career. She worked with 9/11 families, and has presented both nationally and internationally on art therapy, grief, and bereavement. She has published several articles, including 'A legacy of loss: Stories of replacement dynamics and the subsequent child' (2014, *Omega—Journal of Death and Dying 69*, 3, 219–247). She has additionally taught as an adjunct instructor at the graduate level. She earned her MPS in Art Therapy from Pratt Institute and her MS in Social Work from Columbia University.

Sarah Yazdian Rubin, MA, LCAT, ATR-BC, CCLS

Licensed and Board Certified Creative Arts Therapist, Certified Child Life Specialist
Senior Creative Arts Therapy Coordinator at Mount Sinai Medical Center, New York,
New York

Sarah is an art therapist and child life specialist at Mount Sinai Medical Center in New York. Her individual and group creative arts therapy sessions with patients and families facilitate psychological coping, pain and anxiety management, and bereavement support with developmental and cultural sensitivity. Sarah services pediatrics and palliative care departments in both inpatient and outpatient settings. Sarah has also served community centers internationally, facilitating expressive arts groups with disadvantaged youth and women in Dangriga, Belize and in Udaipur, India. Sarah served as an adjunct faculty member at Bank Street College of Education, co-teaching a graduate level course on the therapeutic value of creative arts interventions with hospitalized youth. Sarah has presented nationally and internationally on creative arts therapy in the hospital setting. Sarah received a master's degree in Arts in Art Therapy from New York University.

Marisa Zarczynski, MPS, LCAT-LP

Creative Arts Therapist

Marisa earned her master's degree in Creative Arts Therapy and Creativity Development from Pratt Institute in New York. She has worked extensively with inpatient psychiatric populations but also with pediatric hematology/oncology, individuals involved in the foster care system, and physically and developmentally disabled adults. Marisa works as a psychotherapist/art therapist with the Puerto Rican Family Institute at one of their outpatient clinics in Brooklyn with families and adults. Marisa was recently published in an art therapy adult coloring book and freelances as a fine artist.

Subject Index

Author Index

358